What People Are Saying About
Chicken Soup for the Nurse's Soul . . .

"*Chicken Soup for the Nurse's Soul* is a book long overdue. These stories cannot help but touch the hearts and souls of all who read it, nurses or not. Nurses will recognize their own experiences somewhere in these stories, which affirm the personal nature of nursing and the importance of personal touch involved in the care of others. The authors have done nursing a wonderful service in bringing to light the touching, funny, heartfelt anecdotes shared by those at the bedside."

Sally Russell, M.N., R.N.
educational director, Academy of Medical Surgical Nurses

"Written by nurses, this collection honestly champions the contributions, commitment and sacrifices endured daily by nurses, portraying the compassion, intellect and wit necessary to meet the dynamic, complex and ever-challenging demands of the profession. *Chicken Soup for the Nurse's Soul* will be cherished by nurses and by everyone whose lives have been touched by a special nurse."

Mary H. McMahon, M.S.N., R.N.C.
director of nursing, Maternal Child Services
Salem Hospital, Salem, Oregon

"Nursing, the gentle art of caring, is vividly reflected in this collection of stories. Each provides a snapshot of the caregiving, compassion and depth of feelings encountered in the daily activities of nurses. With all the challenges of workplace issues facing nurses today, this collection of personal stories brings focus back to the motivations for choosing a career in nursing, as well as nourishes the soul of the practicing nurse."

Linda Kubik Goeldner, C.H.E., C.A.E.
executive director, Iowa Nurses Association

"I was inspired and reignited about being a registered nurse as I read these stories. I was overwhelmed with tears, goose bumps, reflection and laughing out loud. In these challenging times we live in, I think these stories are a must for people interested in health care, receiving health care, and most importantly, for nurses of all ages, to be reminded of the importance in the work they do."

Jeannie Eylar
director, Patient Care Services
Pullman Memorial Hospital, Pullman, Washington

"Finally! *Chicken Soup* for the 'angels of mercy' who have always been there for everyone else! Words of encouragement just for us! After that difficult shift at work when the patient load was heavy and the 'moon was full,' kick off your shoes, brew a cup of hot tea and relax in your favorite chair with some inspiring stories that remind us we are not only a blessing—we're also blessed!"

Joan E. Edwards, R.N.C., M.N., C.N.S.
director, Women's & Children's Services
Kingwood Medical Center, Kingwood, Texas

"A powerful and inspiring book! The authors have captured nursing at its very best—demonstrating the art of caring for another human being. These nursing experiences vividly portray the integrity, compassion and intrinsic rewards of the nurse–patient relationship. This book will touch the heart and soul of novice and experienced nurses alike who share a common value of preserving human dignity—in health and in illness."

Martha G. Lavender, R.N., D.S.N.
professor, dean of nursing
Jacksonville State University

"To my nurse colleagues: I urge you to read this book from cover to cover. It will inspire you to remember all those reasons why you became a nurse—an exercise that will result in a warm glow of happiness and the self-satisfaction of knowing you made the right career decision."

Mary Henrikson, M.N., R.N.C.
chief operating officer
Sharp Mary Birch Hospital for Women
San Diego, California

"These inspiring stories illustrate the incredible difference we, as nurses, get to make in people's lives every day. Thank you for reminding me of the honorable profession of nursing."

Diane Sieg, R.N., C.L.C.

"These stories gave me a wonderful sense of community among other nurses. I was able to relate to almost every story with a similar experience of my own. I was reminded over and over why I went into nursing and why I love what I do. I feel an increased pride in my profession and a great sense of belonging to a universal community of caring."

Susan Goldberg, R.N.

"Why did I become nurse? I didn't choose this profession for the big bucks or my name in lights! These stories convey the spirit of what it means to be a nurse!"

Suzanne Phelan, R.N., B.S.N.

"Nurses are the heart and soul of health care. In this book, our colleagues have shared brief glimpses into our profession, opening this heart and soul to the world. *Chicken Soup for the Nurse's Soul* gives us all a chance to laugh and maybe even cry, as we see ourselves provide our unique brand of care and caring to those we serve. So kick back and enjoy this marvelous book!"

Lynn Komatz, R.N., C.N.O.R.

"These stories refresh my spirit as a nurse and inspire me to stay on in this great profession."

Kristina Winch, L.P.N.

"As I read *Chicken Soup for the Nurse's Soul,* I was reminded of the many adventures, challenges, joys and sorrows of the career. It has not always been easy, but certainly rewarding. It forced me to grow up and see the real world. I have always believed that nursing is a blending of art and science. This book certainly illustrates that profound blending of two essential pieces of 'who we are.'"

Jery Sigl, R.N.

"*Chicken Soup for the Nurse's Soul* reminds me why I am so grateful to nurses for supporting me in my work and helping me to become the doctor I am today. Decades ago, when I began listening to patients' stories and helping them to heal, the nurses knew I was on the right path. They were into intensive caring while most medical professionals were into diagnosing and treating the disease, not appreciating the patients' experiences. Nurses taught me that a good doctor is one who is criticized by nurses, patients and families. Their criticism polished my mirror. So, let me take this opportunity to say 'thank you' to all the nurses who trained me."

Bernie Siegel, M.D.
author, *Love, Medicine and Miracles*

"*Chicken Soup for the Nurse's Soul* pays grateful tribute to nurses—those exalted and capable servants who selflessly tend the sick, injured, aged and downhearted with deep compassion and unceasing dedication. Containing more than one hundred true stories of service and sacrifice, this uplifting book tugs on your heartstrings and tickles your funny bone, while artfully honoring the noble profession of nursing. Anyone who has ever been the recipient or the provider of health care will be challenged, motivated and enlightened by these inspiring, true-life examples of exceptional courage, commitment and caring."

"Dr. Mom" Marianne Neifert, M.D.
speaker, author and clinical professor of pediatrics
University of Colorado School of Medicine

"Each story will fill nurses with a sense of pride in their chosen profession, helping them feel good about the work that they do, enabling them to thrive, not just survive, in this health-care arena."

Mary Garlick Roll, R.N., M.S.

CHICKEN SOUP FOR THE NURSE'S SOUL

Stories to Celebrate, Honor and Inspire the Nursing Profession

Jack Canfield
Mark Victor Hansen
Nancy Mitchell-Autio, R.N.
LeAnn Thieman, L.P.N.

Backlist, LLC, a unit of
Chicken Soup for the Soul Publishing, LLC
Cos Cob, CT
www.chickensoup.com

Chicken Soup for the Nurse's Soul
Stories to Celebrate, Honor and Inspire the Nursing Profession
Jack Canfield, Mark Victor Hansen, Nancy Mitchell-Autio, R.N., LeAnn
Thieman, L.P.N.

Published by Backlist, LLC,
a unit of Chicken Soup for the Soul Publishing, LLC. www.chickensoup.com

Cover artwork by Lisa Camp
Originally published in 2001 by Health Communications, Inc.

Back cover and spine redesign & layout, and interior production by Pneuma Books, LLC

Distributed to the booktrade by Simon & Schuster. SAN: 200-2442

Publisher's Cataloging-in-Publication Data
(Prepared by The Donohue Group)

Chicken soup for the nurse's soul : stories to celebrate, honor and inspire
the nursing profession / [compiled by] Jack Canfield ... [et al.].

p. : ill. ; cm.

Originally published: Deerfield Beach, FL : Health Communications, c2001.
ISBN: 978-1-62361-102-6

1. Nursing--Anecdotes. 2. Nursing--Popular works. 3. Nurses--Anecdotes.
4. Anecdotes. I. Canfield, Jack, 1944-

RT61 .C376 2012
610.73   2012944875

PRINTED IN THE UNITED STATES OF AMERICA
on acid free paper
21 20 19 18 17 16   07 08 09 10

Contents

5. CHALLENGES

6. MIRACLES

9. THANK YOU

Introduction

How many times over our years of working with patients have we exclaimed, "I could write a book!" Well, now, together, we have. Nearly three thousand health caregivers from all over the world shared their stories—their hearts, their souls. While we at *Chicken Soup* have been compiling stories for three years, they have been a lifetime in the making. Now your book, *Chicken Soup for the Nurse's Soul,* shares the love, the challenges and the joys of being a nurse.

Most of us didn't choose this career because of the great hours, pay and working conditions! This book reminds us why we did. Stories from students help us recall why we entered this profession in the first place. Stories from seasoned nurses reveal why we stay. Some stories reflect on the "good old days" (many of which didn't seem all that good at the time!), but all of them give us hope for the future.

Regardless of our ages or areas of practice, all of us in health care will find our own hearts and souls in these pages. We'll see the universality of what we do—the power of our skillful hands and devoted hearts.

These stories, like nursing, celebrate life and death. Read them one at a time, savoring the hope, the healing, the happiness they offer. We envision this book in every break room (or bathroom—some days they're the same thing!). Or after a long, hectic day (or night!), we recommend a prescription of a little "Chicken Soup," prn, ad lib.

We honor you for your ministry to humankind and offer this book as our gift to you. It is our sincere wish that *Chicken Soup for the Nurse's Soul* gives back to you a portion of the love and caring you've given to others. We hope it inspires you to continue your compassionate service. The world needs you.

The Florence Nightingale Pledge

I solemnly pledge myself before God and in the presence of this assembly to pass my life in purity and to practice my profession faithfully.

I will abstain from whatever is deleterious and mischievous and will not take or knowingly administer any harmful drug.

I will do all in my power to maintain and elevate the standard of my profession and will hold in confidence all personal matters committed to my keeping and all family affairs coming to my knowledge in the practice of my calling.

With loyalty will I endeavor to aid the physician in his work and devote myself to the welfare of those committed to my care.

1
THE TRUE MEANING OF NURSING

Many persons have the wrong idea about what constitutes true happiness. It is not attained through self-gratification but through fidelity to a worthy purpose.

Helen Keller

Working Christmas Day

If a man loves the labor of his trade, apart from any questions of success or fame, the gods have called him.

Robert Louis Stevenson

It was an unusually quiet day in the emergency room on December twenty-fifth. Quiet, that is, except for the nurses who were standing around the nurses' station grumbling about having to work Christmas Day.

I was triage nurse that day and had just been out to the waiting room to clean up. Since there were no patients waiting to be seen at the time, I came back to the nurses' station for a cup of hot cider from the crockpot someone had brought in for Christmas. Just then an admitting clerk came back and told me I had five patients waiting to be evaluated.

I whined, "Five, how did I get five? I was just out there and no one was in the waiting room."

"Well, there are five signed in." So I went straight out and called the first name. Five bodies showed up at my triage desk, a pale petite woman and four small children in somewhat rumpled clothing.

"Are you all sick?" I asked suspiciously.

"Yes," she said weakly and lowered her head.

"Okay," I replied, unconvinced, "who's first?" One by one they sat down, and I asked the usual preliminary questions. When it came to descriptions of their presenting problems, things got a little vague. Two of the children had headaches, but the headaches weren't accompanied by the normal body language of holding the head or trying to keep it still or squinting or grimacing. Two children had earaches, but only one could tell me which ear was affected. The mother complained of a cough but seemed to work to produce it.

Something was wrong with the picture. Our hospital policy, however, was not to turn away any patient, so we would see them. When I explained to the mother that it might be a little while before a doctor saw her because, even though the waiting room was empty, ambulances had brought in several, more critical patients, in the back, she responded, "Take your time; it's warm in here." She turned and, with a smile, guided her brood into the waiting room.

On a hunch (call it nursing judgment), I checked the chart after the admitting clerk had finished registering the family. No address—they were homeless. The waiting room was warm.

I looked out at the family huddled by the Christmas tree. The littlest one was pointing at the television and exclaiming something to her mother. The oldest one was looking at her reflection in an ornament on the Christmas tree.

I went back to the nurses' station and mentioned we had a homeless family in the waiting room—a mother and four children between four and ten years of age. The nurses, grumbling about working Christmas, turned to compassion for a family just trying to get warm on

Christmas. The team went into action, much as we do when there's a medical emergency. But this one was a Christmas emergency.

We were all offered a free meal in the hospital cafeteria on Christmas Day, so we claimed that meal and prepared a banquet for our Christmas guests.

We needed presents. We put together oranges and apples in a basket one of our vendors had brought the department for Christmas. We made little goodie bags of stickers we borrowed from the X-ray department, candy that one of the doctors had brought the nurses, crayons the hospital had from a recent coloring contest, nurse bear buttons the hospital had given the nurses at annual training day and little fuzzy bears that nurses clipped onto their stethoscopes. We also found a mug, a package of powdered cocoa and a few other odds and ends. We pulled ribbon and wrapping paper and bells off the department's decorations that we had all contributed to. As seriously as we met the physical needs of the patients that came to us that day, our team worked to meet the needs, and exceed the expectations, of a family who just wanted to be warm on Christmas Day.

We took turns joining the Christmas party in the waiting room. Each nurse took his or her lunch break with the family, choosing to spend his or her "off-duty" time with these people whose laughter and delightful chatter became quite contagious.

When it was my turn, I sat with them at the little banquet table we had created in the waiting room. We talked for a while about dreams. The four children were telling me about what they wanted to be when they grow up. The six-year-old started the conversation. "I want to be a nurse and help people," she declared.

After the four children had shared their dreams, I looked at the mom. She smiled and said, "I just want my family to be safe, warm and content—just like they are right now."

The "party" lasted most of the shift, before we were able to locate a shelter that would take the family in on Christmas Day. The mother had asked that their charts be pulled, so these patients were not seen that day in the emergency department. But they were treated.

As they walked to the door to leave, the four-year-old came running back, gave me a hug and whispered, "Thanks for being our angels today." As she ran back to join her family, they all waved one more time before the door closed. I turned around slowly to get back to work, a little embarrassed for the tears in my eyes. There stood a group of my coworkers, one with a box of tissues, which she passed around to each nurse who worked a Christmas Day she will never forget.

Victoria Schlintz

Reprinted by permission of Benita Epstein.

Proud to Be a Nurse

How wonderful it is that nobody need wait a single moment before starting to improve the world.

Anne Frank

I just saw another television show where the nurse was portrayed as an overly sexed bimbo. It's obvious the image of the nursing profession still needs some good public relations. Once in a while, we have an unexpected opportunity to educate the public to what nursing is all about.

My chance came on a warm Saturday morning when I had a coveted weekend off from my job in a long-term care facility. My husband and I headed for the Cubs ballpark via the train. Just as the train arrived at the final station, the conductor curtly shouted for all the passengers to immediately leave the car. He hustled us toward the door. On the way, I glimpsed some people huddled around a man lying limply in his seat.

The conductor talked excitedly into his walkie-talkie.

I heard fragments of "emergency" and "ambulance." Surprising myself, I approached him and said, "I'm a nurse. Could I be of any help?"

"I don't need a nurse," he rudely snapped back, loud enough for the crowd to hear. "I need a medic!"

His public put-down to nurses was a punch in the stomach. I was incensed. My adrenaline kicked in, and I abruptly elbowed my way through the crowd, past the insulting conductor and back on the train.

Three men were standing like statues staring at a young man crumpled over in the seat. His face was the color of a ripe plum. Fortunately, the ABCs of cardiopulmonary resuscitation clicked into my brain. The man was obviously obstructing his own airway. I was relieved to find a pulse.

"He had a seizure," one man offered.

"Help me sit him up," I instructed the bystanders, as I loosened his collar and tie. We hoisted him to an upright position, and I quickly did a jaw thrust and tilted his head to the side. Mucous and blood oozed out. With a wadded tissue from my pocket I cleared more thick mucous from his mouth and throat. A thump on the shoulder caused him to take in a big breath of air. Within seconds, his color changed to pink and his eyes opened. His tongue was bruised and cut from biting it, but he was breathing well.

I heard the ambulance siren in the background.

Shaking now, I returned to my husband, praying the man didn't have AIDS and searching for something to wipe my sticky hands on.

"Hey, you did a good job," one of the men who had been a bystander called to me.

"Thanks," I replied with a pleased smile, as I stared directly at the conductor who still clutched his walkie-talkie and looked surprised. He stammered, "I guess a *nurse* is what I needed after all."

Triumphantly, I marched off, hoping at least one person had a new insight into the capabilities of the nursing profession. Because, at that moment, I was especially proud to be a nurse.

Barbara A. Brady

"Do you want to speak to the man in charge—or the nurse who knows what's going on?"

Reprinted by permission of Chris S. Patterson.

Nellie

Children are God's apostles sent forth day by day to preach of love, hope and peace.

J. R. Lowell

Nellie was only two years old, the only child of a single mother whose boyfriend walked out when he found out she was pregnant. Not an unusual story in an inner city—but Nellie was unusual. She wrapped your heart around her little finger the moment you met her. Her eyes, huge ovals and black as shiny metal, looked out of a pale, round face. I was told her hair was once dark and curly, but when we met she was bald from chemotherapy.

Nellie had leukemia. During her six months in the hospital, doctors had tried one chemotherapy regimen after another, trying to save her life. I was Nellie's primary nurse at a time when primary nursing was not the norm. We all felt Nellie needed someone constant in her life. Her mother, unable to cope with Nellie's devastating illness, rarely visited. Whenever a care conference was scheduled to discuss the next mode of treatment, Nellie's mother came to be included in decisions. She wanted to make sure everything possible was being done for her daughter. But she just couldn't visit. I always thought she had already said good-bye.

When I first met Nellie she had just started the fifth round of chemotherapy. Her face and body were swollen from steroids. She had a Broviac line in her chest for medications and IV fluids; she had severe stomatitis and was unable to take anything orally; her perirectal area was red and raw from constant diarrhea. Yet she had the most beautiful smile I had ever seen, reaching all the way to her eyes. I wondered when she had decided that pain was just a part of everyday life and decided to smile anyway.

Two things made Nellie happy: being rocked while I sang soft lullabies, and going bye-bye in the red wagon. With a fireman's cap on her head, a face mask on to protect her from anyone else's germs, and the red light flashing on the wagon's front end, we walked around and around the unit saying "hi" to all the "'ick babies." Nellie had a problem with her S's.

And she had a faith in God only a child could have. "Unless you become as little children . . . " Nellie bowed her head each time she said his name. She called him "'oly God." H's were a problem, too. When I would finish doing her morning bath and dressing her in a soft fuzzy sleeper, she would snuggle into my lap and ask me about "'oly God."

"Is his 'ouse big?" she would ask with wonder in her voice. "How big is it?" Then, "Tell me again about the 'treets of gold." She remembered all the children's Bible stories her mother had read to her.

One morning she surprised me with the simplicity of her trust. "Pretty soon I go to 'oly God's house."

"Everyone will go to Holy God's house someday," I replied, trying to deny the truth that she had already accepted.

"I know that," she said with all the assurance of a two-year-old who understands the mysteries of the universe, "but I'm going firstest."

"How do you know that?" I asked, choking back tears.

"'Oly God. He told me," she said matter-of-factly.

When the fifth series of chemotherapy drugs failed to have the desired effect, the doctors coordinated a care conference. Nellie's mother was coming and the plan was to get permission to try a new set of experimental drugs, not yet approved for use in pediatric patients. I was surprised at my angry response. "When are we going to say that's enough? It's time to let Nellie go." I couldn't believe this was me speaking. I never thought there would come a time when I would think it was not only okay, but the only right thing to do, to stop treatment on a child. I was more pro-life than the Pope, yet in the deepest part of my spirit I knew someone needed to fight for Nellie's right to die.

My worry was needless. When I returned to work the next night, Nellie was off all drugs. The plan was to keep her as comfortable as possible. She was my only patient that night. In the past twenty-four hours, her already swollen body had become even more edematous. I'm not sure why, but for the first time, Nellie didn't want to be held or rocked. I sat alongside her crib and stroked her puffy face. The short stubble of hair on her head was scratchy under my fingers. Nellie laid awake the first part of the night. I never left her side.

Somewhere around three in the morning, she turned and said, "You hold Nellie now. Nellie going bye-bye."

"The wagons are put away for the night, Nellie," I said, clinging to my denial.

"You hold Nellie now," she repeated. "Nellie going bye-bye."

Gently, I lifted her fragile body from the crib and cradled her in my arms. I held her on my chest with her head resting on my shoulder, her warm breath on my neck. We rocked back and forth, back and forth, as I stroked her and sang, "Jesus loves the little children."

After several minutes, Nellie lifted her head, using all the strength she had left and said, "He's here," then lay her head back down on my shoulder. I could no longer feel her soft breath on my neck. I'm not sure exactly how long I held and rocked her as the tears ran down my cheeks. Finally, I put on the call light to let someone know that Nellie had gone bye-bye with 'oly God.

Joan Filbin

All in a Day's Work

If I can ease one life the aching,
Or cool one pain,
Or help one fainting robin
Unto his nest again,
I shall not live in vain.

Emily Dickinson

Emergency-room personnel transported him to the cardiac floor. Long hair, unshaven, dirty, dangerously obese and a black motorcycle jacket tossed on the bottom shelf of the stretcher—an outsider to this sterile world of shining terrazzo floors, efficient uniformed professionals and strict infection-control procedures.

Definitely an untouchable!

The nurses at the station looked wide-eyed as this mound of humanity was wheeled by—each glancing nervously at my friend Bonnie, the head nurse. "Let this one not be mine to admit, bathe and tend to . . . " was the pleading, unspoken message from their inner concern.

One of the true marks of a leader, a consummate professional, is to do the unthinkable. To touch the untouchable. To tackle the impossible. Yes, it was Bonnie who said, "I want this patient myself." Highly unusual for a head nurse—unconventional—but "the stuff" out of which human spirits thrive, heal and soar. As she donned her latex gloves and proceeded to bathe this huge, filthy man, her heart almost broke. Where was his family? Who was his mother? What was he like as a little boy?

She hummed quietly as she worked to ease the fear and embarrassment she knew he must have been feeling. And then on a whim she said, "We don't have time for back rubs much in hospitals these days, but I bet one would really feel good. And, it would help you relax your muscles and start to heal. That is what this place is all about—a place to heal."

All in a day's work. Touching the untouchable.

His thick, scaly, ruddy skin told a story of an abusive lifestyle. Probably lots of addictive behavior, to food, alcohol and drugs. As Bonnie rubbed the taut muscles, she hummed and prayed. Prayed for the soul of a little boy grown up, rejected by life's rudeness and striving for acceptance in a hard, hostile world.

The finale—warmed lotion and baby powder. Almost laughable—such a contrast on this huge, rugged surface. As he rolled over onto his back, tears rolled down his cheek. With amazingly beautiful brown eyes, he smiled and said in a quivering voice, "No one has touched me for years." His chin trembled. "Thank you. I *am* healing."

In a day when we have increasing concern about the appropriateness of touch, Bonnie taught this hurting world to still dare to touch the untouchable through eye contact, a warm handshake, a concerned voice—or the physical reassurance of warmed lotion and baby powder.

Naomi Rhode
Previously appeared in Chicken Soup for the Soul at Work

Jack

After working many years in a large metropolitan hospital, with state-of-the-art conveniences, my work as P.M. charge nurse in a small, local convalescent hospital yielded many frustrations. Occasionally, we lacked supplies or equipment, and sometimes the food was less than desirable. The biggest problem was the lack of qualified help. Still, everyone working there genuinely loved the patients and did their best to care for them.

Alice, a tiny, alert, elderly lady with bright blue, twinkling eyes was everyone's favorite. Her only living relative was her son Jack, a large, tough man. Tattoos covered his arms and a scraggly beard grew haphazardly on his chin. No matter how cold the weather was, he always wore a tank-top shirt so the dragon and snake artwork could be admired by all. He wore faded jeans, so stiff with grime, they could have stood alone. His loud and gruff manner terrified most of the staff.

But this monstrous man loved his tiny mother. Every day, he roared up to the hospital entrance on his old motorcycle, flung open the front door and tromped down the hall to her room, his clacking boot heels loudly announcing his arrival. He visited at unpredictable hours so he could surprise anyone he suspected of not taking proper care of his mother. Yet, his gentleness with her amazed me.

I made friends with Jack, figuring I'd rather be a friend with a man like him, than an enemy. And I, like everyone else, truly loved his mother.

One particularly bad evening, three aides called in sick, the food carts were late and cold, and one of the patients fell and broke his hip. Jack came in at suppertime to help his mother with her meal. He stood gawking at me in the nurses' station as I busily tried to do the work of three nurses. Overwhelmed and near tears, I avoided his stare.

After the patients were finally fed, bathed and put to bed, I sat at the desk and put my head down on my arms for a few moments' relaxation before the night shift arrived. Suddenly, the front door burst open. Startled, I thought, *Oh, no! Here comes Jack, checking up on us again!* As he stomped to the desk, I looked up to see his burly hand gripping a pickle jar with a bit of colored yarn tied in a bow around the neck. And in the jar was the loveliest, long-stemmed red rose I'd ever seen. Jack handed it to me and said, "I noticed what a bad time you were having tonight. This is for you, from me and my mother."

With that, he turned around, marched back out the door, and with a roar from his motorcycle, rode out into the darkness.

I've received many gifts and cards from many grateful patients and their families, but never one that touched me more than the red rose in the pickle jar given to me that night so long ago.

Kathryn Kimzey Judkins

Olivia

There is no fear in love, but perfect love casts out fear.

John 4:18

"Please drink," De Lewis coaxed, holding an eye-dropper of water to the tiny infant's parched lips. The four-month-old Haitian baby was badly dehydrated and malnourished. She also had pneumonia and a raging stomach virus.

Cuddling the listless infant in her arms, De remembered a seven-year-old girl from North Carolina who once told her mom and dad, "When I grow up, I want to go to a poor country and help care for sick children." Well, here she was in Haiti, where the conditions were ten times worse than she ever dreamed possible. What De never once dreamed, however, was that her very first day in Haiti she would fall hopelessly, helplessly, head-over-heels in love with a sick baby girl named Olivia.

After her divorce in 1994, De had moved to Anchorage, Alaska, where there was a call for her skills as a pediatric physical therapist. She joined a local church, and in September of 1995, De left her patients in a colleague's able care and volunteered for three months of mission work in a Haitian orphanage.

De cried when she reached Port-au-Prince and saw thousands of hungry Haitians teeming in the streets, smoldering piles of garbage everywhere and not a tree in sight. The walled orphanage seemed like a tranquil oasis. Still, there was never enough food or money to buy medicines for the dozens of sick children who lived there.

Olivia was to be the very first Haitian infant De held in her arms.

"A bread vendor found her abandoned in the street only hours after she was born," the orphanage director explained. "She's very sick. We've done all we can with our limited resources."

De couldn't put Olivia down. The moment their eyes locked she'd felt an inexplicable bond with this tiny baby who was so weak she could hardly move her head.

Over the next several days, De pitched right in and helped change diapers and administer medicines to the orphanage children. But whenever she had a spare moment, she always hurried to Olivia's side. De carried the infant to see the doctor every morning, and every night she slept holding Olivia in her arms. "Why, of all these sick children, do I love this baby so much?" she wondered, but De knew it was a question only God could answer.

De's itinerary called for her to spend just a few days in Port-au-Prince before moving on to another orphanage in the remote Haitian countryside. Because of Olivia she delayed her departure for several weeks, and then one night she told the orphanage director, "I'm not going at all unless I can take Olivia with me."

Tears spilled down the director's cheeks. "You really

love that baby, don't you?"

"Yes, I do," De replied.

At the smaller, remote orphanage, De used an old towel to make a sling and carried Olivia snuggled against her chest wherever she went. On those rare occasions when she did put her down, even for a moment, Olivia flailed her arms and cried until De picked her up again. "You're getting so strong and healthy," De marveled when she heard Olivia's lusty cries.

When the other children called her "Olivia's Mama," De began dreaming of adopting Olivia and taking her home to Alaska. She tried to initiate adoption proceedings, but was thwarted at every turn. Rocking Olivia in her arms, she lamented, "Maybe it's not meant to be."

De extended her stay in Haiti until the beginning of February to be with Olivia, but finally she knew it was time to return to the many sick children in Alaska who also needed her care. Before she left, she carried Olivia back to the main orphanage in Port-au-Prince and implored newly-arriving missionaries, "Please take special care of Olivia, and show her to anyone who comes looking for a sweet baby to adopt. If I can't adopt her, I want more than anything for her to find a loving home."

De sat up the whole night before she left, cuddling Olivia. "Will I ever see you again?" she wondered. "Please God, keep this precious child healthy and safe."

Back in Anchorage, De ran up huge phone bills calling the orphanage every other day to ask about Olivia. "She's doing wonderfully," reported the orphanage workers who all knew how much De worried about Olivia.

Then, one morning at 4:00 A.M., De awoke shouting, "Olivia!"

Somehow she knew she had to call right away.

It was four hours later in Haiti. The woman who answered the phone was a stranger to De. When De asked about Olivia the woman said, "Oh, that poor baby is so sad. Ever since her American mama left, she just cries and cries."

"I'm Olivia's mama!" she sobbed into the phone. "Tell my baby I'm coming back for her. Tell her if they won't let me adopt her, I'll move to Haiti to live."

De called the adoption agency only to receive more devastating news. A family from British Columbia had already expressed interest in adopting Olivia.

De felt torn in two. More than anything she wanted to adopt Olivia herself. "But what if that isn't what God intended?" she asked her own mother over the phone. "What if God only meant for me to take good care of Olivia until the family she was meant to be with could find her?"

De prayed for a sign from God, and that Sunday she got one.

It was Mother's Day, and during the service the pastor presented heart pins to all of the congregation's moms. Then he walked straight to De and handed her a pin, too. "This is for Olivia's mother," he announced.

De burst into tears. She knew exactly what she had to do.

Soon she was back in Port-au-Prince. At the orphanage, all of the children gathered around cheering, "Mama Olivia! Olivia's mother is here!"

Inside, De barely recognized little Olivia. She had nearly stopped eating, and her hair had turned red from lack of protein.

De sobbed over the tiny crib. "Olivia, it's me—your mama." Slowly, Olivia opened her brown eyes. And then she smiled.

De lifted Olivia into her arms and hugged her. "First, I'm going to get you well again," she vowed. "Then I'm going to take you home with me to Alaska."

This time the red tape practically cut itself. Olivia's

adoption was quickly approved, and in less than six weeks De was back in Alaska with her brand-new daughter.

Today, Olivia is a happy, healthy little girl who loves hiking and camping with her mom in the scenic Alaskan wilderness. In their cozy home, she carries her toys and picture books to De and snuggles in her arms while her mama reads to her. Wherever De goes, Olivia is sure to be close behind. Her wide brown eyes follow De's every movement as if to say, "I lost you once. I'm never going to lose you again."

It's a sentiment her mama shares with all her heart.

Heather Black

A Matter of Believing

There is something in the nature of things which the mind of man, which reason, which human power cannot effect, and certainly that which produces this must be better than man. What can this be but God.

Cicero

The school bell rang loud and clear at the elementary school. Amidst much shouting and laughing, the children raced out the door for summer vacation. Johnny raced through the crowd to his bike, hopped on and headed home.

From nowhere, a car careened into him, knocking him off the bike and into the street, unconscious. The paramedics arrived and rushed him to the hospital, where doctors whispered behind closed doors and shook their heads solemnly. They had little hope the ten-year-old boy would make it.

News of the accident spread quickly. Teachers, friends and relatives came to the hospital to see their beloved

Johnny and to pray and wait. He was conscious, but couldn't walk or talk. Johnny's mom stayed by his side day and night, praying and holding his little hand.

Slowly, he began to recover, trying to form words and even sitting up in bed. A nurse named Julie came by often to check on him and give him candy. But the doctors still doubted he would ever walk again.

Late one evening, Nurse Julie stopped in Johnny's room. She found him struggling to get out of bed. She rushed to help him, and soon Johnny's feet were on the floor. Julie looked him square in the eyes and said, "It's time for you to walk."

He took one step and stumbled. Julie reassured him: "Have faith, I'm here to help you. Believe you can do it, and you will." A few more steps led to a few more steps, and Johnny was walking. It was a miracle!

Johnny was standing by the window when his doctor came in. "How did you get over to the window?" he asked.

"Nurse Julie helped me," Johnny answered.

The doctor looked puzzled. "Who helped you?"

"Julie. She said all I had to do was believe, and I would walk again."

The doctor walked out of the room, mystified. There was no nurse named Julie. A thought crossed his mind. He shook it off. "No, I don't believe in angels." And he continued down the hall.

But it still puzzled him. He finally asked Johnny what the nurse looked like. From this description, he talked to the nurses, and learned that a nurse named Julie did work there—twenty-five years ago. After a bad accident she, also, was told she would never walk again. A few hours later, Julie died of heart failure.

The doctor talked with Johnny's parents, explaining the history of Nurse Julie. Johnny's mother smiled and said matter-of-factly, "Well, if God sent one of his angels, that's fine with me."

I met him at a charity bike-a-thon. After sharing his story with me, his faced beamed. "Today, I'm flying high because an angel of God touched me." I watched him ride, his muscles straining with the effort and his T-shirt blowing in the wind. He was on a bike again and truly flying high.

Scot Thurman

Wake Up!

Next to a good soul-stirring prayer is a good laugh.

Samuel Mutchmore

Of Midwestern blood, I was schooled as a registered nurse in Fargo, North Dakota. Three years into my working career, my husband and I packed our few belongings and moved south to Fort Worth, Texas.

My initial job was in a Post-Anesthesia Surgical Care Unit. It was an exciting change from my neuro-orthopedic experience, and my clinical skills adapted smoothly. Despite this blanket of comfort, there existed a neoteric aspect of patient care that Fargo had not prepared me for.

Fort Worth was largely populated by persons of Hispanic descent. Fargo was not. In Fargo, the Norwegian dialect asks, "How ya doin'?" Whereas, in Fort Worth you hear, *"Como esta?"* And, the days of *"Uf da"* were now but a dear sweet memory. Soon, my fingertips scrambled through the pages of the Spanish-English dictionary close at hand in my locker. Fortunately, many of my nursing colleagues were already armored with conversational Spanish—at least enough to manage a patient through the recovery-room process. I was assured that I, too, would soon gain such competency.

One afternoon, Mr. Mendoza was wheeled into recovery, still lightly anesthetized. I was given the report: "Fifty-one-year-old Hispanic male, married wife out in the waiting area, non-English speaking . . . right inguinal hernia . . . general anesthesia . . . extubated without difficulty. . . . "

I engaged myself in the care of my new patient, dressing Mr. Mendoza in the standard patient attire of EKG, blood pressure and oxygen monitors. His physical assessments were normal: vital signs checked out normal sinus rhythm; blood pressure stable; respirations nonlabored; breath sounds clear; oxygen saturation at 99 percent; good capillary refill in all four extremities; abdomen soft, with bowel sounds present; surgical dressing was clean and dry.

But his neurological status remained in question: "Mr. Mendoza, Mr. Mendoza." Not a stir. Not a flinch of a response to my voice or to touch.

His wife came in to see him. Mr. Mendoza didn't respond to her either. I continued closely monitoring my sleeping patient, charting, "clinically stable, assessment unchanged . . . remains nonresponsive to voice or touch at this time. . . ." Definitely, it was not prudent to chart, "Responds like a brick wall." I continued to engage every effort to waken him.

"Mr. Mendoza, Mr. Mendoza," I called over and over again. Soon I had an uncomfortable sense of an audience. The other half-dozen or so semi-conscious patients and their nurses were clearly annoyed with the echo of my persistent badgering.

Yet, I was determined to get any elicited response—a

groan, a hand squeeze, a bat of an eye. Art, my trusted and bilingual colleague, finally came to my aid. He suggested I ask Mr. Mendoza to "wake up" in Spanish. I nodded my head as Art repeated the Spanish phrase I was to repeat to my patient. Art assured me it would elicit a response.

Trusting my rescuer, I didn't question Art for the English translation of his tutorial. As I repeated it in my head, I was comforted by the cohesive support I felt from the other patients and staff looking on with eager anticipation. I assumed they sensed the emergent need for Mr. Mendoza to respond, lest he fail his neurological assessment.

With my hands on his shoulders, I leaned over the side rail, twelve inches from his face. In my Midwestern dialect, I articulated the Spanish words in a desperate cry, *"Beso mi, Senor Mendoza, beso mi!"*

To this day, I am not sure what startled me more: the chorus of laughter of my colleagues or Mr. Mendoza, eyes wide open, shooting up in bed! Dazed, I turned to question my instructor, Art, who was buckled over in laughter. In between breaths, he provided me the English translation: "Kiss me, Mr. Mendoza, kiss me!"

Kathleen Dahle

The Night Al Heel Broke Loose

The ability to laugh at life is right at the top with love and communication, in the hierarchy of our needs. Humor has much to do with pain; it exaggerates the anxieties and absurdities we feel, so that we gain distance and through laughter, relief.

Sara Davidson

In a certain northern city, in a certain regional hospital, a story is still whispered about the "Legend of Wanda May." It has grown some over the years, but as one of the few witnesses to the entire chain of events, I will try to stick to the facts.

Wanda, a rookie nurse, was a mighty mite of sorts. Standing four feet, eleven inches, she couldn't have weighed more than ninety pounds, yet every inch of her screamed spitfire! With her green eyes and shiny black hair, Wanda was a looker. Even her cap, which conjured visions of the flying nun, and her oversized scrub suit added to her allure.

Our fifteen-bed ICU ran like organized chaos. With whirring ventilators, beeping monitors, blaring code sirens, ringing phones, glaring lights and chatting nurses, sensory overload was a common problem for our patients. A unique phenomenon known as ICU psychosis afflicts about 10 percent of those treated in this environment. Without warning, a sweet and kindly grandmother could morph into a Linda Blair clone right before your eyes. With proper medication, the condition usually lasts only twenty-four hours. Still, the poor patients are often mortified by their reported behaviors.

On the night in question, the unit was unusually quiet. With only three patients, I stayed at the desk to read the cardiac monitors while Phyllis, a jolly seasoned nurse, looked after two patients. This left Wanda to care for Alan Heel. Al looked much older than his twenty-seven years; he'd lived a hard life. Kidney disease and his penchant for alcohol proved a difficult combination. His heart strained to pump the extra fluids his body couldn't eliminate. Weekly dialysis is a hard lot in life. Long deserted by family, you could almost understand the root of Al's addiction. He was a frequent patient in our unit, and we all knew it would be a miracle if Al saw thirty. This huge grinning fellow with an unruly shock of black hair loved the attention he received in the unit. And he was never happier than when Wanda was his nurse. He swore she looked exactly like his favorite stripper, and we teased and regaled him with "Hey Big Spender" whenever Wanda was at his bedside. In spite of all of his shortcomings, Al was easy to like.

By midnight on this particular night, the patients were settled and the checks were done. Sitting at the desk, Wanda entertained us with the latest chapter of her ill-fated romantic life. Suddenly, multiple monitor alarms screamed. In the time it took to look up, there was Al, looming over us, huge and naked—except for the monitor leads flapping from his chest. We could have taken his pulse by watching the blood spurting from his thigh where he'd yanked the arterial line. If not for the blood, the absurdity of Al dragging his urine bag might have been comical—but there was nothing funny in his eyes.

Wanda and Phyllis tried to cajole him back to his room. Grabbing the phone, I paged security and then put in a call to his doctor. The next few moments unfolded like a scene from the Keystone Kops!

Al ran, followed by Wanda, Phyllis, two seventy-year-old security guards and several nurses from the step-down unit. He charged from room to room, fleeing a demon only he could see. Patients screamed, guards yelled, staff raced in all directions. The arrival of three police officers and his doctor only added to the chaos. Cornering him in the hallway, they nearly subdued him, but the power of his psychosis proved too great.

When he darted into the four-bed ward in the adjoining step-down unit, panic reigned. The screams of the four elderly female occupants almost drowned out the alarms from their collective heart monitors.

Jumping on top of the nearest bed, Al took a hostage. Now debate often ensues about the weapon Al used. I hear tell now that it was a butcher knife, but to the best of my recollection it was a letter opener he picked up from the patient's tray table. Flipping the poor woman so she was perched on top of his naked body, Al held the letter opener to her neck. The frantic look in his eyes gave us all cause to believe he would use it. Backing off as he demanded, we all tried to think of a way of getting a shot of Valium into him. In this truly desperate, life-threatening situation, the legend of Wanda May was born.

Holding us at arm's length, Wanda stepped forward. Slack-jawed, we watched as she flipped off her cap, undid her braid and fluffed her long, luxurious hair. In a sultry voice, she belted the song, "The minute you walked in the joint. . . ." With her eyes focused on Al's, she pulled her scrub shirt over her head and sent it sailing across the room. His wild eyes softened as she shimmied closer. It was plain to see that the occupant with the "knife" to her throat didn't know which of these evils was greater. In two more seductive moves, Wanda was down to her skivvies. With a crooked finger, she beckoned Al to follow her. As if in a trance, he put down his weapon and rose from the bed. In utter silence, the assembled onlookers parted and Wanda, clad only in bra and panties, walked through the center, with a docile Al directly behind. She continued humming the strains of "Big Spender" all the way back to the unit. Patting Al's bed, she prompted him to lie down. Now I was frightened for Wanda's safety. But instead of venting aggression or male energy, Al began to cry. With his head nestling on her chest, Wanda held him and stroked his hair while the doctor and I started an IV and a flurry of drugs. In moments, an exhausted Al drifted off to sleep. Extricating herself from his grasp, Wanda casually asked, "Could someone get my clothes?"

She may have been small of stature, but Wanda May will forever remain a giant to those who continue to whisper her legend.

Elizabeth Turner

Jelly Hearts

The years teach much which the days never knew.

Ralph Waldo Emerson

I was in my second year of nurse's training at Children's Hospital when I fell in love with Jimmy. His eyes were the purple of a full-moon sky. His golden hair tossed rings of curls onto strawberry blush cheeks. He looked like a cherub in the stained-glass cathedral windows. But he had the wail of a lonely, frightened, orphaned baby, which he was.

Jimmy was in the communicable diseases wing, isolated with measles and pneumonia. He had to be enclosed in his oxygen-tent–covered crib most of the time. When he wasn't sleeping, he was crying to get out. But he always stopped crying when I entered his room because he knew I would cuddle, rock and sing to him. The Children's Orphanage had been his only home most of his fifteen months of life. I knew he was well tended there, but no institution care can replace a mother's love.

As I hummed a lullaby, I fantasized. "Jimmy, I promise you that as soon as I finish nursing school, I will find a way to become your full-time mommy. You will be my special little angel."

My mind eagerly formed wedding plans for right after graduation. The man I married would just have to love this beautiful baby as much as I did.

The door opened a crack. My supervisor hissed, "Miss White! Have you completed all of your work and finished charting?"

"Almost, Miss Stickleby."

"It's nearly time to go off duty. Put the baby down now. Check on your other patients, and then go help Miss Nelson. I believe she had an extra patient today." The door closed before I could answer. Suzie Nelson did not have an extra patient. I did. Suzie was assigned as Jimmy's nurse, but I asked to have him added to my patient load. I wanted the extra time with him since I'd be on vacation the next three days.

Deliberately I dawdled, massaging his thin little legs, playing peek-a-boo with his yellow ducky blanket, urging gurgly giggles between his raspy breaths. He was more responsive and playful than I'd seen him before, and his grasp was stronger. A good sign of improving condition.

A loud tap rattled the ward window. Stickleby.

Quickly, I gave Jimmy his favorite squeaky bear and an extra farewell backrub. As his eyelids closed over his pansy eyes, I tucked the oxygen tent around his crib and whispered good-bye.

Back at the nurse's station, Miss Stickleby glared as I signed off Jimmy's chart. *Who was she anyway?* I wondered. We students couldn't fault her as a teacher and supervisor. She saw to it that we were all as conscientious in our duties as she was. But although the hospital policy encouraged staff and students to hold, play with, read and talk to all the children in our care, we never saw her cooing over a baby or reading to a toddler. By the end of the shift, our pink student uniforms were always rumpled and damp. Miss Stickleby's looked as starched and clean as at the start of the day. Unlike my netted unruly locks, no wisps of auburn hair escaped from under her square pillbox nurse cap. She was such a proper, capable nurse. Why did she hide her heart?

I waved good-bye to Jimmy's room as I hurried off duty, excited to have a holiday of mountain fun. But at the same time, I was eager to return to my bright-eyed, nearly recovered Jimmy.

While on vacation, I bought several silly, washable toys for "my little guy." He had only the disposable ones given by the local children's societies. Before he went back to the orphanage, everything would be burned, of course, to prevent cross-contamination.

Holiday over, I rushed back to work and eagerly peeked through Jimmy's window on my way to the ward station. His crib was clean and empty.

"Where did you move Jimmy?" I asked the night nurse.

"Oh, he died Saturday night. Didn't you know?" Such a casual answer.

My body turned to clabbered milk. I fell into the chair, crushing the toy bag.

"I'm sorry, Joy. He was a special little kid." She released a long, exhausted sigh. "Saturday was a bad night."

Beyond consolation, I stumbled into the nurse's lounge where I could release a great wash of tears.

"Miss White!" It was Stickleby's clipped, stern voice. "Time for report. Dry your eyes and get on duty. Now, please."

All of the emotion I felt for Jimmy poured out like boiling oil over this cold, unfeeling woman.

"How can you be so uncaring?" I yelled. "It's bad

enough that Jimmy's beautiful little life is snuffed out, but he didn't even have a mama to comfort him or to care that he died. And you? Do you care about him or any other little life? No! Just 'Miss White, go to work. Pretend everything is the same.' Well, it isn't the same. I care! I loved that little boy!"

Tears spattered down the front of my uniform.

A handkerchief dropped onto my wet lap. I felt a soft touch on my shoulder. Miss Stickleby stood at my side, teardrops softening her stiff uniform.

"Miss White—Joy," her voice was a husky whisper. "There are far too many Jimmys in our profession. They can wreck our hearts if we let them. You and I are jelly hearts. We will always be searching for ways to cope. One thing I know for sure is that we must give equal attention to each child. To single out one child can destroy us and can limit our ability to be an effective nurse."

She blotted her face. "It may give you comfort to know that Jimmy did not die alone. Death took him softly from my arms."

We sat together for a brief time, the seasoned jelly-hearted teacher and the green jelly-hearted student, crying.

Then we put on our fresh nurse faces and went out to love and care for all the little children in our charges.

Joyce Mueller

Boarder Baby

*A sweet new blossom of humanity, fresh-fallen
from God's own home, to flower on earth.*

Gerald Massey

I was working as a pharmacist at the hospital in 1969
when Billy was born with Down's syndrome. His unwed
mother intended all along to put the baby up for adoption. When she was told that the child had been born with
"problems," she didn't even want to see him. She left the
hospital during the night, abandoning the baby.

The law stated that in such cases Children's Services
must be contacted. If no immediate placement was available, the baby would be transferred to a municipal hospital to wait for foster care or adoption. Armed with this
information, the nurses from the maternity floor and
nursery went to the director of nursing.

"Why can't we keep Billy here until he can be placed?"

The director said, "You know he can't stay here. It's
against the rules of the Board of Health. We're not certified
to have a boarder baby. We simply can't keep him here;

there is nothing I can do about it."

"You know he won't be placed easily," they persisted. "It's hard enough to place a baby with no problems, much less a baby like Billy. Please, don't call Children's Services yet. Speak to the administrator first, or better still, let him come up and see the baby. Tell him we will take care of Billy and all the expenses. Just let us keep him up in maternity."

By this time, every employee of the hospital had seen Billy and was aware of the situation. And everybody had fallen in love with him. The administrator, a very religious man, was sympathetic to the pleas of the nursing staff and soon acquiesced.

The problem now was where to keep Billy. He couldn't stay in the nursery because he might subject the other newborns to germs. He couldn't be housed in the pediatric ward because the sick children would expose Billy to their infections. It was decided he would stay on the maternity floor.

One of the three isolation nurseries was commandeered as Billy's private quarters. Through the viewing window Billy could see out, and visitors and nursing staff could see in. Initially he had only a crib, but the employees bought him clothes, a playpen, high chair, toys, a stroller and anything else he needed. The entire hospital staff became his family, constantly showering Billy with affection and attention during breaks, lunchtimes and days off. They took turns taking him outside for walks.

All the maternity and nursery staff mothered him, but no one more than Miss N, who, although she was an excellent nurse, had never shown any maternal instincts. In fact, she was the prototype of a tough army sergeant. Actually, she'd been a captain when she served as an army nurse. Billy's face lit up whenever she approached him. Her coworkers had never seen Miss N even smile before, so they were astounded to see her cooing and cuddling Billy. He truly melted her heart, and she cared for him zealously. She adored Billy and desperately wanted to adopt him. Unfortunately, during the sixties, unmarried women were not considered good candidates as adoptive mothers. Knowing it was hopeless, Miss N didn't even try. But Mrs. B, one of the newborn nurses who loved him specially, applied to adopt him.

Meanwhile, Billy was a happy, gurgling boy thriving as a boarder baby in this nurturing, albeit conspiratorial environment. Every member on the staff was in on the secret. No one even mentioned Billy's name outside the hospital corridors.

One day, the Board of Health came to do an impromptu routine inspection of the hospital. Word of the inspectors' arrival traveled quickly to the maternity ward. The administrator led the inspection team to the opposite end of the facility where each department head delayed the inspectors as much as possible. Billy was spirited away from the maternity ward and taken to the apartment of one of the nurses across the street. Nurses and other staff members emptied his room, moved the furniture to the basement, covered his window with examining-table paper and locked the door.

The inspector arrived on maternity and inquired about that room. The head nurse explained it was one of the isolation nurseries being remodeled. The hospital passed the inspection, the inspectors left, the room was refurbished, and Billy returned to his home.

When Billy was fifteen months old, Mrs. B's application for adoption was somehow expedited and approved. We were all overjoyed when Billy became a sibling of her loving brood. Miss N shared a greater joy when she became his godmother.

Staff members sent gifts and had parties for Billy on his birthdays and holidays. Mrs. B and Miss N kept us informed of Billy's progress with pictures and stories.

And brought him often to visit his family in his "first" home.

Zaphra Reskakis

What Day Is Today?

Sid taught the staff and patients alike that there's room for life and laughter in a hospice. This wonderful man tried hard to cope with a paralysis that left him highly dependent on his family and the nurses. Though this irritated him immensely, he was a born actor with a wonderful sense of theater. Sid knew exactly how to act out his sense of injustice in the face of his terminal illness. Often he played to the gallery—in this case, the three other patients who shared the same room. His roommates tolerated Sid, although "here-he-goes-again" was a much-used refrain.

But Sid was also very religious. One morning, I was giving out the medication in his room when he hoisted himself onto his elbows, looked soulfully across the room and muttered weakly (but loud enough for all to hear), "What day is it today?"

I answered truthfully, "Palm Sunday."

Staring up at the ceiling, Sid blurted dramatically, "Then today is a good day to die." With this he fell back on the bed in such a dramatic fashion, I wondered if he would actually do it then and there! But a few seconds later, he popped opened his eyes, looked at me and sighed.

Later that same week, when I was back in Sid's room, he decided to give a repeat performance. Lifting himself onto his elbows again, he asked, "What day is it today?"

Again telling the truth, I said, "It's Good Friday."

Without looking up from his book, his roommate muttered loudly, "I hope to God he doesn't die today—he might rise again on Sunday!"

Dennis Sibley
As told to Allen Klein

Fresh Sample

Laughter is the closest thing to the grace of God.

Karl Barth

It began as a typical working day. As a registered nurse, I traveled to clients' homes to complete paramedical health assessments for an insurance company.

As I entered this lady's neat, attractive home, I smelled the delicious aroma of pies baking. "Umm, sure smells good in here," I commented.

"I just put a couple of lemon meringue pies in the oven. They're my husband's favorite," my client volunteered.

Returning to the purpose of my visit, we completed the questionnaire quickly. The last section involved collecting a urine sample.

"I collected it earlier and saved it in the refrigerator," she said. "I'll get it for you."

As I emptied the sample into the collection tubes, I noticed the unusual thickness of it. When I tested it with a dip stick, I was shocked at the extremely high protein content.

"Are you sure this is your urine sample?" I questioned. "This almost resembles egg whites."

"Yes, I distinctly remember placing it in the refrigerator in the bottom right-hand corner. Oh! Oh, no!" She wailed. "I've made a terrible mistake. Don't use that. I'll get you a fresh sample."

Not wishing to further embarrass the lady, I asked no more questions. But as I opened the door to leave her home, I heard her removing pies from the oven and the grinding sound of the garbage disposal.

No lemon meringue pie that night!

Donna McDonnall

Codes for the Holidays

'Twas the night before Christmas and in SICU
All the patients were stirring, the nurses were, too.
Some Levophed hung from an IMED with care
In hopes that a blood pressure soon would be there.
One patient was resting all snug in his bed
While visions—from Versed—danced in his head.
I, in my scrubs, with flowsheet in hand,
Had just settled down to chart the care plan.
Then from room 17 there arose such a clatter
We sprang from the station to see what was the matter.
Away to the bedside we flew like a flash,
Saved the man from falling, with restraints from the stash.
"Do you know where you are?" one nurse asked while tying;
"Of course! I'm in France in a jail, and I'm dying!"
Then what to my wondering eyes should appear?
But a heart rate of 50, the alarm in my ear.
The patient's face paled, his skin became slick
And he said in a moment, "I'm going to be sick!"
Someone found the Inapsine and injected a port,
Then ran for a basin, as if it were sport.
His heart rhythm quieted back to a sinus,
We soothed him and calmed him with old-fashioned kindness.

And then in a twinkling we hear from room 11
First a plea for assistance, then a swearing to heaven.
As I drew in my breath and was turning around,
Through the unit I hurried to respond to the sound.
"This one's having chest pain," the nurse said and then
She gave her some nitro, then morphine and when
She showed not relief from IV analgesia
Her breathing was failing: time to call anesthesia.
"Page Dr. Wilson, or May, or Banoub!
Get Dr. Epperson! She ought to be tubed!"
While the unit clerk paged them, the monitor showed
V-tach and low pressure with no pulse: "Call a code!"
More rapid than eagles, the code team they came.
The leader took charge and he called drugs by name:
"Now epi! Now lido! Some bicarb and mag!
You shock and you chart it! You push med! You bag!"
And so to the crash cart, the nurses we flew
With a handful of meds, and some dopamine, too!
From the head of the bed, the doc gave his call:
"Resume CPR!" So we worked one and all.
Then Doc said no more, but went straight to his work,
Intubated the patient, then turned with a jerk.
While placing his fingers aside of her nose,
And giving a nod, hooked the vent to the hose.
The team placed an art-line and a right triple-lumen.
And when they were through, she scarcely looked human:
When the patient was stable, the doc gave a whistle.
A progress note added as he wrote his epistle.
But I heard him exclaim ere he strode out of sight,
"Merry Christmas to all! But no more codes for tonight!"

Jamie L. Beeley
Submitted by Nell Britton

Christmas Magic

When we accept tough jobs as a challenge and wade into them with joy and enthusiasm, miracles can happen.

Harry S. Truman

I wish I could tell you that the whole thing happened because I'm caring and unselfish, but that wouldn't be true. It was 1979, and I had just moved back to Wisconsin from Colorado because I missed my family and Denver wages were terrible. I took a job at a hospice in Milwaukee and found my niche working with the patients and families. As the season changed into fall, the schedule for the holidays was posted:

DECEMBER 24   3-11 Barbara
DECEMBER 25   3-11 Barbara

I was devastated. Newly engaged, it was my first Christmas back home with my family after many years. But with no seniority, I had little clout to get Christmas off while my dedicated colleagues worked.

While lamenting my predicament, I came up with an

idea. Since I couldn't be with my family, I would bring my family to the hospice. With the patients and their families struggling through their last Christmases together, maybe this gathering would lend support. My family thought it was a wonderful plan, and so did the staff. Several invited their relatives to participate, too.

As we brainstormed ideas for a hospice Christmas, we remembered the annual 11:00 P.M. Christmas Eve Service scheduled in the hospital chapel.

"Why don't we take the patients to church?" I suggested.

"Yes," replied another staff nurse. "It's a beautiful candlelight service with music. I bet the patients would love it."

"Great. And we can have a little party afterwards, with punch, cookies and small gifts," I added.

Our enthusiasm increased as we planned the details of our hospice Christmas celebration.

Now, it never occurred to me that all these great ideas may not float so well with administration. It never occurred to me that we might have to get permission for each of these activities—until the director called me into her office.

"Uh, Barb, I'm hearing rumors of a Christmas Eve celebration here at the hospice."

"Well, yes," I replied. Eagerly, I outlined all the plans and ideas the staff had developed. Fortunately for my career, she thought involving our families with the unit activities was a wonderful idea, too.

"But," she said, "certainly you are not serious about taking the patients to church. It has never been done."

"Yes, I'm serious. It would mean a lot to the patients and families."

"Very seldom do you see any patients at this service, and if they do go, they are ambulatory and dressed." She shook her head. "Our patients are too sick to go."

"But a number of them have indicated an interest," I argued.

"I cannot authorize the additional staff needed."

"The family members can help."

"What about the liability?"

Now I felt like saying, "What could be the worst thing that could happen—someone dies in church?" But I didn't. I just kept convincing her, until she begrudgingly gave approval.

Christmas Eve arrived. Family members gathered in the lounge and decorated a small tree, complete with wrapped packages. Then we implemented our plan for the staff and families to transport the patients to the chapel. While most of the patients had family members with them, one young girl had no one. At just nineteen, Sandy had terminal liver cancer. Her mother had died of cancer three years previously, and her father stopped coming long ago. Perhaps he couldn't sit by the bedside of another loved one dying so young. So my family "took charge" of Sandy. My sister combed her hair while my mother applied just a hint of lipstick. They laughed and joked like three old friends as my fiancé helped her move to a gurney.

Meanwhile, other nurses hung IVs on poles, put IVACs on battery support and gave last-minute pain meds. Then, with patients in wheelchairs and on gurneys, we paraded our group into the chapel just as they were finishing "Joy to the World," with the organ and bells ringing out in perfect harmony. Silence descended on the congregation as we rolled slowly down the aisle. The minister just stood there with his mouth open, staring. Everyone turned around to look at us. We faltered in our steps, each movement echoing in the large, crowded chapel.

Then the *magic* began.

One by one, people stood up, filed into the aisle and began to help us. They handed patients hymnals and distributed programs. They wheeled patients to the front so they could see well. They handed out candles to be lit for the closing hymn. One woman adjusted Sandy's pillow and stroked her hair. Throughout the service, the congregation catered to our patients, guiding them through the worship.

The beautiful service closed with a candlelight recessional to "Silent Night." Voices rang in disjointed harmony as the congregation assisted us in exiting the chapel and returning our charges to the unit. Many stayed to share punch and cookies and stories.

As I got Sandy ready for bed that late night, she whispered, "This was one of the nicest Christmases I ever had."

When I shared her comments with my family later, we realized the magic that evening was on many levels. The unit had a special climate we'd never experienced before. Sandy had one of the best Christmases she'd ever known. The congregation had shared in a special, caring way. But we also realized that this evening impacted our family as well. We felt closer, bonded in purpose and spirit.

Since that Christmas of 1979, my family has been blessed with many Christmases together—but I think that one was the best. Like author William Shore, I, too, believe that when you give to others and give to the community, you create something within yourself that is important and lasting. He calls it the "Cathedral Within."

Our family cathedral is a little stronger for the privilege of giving that Christmas.

Barbara Bartlein

2

ON LOVE

It is not how much we do—it is how much love we put into the doing.

Mother Teresa

A Forever Kind of Love

Treasure the love you receive above all. It will survive long after your good health has vanished.

Og Mandino

One of our favorite patients had been in and out of our small, rural hospital several times, and all of us on med-surg had all grown quite attached to her and her husband. In spite of terminal cancer and resulting pain, she never failed to give us a smile or a hug. Whenever her husband came to visit, she glowed. He was a nice man, very polite and as friendly as his wife. I had grown quite attached to them and was always glad to care for her.

I admired their expression of love. Daily, he brought her fresh flowers and a smile, then sat by her bed as they held hands and talked quietly. When the pain was too much and she cried or became confused, he hugged her gently in his arms and whispered until she rested. He spent every available moment at her bedside, giving her small sips of water and stroking her brow. Every night, before he left for home, he closed the door so they could spend time alone together. After he was gone, we'd find her sleeping peacefully with a smile on her lips.

On this night, however, things were different. As soon as I entered report, the day nurses informed us she had steadily taken a turn for the worse and wouldn't make it through the night. Although I was sad, I knew that this was for the best. At least my friend wouldn't be in pain any longer.

I left report and checked on her first. When I entered the room, she aroused and smiled weakly, but her breathing was labored and I could tell it wouldn't be long. Her husband sat beside her, smiling, too, and said, "My Love is finally going to get her reward."

Tears came to my eyes, so I asked if they needed anything and left quickly. I offered care and comfort throughout the evening, and at about midnight she passed away with her husband still holding her hand. I consoled him, and with tears running down his cheeks he said, "May I please be alone with her for awhile?" I hugged him and closed the door behind me.

I stood outside the room, blotting my tears and missing my friend and her smile. And I could feel the pain of her husband in my own heart. Suddenly from the room came the most beautiful male voice I have ever heard singing. It was almost haunting the way it floated through the halls. All of the other nurses stepped out into the hallways to listen as he sang "Beautiful Brown Eyes" at the top of his lungs.

When the tune faded, the door opened and he called to me. He looked me in the eyes then hugged me saying, "I sang that song to her every night from the first day we met. Normally I close the door and keep my voice down so as not to disturb the other patients. But I had to make sure she heard me tonight as she was on her way to heaven. She had to know that she will always be my forever love. Please apologize to anyone I bothered. I just don't know how I will make it without her, but I will continue to sing to her every night. Do you think she will hear me?"

I nodded my head "yes," unable to stop my tears. He hugged me again, kissed my cheek, and thanked me for being their nurse and friend. He thanked the other nurses, then turned and walked down the hall, his back hunched, whistling the song softly as he went.

As I watched him leave I prayed that I, too, would someday know that kind of forever love.

Christy M. Martin

Happy Birthday, Grace

Where there is love, there is life.

Mahatma Gandhi

Several months before my mother's birthday, my father was diagnosed with Parkinson's disease. The crippling illness progressed very quickly. Many Parkinson's patients' speech is affected, so in the early stages, during his first hospital visit, Daddy asked me for a favor. "Please take care of your mother, Honey," he begged. "That's all that I ask of you."

Within six months, Daddy was totally bedridden. The majority of that time, he couldn't speak above a whisper. Dementia is another complication of Parkinson's, and one day his doctor held my hand and broke the news to me. "Your father will not get better, Nancy. It's all downhill from here. In a few months, he won't even remember your name." Unfortunately, the doctor was right. Our entire family was heartbroken, as we began to slowly lose Daddy to this horrible disease.

Since I lived seventy miles away, I couldn't visit with

Dad every day. I called, however, to check on him and Mom every night. I thought I was prepared for the storms that lay ahead of me. I did pretty well, until the holidays and other special occasions crept up on us. Mostly I really dreaded my mother's birthday. I knew how hard it would be for her, and how hard it would be for me to fulfill that favor for my dad. I bought her a present from Daddy, but I knew things still wouldn't be the same for her when her birthday came.

A couple of weeks before her birthday, I began to notice my mother's downcast mood when we talked on the phone. We never mentioned it, however. I didn't know what to say.

Daddy had resided in a nursing home for the previous year. Fortunately, the nurses there loved both Daddy and Mom. Since my mother spent almost every day in Daddy's room, all of the nurses and their assistants knew her well.

Tina, one of Daddy's nurses, sensed my mother's lack of joy and enthusiasm. Somehow, she found out that my mother's birthday was drawing close. I was ever grateful for her, as she went way beyond the call of duty to lift Mom's spirits on her special day. Tina bought a small picture frame and put Daddy's picture inside it. It had a little tape player at the bottom, which would hold a brief message. Daddy still had the capability to speak in a faint whisper, with a great deal of coaxing, if he was coherent. For two solid weeks, after my mother left the nursing home for the day, Tina went into his room and begged Daddy to speak into the microphone.

On her birthday, Mom went to the nursing home just as she did every other day. Through her swollen eyes, she was surprised to see birthday balloons adorning every corner of the room. Sitting on Daddy's lap was a beautifully wrapped box. Tina and some of the other employees slipped into his room right behind my mother. Mom opened her present and pushed the tiny button. Daddy's voice softly spoke. "Happy Birthday, Grace."

The tone of my mother's voice as she told me the story convinced me that we were surely going to make it through the trying days ahead. And it was all because of a nurse who took time from her busy schedule to care about the love between a sick man, his wife and an important birthday.

Nancy B. Gibbs

In the Arms of an Angel

To do the useful thing, to say the courageous thing, to contemplate the beautiful thing, that is enough for one man's life.

T. S. Eliot

I glanced at the clock on the musty green hospital wall. Almost midnight. Had it really been only twenty-one hours since the ringing phone startled me from sleep, spinning my life out of control? Panicked, I had grabbed the receiver, fearing something had happened to my mother. But it was *her* voice I heard on the other end. Rondi, my younger sister . . . brain aneurysm . . . coma . . . surgery . . . could I fly to New York right away?

Before I knew it, I was pacing in an intensive care unit waiting room. The walls, supposedly painted to look soft and welcoming, instead felt cold and threatening. Random chairs sat scattered, while others formed small circles of comfort for families. This room was like no place else on earth. Time stood still here. I walked to the window and gazed from the eighth floor at the people below.

I wanted to scream, "How dare you have the audacity to carry on normal lives! Don't you have any idea what's happening up here?"

Yes, my world had definitely stopped.

On one side of the waiting room, where we'd "made camp," friends and relatives congregated to pray, help, cry, ask "why" and bring food. It felt like we should be gathering for a party, not pleading for Rondi to make it through the night.

Family members were allowed in her room only one or two at a time. We "took shifts" around the clock so she'd never be alone. I walked in, startled by the incongruity of seeing Rondi, peacefully "asleep," quiet, no movement amidst the chaotic activity around her. I counted the rhythmic sounds from monitors and machines—the eerie whoosh of the ventilator—and the steady beep-beeps proving she was still alive.

Nurses, dressed in blue, bustled around, checking lines, gauges and tubing, as if Rondi were the only patient in the whole hospital. I retreated to the background, hesitant to sit in a chair that would be in the way or ask bothersome questions. Then I noticed. All these nurses' faces reflected knowledge, determination and purpose, yet in their eyes I saw softness and patience. I marveled at the realization that Rondi's very life rested in the hands of these souls and God.

I had the midnight to 4:00 A.M. shift. It was 1:56 A.M. Things in the room became quieter as only one nurse cared for Rondi. Through misty eyes I read her name: Linda Plano. The flurry calmed as she dimmed the lights, and the machines echoed their discordant beats. Now, I had time to think. And feel—helpless—with no control. I could do nothing to make my sister better. With tubes and wires all over her, I didn't even know where it was safe to touch her. And how I yearned to touch her, so she'd know I was there, wanting to help. I would do anything, anything, but I had no idea what that should be. If all the medicine, machines and beeping couldn't save her, then what on earth could I do? The frustration welled up inside me as the tears finally let go. I felt so alone.

I gleaned a bit of comfort as I watched the nurse check Rondi's monitor connections with the gentlest touch. Sure, she was performing the tasks necessary to save a life, but there was more. She smiled at Rondi while she worked and talked softly to her even though she was in a coma. How I wished I could connect with Rondi in such an intimate way. Suddenly, I noticed the nurse was talking to me, too. Carefully lifting sections of Rondi's hair, she commented on how sad it was that bed rest caused it to become so mercilessly matted.

Then, out of the blue she looked at me. "Do you have a brush?" Numbly, I retrieved one from my purse. She motioned me to the head of the bed and gently showed me how to brush out small sections of Rondi's hair and lay them on the pillow without disturbing any tubes or wires. My little sister's hair felt so light in my hand as I touched her for the first time. I was helping—actually doing something to care for her. The nurse dimmed the lights and quietly slipped out of the room, but not before she smiled again, this time at *me*.

I felt like Rondi and I were the only two people in the world during the hour I brushed her hair. That precious time meant more to me than any other hour we had ever spent together. With the lights lowered, I talked to her, hoping in an odd way that she would open her eyes and tell me she was going to be fine. But I knew she couldn't do that. If only I could know she was safe and not feeling any pain. As I brushed, I lamented about where people "went" during comas.

As if to answer my questions, a new sound emerged

past the hospital noises. Music. It must have been playing in the background all the time, but I hadn't heard it. I caught some of the words, " . . . you're in the arms of the angels . . . find some comfort there. . . . "

In the arms of the angels—yes! I knew at that moment where Rondi was. She *was* safe, not in pain, being cared for by angels until it was time for her to return to us here in this room.

It's hard to describe the power and beauty of the moment Rondi's nurse insightfully created for us that night. Did she know? After all, she ministers to patients every day, nonstop, during her shifts. It's her job, and this could be just an everyday activity for her, but it meant the world to me. I'm in awe to think that if only one person a week is the recipient of her gift, imagine how many lives she has changed in her twenty-plus years "on the job."

That night, at 1:56 A.M., there was a great deal of healing needing to take place in that room. This wise, wonderful nurse saw that and nurtured it. Rondi was in the arms of more than one angel that night. We both were.

Elaine Gray Dumler

The Greatest of These
Is Love

Though I articulate the contemporary jargon of nursing,
If I have not understanding that touches the heartbeat of
my patients,
I only generate chatter.

Though I boast of diplomas, awards and publications, and
my skills reflect the wonderment of technology,
If I have not mastered the gift of compassion,
My endeavors are hollow.

Though I impress my colleagues with my intellectual
prowess and lofty idealism,
If I offer not the instrument of self,
I serve my patients with mere activity.

Though I devote my very life to the profession of nursing
and forfeit personal desires,
If I become cynical, detached and fatigued to the point of
indifference,
My energy is expended in futility.

Though I integrate the art and science of nursing, translate research into clinical practice, and achieve professional notoriety,
If I do not notice wounded hearts and broken dreams,
My mission is not fulfilled.

I may be competent, dependable, efficient, but if I fail to communicate the language of love,
I practice nursing in vain.

Faith, hope and love—these are all craving of the human spirit—but
The greatest of these is love.

Roberta L. Messner
Submitted by Lisa Riha Strazzullo

You Held My Hand

Absence is to love what wind is to fire; it extinguishes the small, it enkindles the great.

Roger de Bussy-Rabutin

Excruciating, searing pain gripped his stomach and woke Nick from an uneasy sleep. He staggered from underneath his mosquito net, felt for his sandals and, bent double, hurried to the toilets behind the barrack room. He spent the rest of the night there, unable to move, and when the first of the early risers came into the toilet block, he called for help. Two of his friends summoned an ambulance that carried Nick to the British Military Hospital on the outskirts of Poona in India.

The bliss of clean sheets, ceiling fans and quietude was something Nick had not enjoyed for many months. As a trooper in an armoured regiment, he'd known only coarse blankets and barracks full of soldiers.

"So, Soldier, how are you feeling now?" A cool hand took his wrist, and he saw a nurse at his bedside. No ordinary nurse but an army nurse, wearing a crisp white uniform with a belt and a badge carrying the insignia of the QAMNS.

"Not good, Miss," he replied.

"Sister to you. Sister Nichols," she said with a smile. "Doctor will be along to see you soon. We'll know then what to do with you."

About an hour later, an RAMC officer came swinging a stethoscope. He asked a few questions, kneaded Nick's stomach and said, "Dysentery. We'll do a test or two and find out which one. Sister, give him plenty of fluids and a chicken diet."

"Right, Sir," she said, as she straightened the bed.

Within a few days, Nick was feeling better. It was the bacillary dysentery, not the dreaded amoebic, and the medicine dispensed four times a day by Sister Nichols soon eased his discomfort. While he sat on the verandah, shaded from the sun, he watched Sister Nichols, always busy, moving briskly about the ward in her starched uniform. She never failed to stop for a word of encouragement or reassurance to her patients.

"Where are you from, Sister?" asked Nick one day.

"Aldershot," she said with a smile. "We all come from Aldershot."

"No," laughed Nick. "Come on, where's home?"

"Not that it's any of your business," she replied, "but Lincolnshire, near Caistor."

"I'm from Spalding. Country cousins almost, aren't we?"

Sister Nichols smiled and moved on to the next bed.

Nick looked out for her each morning as she busied herself around the ward. She was good to look at: dark-haired beneath her cap, deep brown eyes that crinkled with a ready smile and a neat figure.

There was a radio mounted on the wall of the ward. The reception was not good, but a tune came on most days, a catchy melody Nick had not heard before, about a whistling fisherman.

"What's that tune, Sister?" he finally asked one day.

"It's 'Pedro, the Fisherman.' Comes from *The Lisbon Story*. I saw it in London just before I came out here. Lovely, isn't it?" She smiled that smile again. "Now, Soldier, I've news for you: You'll be discharged tomorrow, back to your unit."

Nick was saddened by this. He knew it was silly but, like so many, he had fallen in love with his nurse. Silly indeed, for she was an officer and he was a trooper. The two could never meet in the strict world of the army. So the next day he packed his kit, held her hand, perhaps a little too tightly, as he said good-bye and went back to the war.

Three years later, Captain Nick Bartlett had been promoted rapidly after fighting in the brutal war in Burma. Now he was stationed in a little coastal town in Malaya, one that had not suffered under Japanese rule. The cafés and shops were open and full of the pre-war goods that had been hoarded by canny Chinese in anticipation of the Japanese defeat. A large dance hall was full every night of the week. A Filipino band played the hit tunes of the war years and slender Chinese girls in cheongsams were employed as dancers. Nick's regiment was based outside the town, but most nights he drove in, parked his jeep, had a meal in the Café 7, then looked in at the New World for a dance or two with the girls.

One night as he sat at the bar, a crowd of people came in. He did not believe what he saw—a dark-haired girl with deep brown eyes that crinkled as she smiled. Gone was the white uniform; jungle green fatigues had replaced it, but those could not disguise the slim figure of Sister Nichols.

Nick headed across the room to the bandleader he'd come to know quite well. "Chan, do you know 'Pedro the Fisherman'? It goes like this," and he whistled a few bars.

"Of course," smiled Chan. "You want us to play it for you?"

Nick smiled his assent and waited for the music to start.

"Pedro, the fisherman, was always whistling," sang the Chinese vocalist as Nick walked across the floor.

"May I have this dance?" he asked.

Sister Nichols looked at her escort, a rather paunchy major in the RAMC, who nodded somewhat reluctantly.

Nick took her hand and led her onto the floor. "Remember me?" he asked. She looked at him quizzically. "Should I?"

"Well," he replied, "you held my hand."

She smiled at this, that same smile that had captivated him all those years before.

"You and a hundred others," she said.

"Poona, 1943 and 'Pedro the Fisherman.'"

"Oh, no!" she said.

"Oh, yes," said Nick. "What about dinner tomorrow night?"

Sister Nichols, or Jane as he soon learned, was with a Field Ambulance Unit only a few miles away. When Jane told the paunchy major she'd be leaving with Nick, he looked somewhat disgruntled. "He's rather sweet," Jane explained to Nick, "more a father figure than anything else."

From that time on, Nick and Jane were inseparable. They had years of experiences to share. The warm, starry nights were never long enough for them. Too soon, Nick was due for repatriation.

As palm fronds rustled above the beach on their final night, he asked, "Marry me?"

"Of course," she beamed. "As soon as we can."

"Aldershot?" he laughed.

"No," she said, "Lincoln Cathedral."

So it was. And a year later, Jane lay in a hospital bed.

"Position's reversed," teased Nick. "Remember Poona?"

"Forever," said Jane, as she held his hand and looked at the tiny baby beside her.

F. A. Thompson

Love in Its Purest Form

Being deeply loved by someone gives you strength; loving someone deeply gives you courage.

Lao-tzu

I looked up at the clock with tired eyes. *Six A.M., one more hour 'til the shift is over,* I whispered to myself. Then there he was, strolling in, head up high, as he walked toward the nursing station. The other nurses turned their heads and smiled as they recognized that old familiar face.

"You're always on time," I commented. He smiled and asked, "Are we ready?"

I nodded my head in reply, and we proceeded to Mrs. Walter's room. "Did you premedicate her for pain already?" he asked.

"Yes, sir," I replied. We knocked at Mrs. Walter's door to let her know we were coming in to begin the procedure. She was bedridden, barely able to move herself. I sighed as I looked at her swollen legs, ulcerated, from ankles to thighs. The oozing, foul-smelling drainage from her wounds permeated the room. Nevertheless, I smiled. I saw the joy in her eyes as she saw him enter the room with me.

"Just let us know if you feel any pain, so we can be more gentle," he told Mrs. Walter.

"Okay," she sighed.

We began the dreaded dressing change. He held her feet off the pillows, so I could undo the old dressings wrapped from her ankles to her thighs. He laid out all the sterile dressings, scissors and tape on the bedside tray in a very organized manner, just as he did yesterday. He was a master at this procedure. He handed me the spray bottle, and I sprayed her wounds to clean them.

"Are you okay?" he asked Mrs. Walter.

She just nodded and bit her lips in pain.

"Hang in there, we'll be done soon," he reassured her.

We began with her right leg. It was a difficult task standing there seeing the worst of all wounds. The stench forced me to hold my breath. And yet he stood there, right beside her, brave and strong, keeping his composure.

"Here, let me help you with that," he said as I struggled to reach over her upper thigh.

Ten minutes had passed and we proceeded with her left leg. It seemed like forever until we were finished. *Thank goodness*, I whispered to myself. I looked up at the clock and it was 6:30 A.M. Was it only thirty minutes?

"Thank you, Nurse," Mrs. Walter sighed in relief. She then turned her head to look up at him and whispered, "Thanks a lot, Honey. You know you really didn't have to come early today to be here, but I'm glad you did."

And it was my turn to thank him, just as I did yesterday, and the day before, and the day before that. "Thanks for your help, Mr. Walter."

He didn't say a word. He just smiled at Mrs. Walter with reassuring eyes and reached out for her hand. I looked at his eyes and saw the meaning of family and true love. I left Mrs. Walter alone with her husband and slowly walked away in silence, overwhelmed to witness love in its purest form.

Maryjo Relampagos Pulmano

A Single Act of Love

The hunger for love is much more difficult to remove than the hunger for bread.

Mother Teresa

His brief but tormented young life was punctuated by recurring visits to hospital emergency rooms for treatment of unexplained, questionable injuries too numerous to count. Despite the unsettled conditions of his family, this small boy always had a smile for everyone.

Only God knows what horrors he was made to endure.

The responsible adults who were supposed to be caring for him and providing love couldn't control their own anger, impulses and frustrations. The family, friends and social system that was intended to protect this young lad failed him miserably. He shouldn't have been allowed to slip through the cracks, but somehow, in this imperfect world, he did.

On his last hospital admission, this battered and wounded youngster received exceptional care and experienced perhaps some of the only loving and caring moments of comfort and safety he would know in his abbreviated life.

One evening, the nurse who was taking care of this broken four-year-old boy climbed into his bed, lay down next to him and cuddled him close to her heart. She gently stroked his forehead and sang soft lullabies in his ear until he fell asleep. That night he closed his tiny eyes for the last time.

Those beautiful lullabies were the last sounds he would ever hear.

This little boy passed into the next life surrounded by love—the love that he so desperately needed and deserved in this life. There is a Bible passage that says, "Whatsoever you do to the least of my brothers, you do unto me." By her actions, this nurse clearly demonstrated the powerful significance of these words.

A single act of love, performed by one special nurse who opened her heart and soul, made a big difference to this precious little angel.

Laura Hayes Lagana

My Promise

When love and skill work together, expect a masterpiece.

John Ruskin

I was working as a house supervisor in a small, rural hospital on a bitter cold Midwestern winter in 1992. I wasn't even supposed to be working the evening shift, but had agreed to swap with a colleague who needed the night off.

Among my many duties was to assist in the emergency room if our lone ER nurse needed help. My pager echoed down the hallway that quiet evening, and I picked up the nearest house phone.

"I need your help now," Nancy said urgently. "We have an ambulance out on a little boy. Not many details, but it doesn't sound good. He was found outside in a snow bank, and the first responders have started CPR."

My heart sank. It was thirty degrees below zero with windchill. The child didn't have a chance.

I immediately thought of my own little three-year-old

boy. It seemed he was always on my mind. He'd been so distant for such a young child, disappearing into his room for hours to read his books. If I tried to sit down and read with him, he threw the book and left the room. I was his mother and loved him more than anything in this world, but he seemed to prefer his silence to my songs. He preferred aloneness to my love.

My attention snapped back as I entered the emergency room. The ambulance was just pulling up, and when the gurney rolled into the ER it was met with dead silence. CPR was in progress. The blond boy lay lifeless and pale, his blue eyes staring vacantly, pupils fixed and dilated. His perfect little hands were frozen so solid, we could not unclench his fists. Because of the circumstances, we were obligated to continue CPR until his core body temperature was raised. I had heard of cases of hypothermia where children were revived, but no one in the room seemed to hold any hope of bringing back this little boy.

The next hour passed quickly as cut-down IVs, chest tubes, peritoneal lavage and urinary catheters all infused warmed saline into his still, frozen body. I stood silently over him, tears running down my cheeks, as I prayed silently for him and his family. I could not even begin to understand the pain his parents were experiencing, and all I could do was bring them periodic reports that we were doing all we could.

He was the same age as my little boy, with the same beautiful blue eyes and blond hair. I thought of how much I loved my son and tried to remember the last time I told him I loved him so. What if he died tonight? Would he die knowing how much I loved him? I realized, watching a group of doctors and nurses desperately trying to do the impossible, that I hadn't even hugged him before leaving for work. And I deeply regretted that now.

Then a miracle occurred. We gave no medicine; we gave no electrical shocks to the heart. All we did was warm him up. His heart began to beat. Slowly at first and then more steadily. Ten beats a minute. Then twenty. We thought about adrenaline, but the physician decided against it. Within two minutes, we had a pulse. In ten minutes, his color turned a beautiful shade of pink and his pupils became reactive.

Stunned silence permeated the room, and I was in awe knowing I had received a very special invitation to witness a miracle.

Over the next few months the child made a full recovery. Other than frostbite to his toes, he was miraculously unharmed.

I made a promise to myself that night. A promise to never again let a day go by that I didn't hug my son and tell him that I loved him. It no longer mattered if he returned my love or if he continued to push me away. He would never leave this Earth without knowing how much I loved him.

In the months and years that followed, I kept my promise. My son was diagnosed with autism shortly after I witnessed this miracle. He has done very well and is today a very happy, loving little boy. Thanks to my special invitation to witness the miracle that taught me unconditional love.

Linda C. Bird

Billy's Good-Bye Gift

You will find as you look back upon your life that the moments when you have truly lived are the moments when you have done things in the spirit of love.

Henry Drummond

When I moved from Ohio to Arkansas, I considered it a blessing. After living up north all of my life, I was ready for a change. My house had burned down, my husband left me after fourteen years, and my very existence had disappeared into a black hole. Moving to Arkansas, nearer my ailing mother, seemed to be a great idea. I had nothing to lose. However, I was not prepared for the gifts I was about to receive.

I was very grateful to land a job right away at a Christian hospital, working on surgery floors. Then one day I was sent up to oncology. I protested to deaf ears. You will work where you are needed, they told me. I thought it was dreadful. I could feel death everywhere, and my heart felt so heavy. Day after day, I was sent to the cancer floor.

To my amazement, after awhile I began to "need" to work on that floor. One day, I stood among my "babies" and realized that God had sent me here. This was my home. My patients were no longer room numbers—they had faces and names. I knew what they liked to eat, how many children they had, at what job they had spent most of their life working and how they felt about their cancer.

As with many nurses, I became close to these very special patients. I loved each and every one of them. At times, it was difficult keeping my emotions in check.

One day, a patient named Billy came to the floor. He was a large man with bone cancer and a great sense of humor. Though he was in great pain, he rarely complained. His loving wife watched over him with the greatest love one can imagine and made certain he received the best care. We all laughed and cried together, and shared family stories and jokes. They became part of our hospital family.

After coming in for chemo treatments and going back home several times, Billy's energy was spent. The last time he was admitted, he looked beaten. So did his wife. He was suffering so much that it was hard for all of us to care for him—we knew there was nothing much we could do. He was now terminal, and his pain so intense that no amount of medicine helped. I think every nurse cried for Billy and his family.

It was nearing Easter, and Billy had so many visitors it was hard for his wife to have any time alone with him. I felt so sorry for her. But she kept smiling.

One night, near the end of my shift, I made my last trip down the hallway and peeked in on Billy. I opened the door to his room very slowly so I wouldn't wake him. The light from the hall shone into the room and lit it up like moonlight. I looked towards the bed and a little gasp escaped from my mouth. There was Billy, lying on his back, the position I knew was most painful for him. Next to him lay his wife, nestled in the pit of his arm, all curled up like a baby deer next to its mother. She was sleeping so soundly, I could hear little whistles coming from her mouth. I stood there, like an intruder. My feet would not move. As I tried to leave, Billy opened his eyes. He smiled a crooked smile and winked at me as if to say, "It's okay."

I closed the door, walked up the now empty hallway, and went to the chapel. I cried a few minutes then thanked God for blessing me with this very special moment.

Billy died soon after that night, but not before he gave me new eyes and a special good-bye gift.

Susan Spence

3

DEFINING MOMENTS

Life becomes harder for us when we live for others, but it also becomes richer and happier.

Albert Schweitzer

All Our Hearts Have to Offer

Death and Love are the two wings that bear the good man to heaven.

Michelangelo

No classroom course I ever took prepared me for one of the most difficult lessons I learned during my nursing career. Feeling fully confident and armed with cutting-edge knowledge of critical care, I embarked into the incredibly exciting field of flight nursing. Life on the helicopter was full of ups and downs—literally. I was constantly placed in a pivotal position impacting the way families dealt with instantaneous life-changing events.

During my first pregnancy, I worked with a pediatric resident who predicted my outlook on my patients would change dramatically when I gave birth to my child. I'd always felt I had compassion for my patients and their families, but her words proved prophetic and have echoed in my mind and heart many times since that day in 1984.

I was called to a small emergency room to airlift a five-month-old who had stopped breathing. I was immediately confronted by a hysterical mother, distraught over the possibility that she had somehow caused this catastrophe. She desperately looked to me for reassurance that all would be well. Based on the lab values, X rays and the child's condition, I could not promise that. In those days, our helicopters were much too small to accommodate a parent, and this child was so critically ill and in need of advanced care, that it became a "scoop and run" situation.

In my haste, I failed to allow a momentary interaction between mother and child. I cuddled the little girl in my arms, and we flew with all the speed the machine could muster to the awaiting pediatric critical-care facility. Her condition proved too critical, and resuscitation attempts were futile. As I realized this sweet mother would never again have the chance to hold her live, breathing, warm baby, a haunting feeling pervaded my soul. A feeling I would not soon forget.

Since that day, and following the arrival of my four beautiful, healthy children, I have been faced with countless opportunities to extend healing to family members. My outlook on my patients has, in fact, changed dramatically. While I still carry charts, calculations, medications, equipment and skill, I have learned there truly is no replacement for the human touch. Since most of the patients I transport are extremely critical, the window of opportunity for technology passes for many of them. Yet families still count on me and countless other flight programs around the world to deliver one last miracle. Thankfully, a God-given feeling of compassion encircles me when I realize the time has come to help heal the nurturers. Now I allow human contact to begin the healing process for family members.

I spent time with a distraught father several days after his daughter was killed in an accident. He came to pick up her purse, left in the back of the helicopter. He begged to know of her last words, to know if she suffered, to know if there was anything he could have done to change the tragic outcome. Tears flowed freely as I reassured him she had been in good hands and given every opportunity available to her. We parted having given each other a small measure of comfort.

I arrived to pick up a three-year-old who had been found submerged in the family pool. Fourteen family members cried out, "Thank God, they're here to save our baby!" A review of his condition soon revealed his little body and brain had been deprived of life-sustaining oxygen for too long a period. His six-year-old sister stepped forward with his stuffed animal; he needed it with him at all times. Kisses were given, touching encouraged, cautions for them to drive safely issued, and we flew to the receiving facility, teddy bear in tow. Gratefully, the little boy survived long enough for the family to arrive. Seeing it was hopeless, the father begged to hold him one last time "while he still feels alive and warm." We disconnected all technology and wrapped his son snugly in a blanket for his daddy to spend precious moments embracing him.

I broke all the rules when I brought family members past the yellow "Caution" tape so they could touch and whisper hasty good-byes before departing from highway accidents, certain they will never again see their loved ones alive. I violated the posted hospital visiting rules and carried small children to their mother's side to kiss, touch, cry and lie next to mommy on the way out to the helicopter.

I'm asked by patients, en route to trauma centers, the status of their husband, wife, friend or sibling. The looks in their eyes indicate their knowledge of the inevitable, and my heart aches as I try to soften the truth.

How grateful I am for all that medicine has to offer, for living in a time when technology changes as rapidly as the second hand ticks. But I am more grateful for those opportunities when soul touches soul, when communication is perfect despite the silence, and when the only thing I have to offer family members is one last memory with their loved ones.

Sixteen years have passed since I listened to words that would shape my care of patients. I have witnessed untold tragedies, but through it all my solace has been the gift of a last touch, a last kiss, a last word, and the hope that these moments would alleviate some of the suffering. I pray that other caregivers will learn this lesson sooner than I did and extend not only all that technology has to offer, but all that our hearts have to offer, as well.

Janie K. Ford

The Touch of Kindness

No love, no friendship can cross the path of our
destiny without leaving some mark on it forever.

François Mauriac

"Why do you want to be a nurse, Patricia?"

The two nursing instructors and the dean of nursing sat at their table, squarely facing me as I sat on my hard, straight-backed wooden chair facing them. "Two thousand young people have applied to our program." The dean's voice came from across the room, "and we will select sixty of them. Tell us why we should choose you." She folded her hands and looked up at me from the stack of application forms.

I hesitated a moment, wondering what the other applicants sitting in this same chair had answered. What did they say that was music to the instructors' ears? I tried hard to imagine what they wanted to hear from me.

I thought my reason for wanting to be a nurse sounded simple and silly, so I hesitated and was quiet. It seemed laughable that I should be applying to nursing school at all. During my childhood I was terrified of doctors, nurses and hospitals. I dreaded every office visit even for an annual checkup! So it was a surprise to many that I now had the desire to become that which I had formerly done my best to avoid. But an incident from my childhood was compelling me, and I drew upon that now.

When I was six years old, my parents were told I needed to be admitted to the hospital for some "tests." They drove me to the children's hospital across town on a cold gray Sunday afternoon. I looked up at the imposing building and then quickly hid my face in my mother's sleeve. I tried to resist going in, but my mother and father were holding my hands and I was whisked along against my will.

We exited the elevator, and my parents led me down a long hallway. When we came to a large room that was divided into cubicles, we stopped. We were directed to one of the cubicles by a stern gray-haired nurse who pointed here and there, showing us where my suitcase should go, where my pajamas and robe should hang, where the button was to press so a nurse would come when we wanted.

My father went downstairs then, and my mother tried to make me feel at home. The gray-haired nurse soon brought a supper tray, but I couldn't eat. Everything here was so different from what I was used to. So my mother picked at the food on my tray while she tried to entertain me. She tried to cheer me by talking about how some of the children there were very sick, and it was nice that I was only there for "tests" and would be able to come home soon.

I wondered why my mother didn't have a suitcase with her. Wouldn't she need some pajamas and a robe, too? After the nurse took the tray away, I learned why. My parents were not allowed to stay with me. They were going home, and I was staying there. They were leaving me, and I'd never been away from them before. As my mother slipped into her coat and prepared to leave, I began to cry.

"No, no, Mama, please don't go, please don't leave me!" I begged. She just smiled slightly and told me she'd be back tomorrow, to be a good girl and do what the nurses told me.

As I listened to her footsteps fade away, I turned over in my bed and curled up in a tight little ball, facing away from the door. I tried to think of something happy. I tried to think of songs I liked to sing. I tried to remember the faces of all my stuffed animals at home. I thought hard, but my thoughts were interrupted by another nurse who said firmly, "Time for bed."

I sat up then, and she removed my robe and pajamas and dressed me in a hospital gown. I lay back down and curled up tighter than ever and wept. The lights were turned out then, and I lay awake in the dark.

Much later, I heard someone enter the room, where I still whimpered in my bed. "You're not asleep yet?" a pleasant, quiet voice asked.

"I can't sleep," I said, trembling.

"Sit up a minute and talk to me," the voice coaxed. I sat up then, and in the dim light I could see it was a nurse, but not one I had seen before.

"I want to go home," I said, sobbing again. The nurse reached forward and held me as I cried. "I think I'm going to be sick," I moaned, and my stomach began to heave.

She held a basin in front of me and wiped my face gently with a damp washcloth. She cradled me then as I calmed down, and I lay limp against her shoulder as she rocked me back and forth.

After what seemed like a very long time, she looked down at me and said, "I have some work to do now, so I can't stay with you." Seeing my dejected look, she added, "But maybe you could come and be with me. Let's see."

In the hallway there were low wooden wagons with

mattresses and pillows that the nurses used to take some of the children outside for some fresh air. She brought one of these to my bedside and beckoned for me to get in. As she lifted me down to the wagon, I looked at her shiny name pin and read "Miss White."

Miss White wheeled me out to the nurses' station and parked the wagon by the desk. I watched as she sat and wrote, and every once in awhile she'd look over at me and smile. "Want something to drink now?" she asked. I nodded and sipped the apple juice she brought, and soon I drifted off to sleep. Early in the morning she rolled me back to my bed, and I was so tired that I hardly noticed when she told me good-bye.

My mother did come to see me later that day, and the next night was not quite as hard to bear. I had to stay in the hospital for only a few days before my brief ordeal was over. But I never forgot how terrified I felt, and I never forgot Miss White's kindness to a desperately lonely and scared little girl.

This incident ran quickly through my mind, and I thought for a moment before I answered the dean's question. Why did I want to be a nurse? I straightened up in my chair and lifted my chin and said, "Being a patient in a hospital is a frightening thing, for anyone. Some people conceal it better than others, but all patients are afraid. I remember being a frightened child in a hospital when I was only six, and there was a nurse there who was very kind to me. She was the one who made my stay bearable."

The room was quiet as I went on. "I have always remembered her, and I want to be the kind of nurse she was. I want to be the one who cheers up a frightened child, holds the hand of a lonely older person, soothes the anxiety of a nervous patient."

I was accepted to the nursing program and worked hard to learn the skills and techniques necessary to provide the best care for my patients. On graduation night as I stepped up to the stage to accept my diploma, I thought of Miss White and smiled. She would never know what a profound influence she'd had on me. She taught me the most important lessons in nursing. She taught me the significance of empathy for the patient and his or her plight, of compassion in easing the difficulty of another. What she gave to me was now my own to give, the gentle touch of kindness that makes the difference to our patients and to our world.

Tricia Caliguire

THE FAMILY CIRCUS   **By Bil Keane**

"I can't sleep in here very good 'cause I can't hear Daddy watchin' TV or Mommy doing the dishes or Barfy barking or PJ crying . . ."

Reprinted with permission from Bil Keane.

A Part of the Team

A teacher affects eternity; he can never tell where his influences stop.

Henry Adams

In the summer of 1945, my father directed a camp for inner-city children and teens. He hired two young women to be the nurses for that camping season. They allowed me to be their shadow, and I watched everything they did and listened to everything they said. I sat quietly in a corner of the infirmary each morning as campers came through for treatment of sore throats, cuts and bruises, poison ivy, mosquito bites and homesickness. Some days they even let me help clean up the infirmary after sick call. If I was really good, they took me with them on cabin visits to check on the sick campers.

My father was alone one morning when he drove a truckload of garbage to burn at the dump. When the trash was emptied from the truck, he lit a match and threw it onto the pile of rubble. He stepped back, expecting the garbage to slowly burn. He waited. No flame; nothing was burning. Dad bent over and lit another match.

An explosion wrapped him in flames.

He rolled alone on the ground to put out the flames, got into the truck and sped back to the campgrounds. He drove up the road toward the dining hall, blasting the horn. People came running from everywhere. Orders were shouted to those around. I watched, frightened and confused, hardly able to believe what was happening around me.

Suddenly, a station wagon came to a screeching halt right behind the garbage truck. The doors flew open and out jumped the two camp nurses. They guided my father into the back seat of the station wagon, got in the car and sat on either side of him, and wrapped his arms in wet towels. The car sped off to the nearest hospital emergency room where he was treated for several days.

When he returned to the camp, he resembled a mummy. His arms, hands, neck and head were covered with large white bandages, with only his mouth and eyes showing. His bed was moved into the living room of the family cottage where the two nurses and my mother cared for him day and night. Each day they removed the large white bandages from his arms and neck, treated the areas and applied fresh dressings to the wounds. Dad groaned with pain but never complained. When they finished this routine, he was always able to rest. That was the only time he could tolerate anyone touching him.

On the day he came home, I stood in the shadows of the room watching as they cared for him. I heard my name. One of the nurses was calling me. She told me they were giving me the responsibility of seeing that he had plenty to drink. I was also to feed him the meals the camp cook sent down to the cottage for him. So each day I sat at his bedside, ready to get whatever he needed. Sometimes he would have me read to him as he rested. Mother and the nurses praised me for being part of the team. Every day they told me my father was getting better because I gave him such "good nursing care." I felt pride and satisfaction in being able to do something for someone hurting.

Those feelings stayed with me forever. I wonder if those camp nurses knew how they influenced the life of an eight-year-old child. I wonder if they ever imagined the impact they had in molding my forty-year career in nursing—forty years as a member of healing teams.

Viola Ruelke Gommer

THE FAMILY CIRCUS By Bil Keane

"I wanna be a nurse, Mommy!
So when I grow up, can I go to nursery school?"

Reprinted with permission from Bil Keane.

To Care for Them

Knowledge comes, but wisdom lingers.

Alfred Lord Tennyson

It's funny how the most unexpected circumstances can change our lives forever. In April of 1991, my friend Jason was diagnosed with leukemia; we were in the seventh grade. I went to visit him a few times at the Miami Children's Hospital, and the first time I went there, I noticed something. Jason's room was filled with balloons and flowers; cards and pictures were scattered everywhere. People called him and visited him and wrote him letters. Something was always going on in his room; someone was always there for him. We came from a small town in the Florida Keys, and everyone was wonderful when it came to Jason. People who didn't even know him got together and sent get-well baskets. The town held blood drives in his honor. The support was endless.

Jason's room was at the end of the hall and visiting him meant walking by all the other rooms where the walls were bare. The televisions were turned off and the children lay quietly in their beds, alone, facing what I'm sure was the most frightening experience of their lives. Not all those children had what Jason had. That's where my uncle's idea came from.

When we got home after that visit, the two of us went to work. My uncle called on some people from our community for help, and he phoned the oncology ward of the hospital and got every child's name who was staying there. The next time the two of us went to visit Jason, we stepped on to that floor pushing a cart of buckets filled with candy, magazines, hats and games. The two of us wore multicolored beanie caps with propellers on them that spun around like the props to a helicopter as we walked.

We said hello to Jason and then made a procession down the hallway, stopping at every child's room, delivering the gifts that my uncle and the rest of our little community had donated. In each child's room, we hung a banner with his or her name on it, wishing each child a speedy recovery. The expressions on their faces were priceless.

We walked in, acknowledging the child by name, and at first they had no idea what we were doing in their room wearing those silly hats. When we started decorating their rooms and handing them their buckets of candy and toys, the smiles that spread across their faces were the biggest I've ever seen. To have interaction with someone, to know that someone cared about them, to know that they weren't alone, seemed to really make a difference to those children.

The last patient we planned to visit was in isolation, so my uncle and I were not allowed inside. A caring nurse donned the necessary garb and brought in the gifts we had for the little boy. The boy came to the door, looked out the window of it with a huge smile, and mouthed "thank you." It was a moment in my life that I will never forget.

My past experiences have led me to the place I currently find myself—finishing my first year as a nursing student. It has been exciting to learn about medicine and machines, how things work, and what to do when they don't work. Learning how to create a sterile field, change dressings, set up IV lines and administer meds are all so exciting to someone who is just starting off. Only, this is not the reason I decided to become a nurse.

There is more to our profession than beeps and clicks, procedures and results. We may not have the ability to "fix" everyone, but we definitely have the capability and responsibility to have compassion for them, to make them comfortable, to be their advocate, and to be the person who comes into their room and makes them feel like a human being.

I decided to become a nurse so that I would have the chance to feel the same as I did that day when I saw the life spring back into all those children when some attention was paid to them. A little smile, some small talk or a pat on the hand may be all our patients need to lift their spirits. I may be inexperienced and naive, but I do know that those children lit up when we came into their rooms. I also saw that the nurses who made them laugh, or took a minute to play with them, got the same reaction that we got from giving candy and games.

We need to bear in mind that while our patients need procedures done, they also need a warm touch. They may need tests run, but a soothing voice may be just as important to them.

When I graduate from school next year and enter the white-scrubbed and gloved world of medicine, I vow to remember that as a nurse, I will not only have the ability to give care to my patients, but also to care for them.

Christine Ehlers

In memory of Jason McGraw (1978-1991)
The Hip in 46B

The supreme happiness of life is the conviction that we are loved.

Victor Hugo

As medical caregivers in hospitals and nursing homes, we sometimes become a bit callous in how we identify our patients. I mean, after all, we do see lots of them. And over the years they seem to blur together a bit. How could we remember each name?

I learned how when I was a physical therapist starting a small private practice in a skilled nursing facility. We had minimal equipment, funding, personnel and space, but we were inspired by the rehabilitation possibilities in the elderly.

One day I asked my aide, Bobby, to go and get "the hip in 46B" because he had a repaired hip fracture and needed to walk in the parallel bars. She went off to retrieve him in his wheelchair.

Momentarily, Bobby returned and stated that "the hip

in 46B" did not want therapy today. I said, "Well, he has to become weight bearing. We need to work on his balance, and we need him down here in the parallel bars to do that. Please go ask him again."

A second time she went to convince him. Soon she returned stating, "He says he is not getting out of bed and is not coming to therapy today."

"Okay, I'll go down and talk to him," I said.

I will never forget walking into that lovely gentleman's room and suddenly seeing the man. The person. Next to him, on his nightstand, was a magazine my father used to receive, *The Nebraska Rancher and Farmer*. A book title read, *Who's Who in Hotel and Restaurant Management*. I picked it up to see his name honored there. He had been more important in his life than I would probably ever be in mine. And now he was confined to a bed in a room where all his choices had been taken from him: when to go to the bathroom, when and where to go to meals, when to go anywhere—including therapy. He had been stripped not only of his belongings, but also of his independence and self-worth. And now all he wanted to do was assert some sense of control over his own body; make a choice or two on his own time.

I took his hand. "Good morning, Mr. Carlson. What time would you like to go to therapy today?"

Linda McNeil

I Baptize You . . .

Blessed be the hand that prepares a pleasure for a child, for there is no saying when and where it may bloom forth.

Douglas Jerrold

Years ago I attended a Catholic nursing school, but no one in our class was Catholic. This posed a problem with some of the church doctrines. In our first year, the entire class almost missed being "capped" because we refused to do a procedure: baptize a fetus or person after death. Since we were all Baptist or Pentecostal, this was contrary to our religious beliefs.

As president of the class, I took the brunt of the lecture from Sister James Cecilia. "Miss Sanefsky, you knew this was a Catholic school when you applied. You should also have known that you would have to adhere to our teachings." I wasn't convinced, but I wanted my cap as much as my twenty-three other classmates did, so we compromised. We agreed to learn it if we could be assured we would never have to take part in this procedure.

Years went by. I married Harley and moved to Ohio where I worked in a small eighty-bed hospital. There were many Catholics employed there, so I never worried about having to perform last rites or baptisms until one stormy night.

The rain came down in buckets and lightning flashed as I worked second shift in the nursery. A woman came in and delivered two months prematurely, giving birth to a baby weighing two pounds and one ounce. We knew this little person had little chance of surviving. Our nursery was primitive. We had no neonatologists; only incubators, oxygen and prayer.

As the tempest raged, we worked to clear this little guy's lungs. All we knew to do to keep him alive was to keep the incubator at 98 degrees.

I took him to see his mother and her first words were, "I want him baptized." When I phoned her priest to come, he told me he had no transportation on this stormy night. He would be there first thing in the morning.

This gave us cause to panic. We knew this baby had a slim chance of surviving the night. I went back to the mother and let her know what the priest had said. She was devastated as she repeated the doctor's prediction that her baby may not be alive in the morning. Desperately, she begged me to baptize him. I paged my Catholic supervisor. She was off. I called all over the hospital. Not one single Catholic was on duty. It was falling back on me. I prayed, "Oh no, God, you know how I feel about this. I can't do it."

After talking to the mother once more and seeing her desperation, I conceded. I would baptize him "conditionally" as I was taught years before. I explained that I was not Catholic and how my faith viewed infant baptism. I told her I would do it if she really wanted me to, or we could pray that the baby live until the priest came in the morning. Adamantly, she insisted she wanted it done right then. So I proceeded to the nursery and the task I felt unprepared to do.

I prayed as I got a sterile medicine cup, sterile water and sterile cotton balls. Gently, I lifted this precious baby's head in the palm of my hand. With my other hand, I poured the sterile water over his head. "Joseph Sanchez, I baptize you, conditionally, in the name of the Father, the Son and the Holy Spirit." With tears running down my face, I wiped this angelic little head with the sterile cotton, changed the wet towel beneath him and took him back to his mother.

Overwhelmed, she cradled this tiny gift of God in her arms. I knew then I had done the right thing. I brought peace to this young mother so she could give him back to God, if that was in the scheme of things.

The story doesn't end there. Over the months that followed, this baby became "Little Joe" to us in the nursery. Each day we prayed he would live through our shift, then we gave the responsibility to the next.

One afternoon, I was met in our staffing room with, "Little Joe had a bad day, and he may not live through the night." I prayed, "Please Lord, don't take him on my watch." I made rounds on all the babies in the nursery and came to the incubator. The temperature gauge read 80 degrees. The temperature had to be at a constant 98 degrees or he would die! I went around to the back of the incubator, and I found the electrical plug lying on the floor. I quickly plugged it back in, called the doctor and then my pastor. I asked him to pray. We worked frantically to bring Joey's temperature back up, placing warm towels on his body. Prayers went up to heaven for him. He lived through the night.

I was off for three days. When I came back, he was gone. He had reached five pounds and was sent home at three months of age. After having cared for him all those months, I was crushed I didn't get to say good-bye.

The Bible says, "Some plant, some water and then some harvest." I prayed that this little boy would grow and be nurtured in the love of God for he was indeed a miracle baby.

But the story doesn't end there, either. Years went by and then one night, my husband, Harley, came home from a men's church dinner. "Wait 'til you see what I have for you." In his hand was a picture of a young boy. On the back was this message:

> *Dear Ms. Houseman,*
>
> *My name is Joseph Sanchez. I am fourteen years old and weigh 140 pounds. Thank you for taking care of me when I was born.*
>
> *Little Joe.*

God puts us in places to do special things, and we may not always agree, but we better be obedient.

Beverly Houseman

CLOSE TO HOME   JOHN McPHERSON

"Sorry about the mix-up, Mr. Bixford.
We'll be moving you to a semi-private room shortly."

A Visit from an Angel

A patient came into my office this week to have a physical exam and to get a refill on high-blood-pressure medicine. My heart filled with great pity as she undressed, revealing a frail, stooped body. Every joint was deformed from years of arthritis. Her thinning hair was gray and lifeless; her brown eyes were clouded by cataracts.

As I asked her the usual questions, every answer she gave surprised me.

"No, I don't hurt much."

"Yes, I still cook and clean my little house."

"No, I don't sleep much, but that gives me more time to read my Bible."

I proceeded to talk to her about getting her cataracts removed and to accept a referral to an arthritis specialist. I pleaded with her to join the senior citizens group for companionship. As I knelt down to help her tie her worn, frayed shoes, I stressed how concerned I was about her living alone in the shape she was in. She took my hand in her crippled grasp.

"My little nurse," she said, "don't you believe in God?"

"Oh yes, Ma'am, I do."

"Well, believe in him a little harder and you won't worry about me so."

She limped out of my office with her paper sack for a purse, and for a moment I thought I saw angel wings on her back.

Sarah Webb Johnson

New Job

If you think about what you ought to do for other people, your character will take care of itself.

Woodrow Wilson

Finding a new job when I moved to another state proved to be more daunting than I'd anticipated. At the hospital closest to my home, there were no immediate openings. The nurse recruiter suggested I try the new adjoining continuing care facility. "They're always hard up for nurses," she mumbled under her breath as I left the office.

I'll bet, I thought to myself. In reality, it was a nursing home. Being called by another name didn't erase my dismal image about such places. I wasn't eager to "step down" to that type of nursing. However, I felt I owed the recruiter the courtesy of at least touring the place she'd offered.

A young woman from the office took me to the third floor. She explained that the residents were waiting to go to the dining room for their noon meal. I was appalled by what I saw. The hallway seemed endless and dark as a train tunnel. Wheelchairs containing the harnessed flesh of old people lined the walls. Heads bobbed, arms flailed and legs hung limply or kicked at random. Foreign sounds filled the air: grunts, groans, mutters, mumbles, sniffles and sobs.

Dejected faces stared into space. Pairs of eyes filled with loneliness followed us as we walked down the corridor. My tour guide cheerfully greeted each resident. Most responded with a timid smile. I was overwhelmed.

As we passed by one old woman, she reached out and grabbed my skirt. "Help me, help me," she chanted as she held me in a grip that was amazingly strong. I was tempted to pull away from her grasp and run to the quiet sanctuary of my car. Instead, I stood still. My conscience prodded me to look closely at her face. Suddenly, the cluster of residents became just this one. I leaned close and asked, "What is your name?"

"Rosemary," was the reply.

Her face was wrinkled and lined from years of valiant struggle. In her faded blue eyes, I saw tiny sparkles of hope. Revealing dentures too large for her face, she grinned and clutched my hand. I held her gnarled hand, laced with blue veins, in mine. As our hands connected, so did my heart. No longer were they pitiful old people, but elderly human beings worthy of my respect and understanding. Tomorrow I will be on duty at my new job. I'll do my best to give compassionate care to each one—starting with Rosemary.

Barbara A. Brady

The Depth of This Career

Have patience with all things, but chiefly have patience with yourself. Do not lose courage in considering your own imperfections, but instantly set about remedying them—every day a task anew.

St. Francis DeSales

I was such a young nurse, I had nothing in common with the grannies and grandpas on the orthopedic surgical floor. I was glad of that and glad to leave them at the end of my shift.

Nothing rattled me much, until I was assigned to the gangrene lady. Both her calves were decaying. In days past, I'd helped other nurses change her dressings. I held her heels up while the attending nurse irrigated the wounds and wrapped the bandages. I tried to look out the window. The stench was unbelievable. I breathed from the corner of my mouth to avoid it. After I left the room, the sickening smell clung to my clothes.

I knew I'd been lucky not to get the gangrene lady until

now. Lucky, or else the charge nurse had been kind to me because I was new. In any case, it was my turn today, and I would handle it, though the mere thought of those wounds made me cringe.

"She had her dressings done at six," the charge nurse told me, "and she's going to surgery at ten."

Wow—so I didn't have to mess with her legs. What luck. The night nurse even got her to sign the surgical consent for a double amputation above the knees. What a relief. I could be practically stress-free, just finish the paperwork.

I held my breath against the odor as I entered her room. "How you doing there, Mrs. Palmer?"

"Hmm?" She glanced at me and looked away. She was thin, her skin browned by the sun and robbed of moisture. Her long white hair fanned out behind her head. Long hair on an old woman was in a way charming, like a lady at court in more chivalrous times. In another way it seemed strange, because all her peers had cut theirs short, and she still grasped at youth and vanity.

I helped her sit forward and placed my stethoscope against her back. "Take a deep breath," I said. I decided not to peel back the covers to check her legs. No need. She'd have fresh healthy stumps this afternoon.

"Surgery's at ten o'clock," I said. "You're going to feel a lot better by tomorrow."

"Why do you say that?" She turned her eyes on me. "My legs don't hurt."

"You'll be healthier."

"Hmm."

"It's all for the best. There's really no other choice. They'll teach you how to walk again." I gave her hand a quick squeeze.

Tears welled up in her eyes. This I couldn't handle.

"I'll be back in a little while," I blurted and went to pass pills to my other patients.

Dolores was working my side of the hall that day. She was an older nurse, competent in every way, though she wore false eyelashes and a big poofy hairdo with ringlets. I always felt apprehensive working alongside her because she was a much better nurse than I. She gave me occasional suggestions. She was always right. I hated to be wrong. I knew I was still learning, but it disturbed me to be corrected by one whose appearance I considered ridiculous.

It was nine o'clock when Dolores caught me in the hall and asked how my morning was.

"Good," I replied. "I've got everything under control."

Dolores smiled as we walked toward the nurses' station. I had an itch to get away.

"How about that surgery?" she asked softly. "Emma Palmer?"

"It's all ready."

"I took care of Emma yesterday," said Dolores. "Such a shame, what's happening to her."

We both glanced into Palmer's room. To my embarrassment, she was dangling at the foot of her bed, weeping and watching the hallway for help.

"Oh, she's crying!" Dolores walked right into the room as if pulled by a magnet.

I followed reluctantly. What was I supposed to do now? I couldn't stop her tears.

"Here, Honey, let's put your feet up." Dolores put one arm around Palmer's neck, the other arm under her bandaged legs, and scooped her gently into bed.

I couldn't imagine getting that close to those legs with my bare arms.

"Didn't your family come to see you yet?" Dolores asked.

"N-no," she sniffled. "I don't have any family."

"Oh, Honey!" Dolores sat down on the mattress and hugged her close.

Emma Palmer sobbed aloud and hung her head on Dolores' shoulder.

I stepped back and swallowed.

"Oh, Emma." Dolores began to rock her soothingly. "It's all right. No, it's really not all right, is it?"

Emma let loose a bigger flood of tears. Her mouth opened wide but speechless.

I could hardly tolerate all the pain in that room, all the loss Emma had to bear.

"Yeah, it's the pits, it sure is," said Dolores, her strong arms wrapped around those frail shoulders.

"It . . . is," said Emma.

"But you know your legs are so far gone, Honey, you're better off without them." Dolores stroked her back again and again.

Emma's intake of breath was staccato from weeping. Dolores kept rocking her, comforting her until she calmed.

Emma said, "How will I manage, at my age?"

"Oh, you'd be surprised. They've got wonderful prosthetics these days."

Dolores leaned back and looked at Emma. Her hands gently brushed down from Emma's shoulders to her fingers. "It will work out."

Emma cried. "How?"

I felt awkward and useless. I began to understand the depth of this career, and how shallow I had chosen to make it. Would I ever be able to give from the heart as much as Dolores did, so easily, so naturally?

I patted Emma's leg. "I know how. I'll help you."

Diane Stallings

How Could I Stay in This Profession?

In my early years as a relatively new graduate R.N. working in neurotrama intensive care unit (ICU), I hoped to save the world. While it was exciting to see the young trauma victims make rapid recoveries from their comas, it was devastating to work with those who did not.

I stood at the bedside of a young comatose car-accident victim and performed passive range-of-motion exercises on her extremities, while playing tapes of her three-year-old son talking to her. The chief neurosurgical resident entered and blurted out sarcastically, "What are you doing?"

"I'm allowing her brain to process her child's voice as best as her neurons can, while I speak softly to her and play tapes. And I'm doing my best to be sure her joints remain limber so she can walk again."

He laughed at me. "She will never walk again! You're wasting your time. As a matter of fact, we are taking her off the ventilator tomorrow, and if she breathes on her own she will be transferred out of ICU to the neurosurgery floor where she will most likely die."

Something didn't seem right to me. It was too soon after her injury. They needed to give her a chance. She had damage to the axons of the neurons. In my limited experience, I knew most of those patients did poorly. But some did not. CAT scans were the main diagnostic study at the time, and I knew it was difficult to assess how badly the neurons were damaged.

I contacted my head nurse to tell her I disagreed with the neurosurgeon's decision. Then the patient's family begged me to help them fight to keep her in the ICU a little longer. I don't know who I thought I was, fighting orders of the powerful, well-known attending neurosurgeon, especially since I was just a new grad. We succeeded in delaying her transfer out of the ICU until we could wean her slowly off the ventilator. She was eventually transferred out of the unit when she was stable enough—much later than the neurosurgeon advised.

As I heard stories of her being in a chronic vegetative comatose state, I began to feel stupid for disagreeing with her doctor. Who was I to challenge one so well known for his brain-injury research? Would it have been more merciful to have just let her go?

How could I stay in this profession? I started looking at law school for a career change.

Months later, I was on duty in ICU and thinking about quitting when someone asked, "Are you Kathy?"

I looked up as a young woman I didn't recognize threw her arms around me.

"Yes."

"Thank you for everything you did! I heard you would not allow them to just let me die."

I stood, still perplexed, until I saw her family come around the corner with big smiles on their faces. Without the intracranial pressure monitor in her head and the endotrachial tube in her mouth, I hadn't recognized her.

Her hair had grown in beautifully and she was walking on her own. I was so glad I'd done those range-of-motion exercises! I was glad I had fought for her. But most of all, I was glad I had done what she'd wanted me to do.

She and her family gave me a lovely necklace with my initial and a diamond on it. As they walked out the door of the ICU, I had a sense of renewed strength and the emotional energy I needed as I looked at the current comatose trauma patients.

Later, her neurosurgeon made rounds. He reviewed a chart and asked me, seriously, "When do you think this one will be ready to be transferred out of the ICU?"

The law-school applications were quickly replaced by applications for graduate schools of nursing.

How could I leave this profession?

Kathleen Brewer-Smyth

Reprinted by permission of John Wise, R.N.

Women in the Military

All these were honored in their generations
and were the glory of their times.

Ecclesiasticus 44:7

The first military women to arrive in Vietnam were
nurses, in 1956. As the American presence in Southeast
Asia grew, so, too, did the number of young women who
served. In all, nearly eight thousand military women were
there, along with thousands more who served in the civil-
ian sector.

Eighty-three percent of us were nurses; the rest held
positions in special services, supply, air-traffic control,
cartography, the USO, American Red Cross and many
other jobs in support of our combat troops.

We were all fairly young when we volunteered to serve
our country. And many of us were woefully naive in
believing our recruiters' promises; mainly that we could
be stationed anywhere in the world that we wanted, and
that Vietnam was "strictly voluntary."

Still, when our orders arrived sending us to war, most

of us believed in our hearts that we were needed, that what we were doing was important, and that it was our duty to go. We did our jobs, facing the perils of enemy fire, horrific heat and humidity, disease, insects, isolation, long work hours and sleepless nights. Then we managed to pull ourselves together, dab some perfume behind our ears and do it all again the next day.

We learned a lot about ourselves. We discovered our strengths and tried to survive our weaknesses. We were ordinary young women trying to function in the most extraordinary of circumstances; dealing in life and death and seeking not just to survive, but to understand.

We did the best we could with who we were and what we had. And daily we collected our memories and stored them away someplace safe, out of our conscious minds where we thought, "I'll deal with this later."

And after a year, we came home, back to "The World." In one plane ride, we went from war to peace. In one year, we had gone from childhood to irrevocable adulthood. We knew we had changed, that our lives would never be the same, and that we could never explain any of it to the folks back home. We couldn't, and we didn't. For as unacceptable as it was for the guys to talk about the war when they came home, no one wanted to acknowledge that young women had been there. Even as the Women's Movement was making its voice heard, the underlying message was clear: "Nice girls wouldn't have gone to war."

So we came home quietly, went back to our homes, our families, our jobs and never spoke about the war to anybody. Many of us quit nursing and never knew why. Some of us had recurring nightmares, flashbacks, unexplained illnesses, depression, or abused drugs or alcohol. Many women applied themselves with a fury to school, attaining one degree after another, to work, rising to the top leadership positions in their companies, to their church, their social organizations, their families—anything to avoid the memories they had stored away "to think about later." The memories had created a deep, impenetrable wound that needed to be healed.

In 1982, the initial healing ground was laid in the form of the Vietnam Veterans Memorial—The Wall. The women, just like men who had served, were drawn to it. The healing power of that sacred place is evident to all who have been there. We could go to The Wall, and mourn, and cry, and reach out for comfort if we chose, and yet it was so easy to be invisible there.

Women simply weren't recognized as veterans.

Then, on Veterans Day 1993, the Vietnam Women's Memorial is dedicated in Washington, D.C. Thousands of women vets attend, and we are overwhelmed. We lead the parade: the nurses, Red Cross workers, entertainers, women who worked in administration, logistics and intelligence. The streets are lined with people applauding and crying. A vet sits high up in a tree yelling, "Thank you! Thank you!" A man in a flight suit stands for over two hours at attention, saluting as the women pass by. People hand us flowers and hug us. One G.I. has a picture of his nurse taken "July 1964." He is trying to find her.

We find each other. We know, at last, that we are not alone; that we are not crazy or paranoid, but that we have a lot of work to do in order to heal. We talk to each other and find comfort as well as pain in our words and our tears. Words and tears, that now, finally we share. Now, after so many years, the process has finally begun, and we hold each other close and say, "Welcome home!"

Janis Nark

4

ON TEACHING AND LEARNING

True teaching is only achieved by example.

Plato

Reprinted by permission of Benita Epstein.

Diabetic Teaching

No tempting form of error is without some latent charm derived from truth.

Sir Arthur Keith

As a part of the discharge teaching, the newly diagnosed diabetic patient was taught how to give his own insulin. The nurse who had been giving him the injections during his hospital stay instructed him on preparing the insulin syringe, then gave him the equipment and an orange to use to practice the technique. She also instructed him about diet, activity and monitoring his blood sugar, as well as what to do if his blood sugar was too high or too low. He had no questions when he was discharged and said he felt confident in administering his own insulin.

At his next doctor's appointment, his blood sugar was very high. The doctor asked him if he took his insulin every day as instructed and if he followed his prescribed diet. The patient said he knew, from the diet teaching he received from the nurse in the hospital, that the juice of the orange was important in controlling his blood sugar. Then he proudly described his insulin administration technique: He drew up the insulin, injected it into an orange every morning and ate the orange.

Johanna Tracy

"That's not the sliding scale I ordered!"

First Injection

He who laughs, lasts.

Norwegian Proverb

From the time I was four years old, I announced to anyone who asked, "When I grow up, I'm going to be a nurse." My parents tried to nurture this dream. They would surprise me with little nurse's kits. Contained in a small plastic case latched at the top was all the equipment needed to be a nurse: a thermometer permanently marked to 98.6, a pill bottle filled with candy (which would be gone in two hours), a stethoscope that didn't work and, best of all, a syringe.

I loved that syringe. I would spend hours filling it up with water and "injecting" my little sister. I would "inject" the family dog and a very reluctant cat. No other single function represented nursing to me as well as giving injections. To me, giving shots was the epitome of what nurses do.

You can imagine my excitement, therefore, when we reached the part of my nurses' training where we learned injections. I studied the techniques carefully and practiced on peaches. I practiced so much that the fruit at my house had little water blisters all over that looked like scabies. I participated in the "return demonstration" with my fellow nursing students. I always claimed that my partner's injection was painless so that she would make a similar claim when it was my turn.

The following week, I began my emergency room rotation at Penrose Hospital in Colorado Springs. One day, a handsome, tanned construction worker was admitted with a large laceration on his right arm. About six feet, five inches tall, 250 pounds, he had huge muscles and a grin to match. "I just sliced this a little with some sheet metal, Ma'am," he reported. He lay on the exam table while the doctor sutured him with a dozen stitches. He listened intently while the doctor gave instructions for wound care.

And then the magical moment occurred. The doctor turned to me and said, "Nurse Bartlein, would you please give this gentleman a tetanus shot?" *My big chance!* A real injection on a real patient. I practically floated on air as I scrambled to the refrigerator and took out the tetanus vaccine. I carefully drew up the prescribed amount and returned to the patient. I meticulously swabbed the site with an alcohol wipe and then expertly darted that needle deep into the deltoid muscle. I aspirated as taught and slowly injected the vaccine.

With a grin, the construction worker said, "Thank you, Ma'am" and stood up. I winked at him, and he winked at me. He stood there for a minute and promptly crumpled to the floor unconscious. *Oh, my God, I killed him! My first injection and I killed the patient.* My impulse was to run out the door as far into the mountains as possible. *Forget about being a nurse, forget about injections, I'll live off the land. No one will ever find me.*

Everyone else came running and slowly helped the

patient to his feet. The doctor could see that I was quite shaken. He reassured me with a smile and said, "Don't worry, he's fine. The big ones always faint!"

Barbara Bartlein

CLOSE TO HOME   JOHN McPHERSON

"Dr. Bigford is trying out a new inoculation method he found out about when he was traveling in Borneo."

Peppy

Happiness is a warm puppy.

Charles M. Schulz

I was a new graduate nurse, on probation in my first job, when I met Mrs. Oldman, a charming lady of about eighty who'd never been ill or in a hospital.

One day, I saw her staring outside with tears in her eyes.

"Are you in pain?" I asked.

She looked up, startled, and shook her head. Smiling, she apologized. "No, I'm just silly. I'm lonesome for Peppy. I must be getting senile to cry for a little dog, but he's always around me at home. I forget he's not human. I talk so much to him, and somehow he gives me the impression that he understands me." She wiped her eyes and looked helplessly up at me. "Do you think I'm silly?"

"Not at all," I assured her.

"I'd do anything if I could see and hold him for a moment." She questioned me with her eyes. Reading the hopelessness in my response, she said tonelessly, "No, I guess it's impossible."

"Some people are allergic to dogs," I tried to explain, visualizing a dozen dogs, cats and heaven-knows-what other pets chasing each other under the beds during visiting hours.

She nodded sadly. "Of course."

After that crying spell, she favored me with stories about Peppy. Her neighbor, Mrs. Freund, was taking care of him and claimed he knew she'd been in the hospital. Wasn't that smart? Then she said sadly, "Yes, Peppy, he misses me. I miss him."

She grew despondent as the days passed. I tried everything to draw her out and cheer her, but to no avail. Even the other ladies in the ward noticed my efforts and Mrs. Oldman's silence. They offered snacks, refreshments and suggested they play cards with her. She thanked them gratefully, but her eyes had that lost expression and she politely refused everything. Patients came and went every day, and soon Mrs. Oldman was an old-timer, and one who'd grown dear to me. I'd often been told that a person could die if he or she lost the will to live. I feared Mrs. Oldman would give up and die if I didn't find something to give her life meaning, a reason to live. It was then I thought of Peppy. Taking my camera, I went to Mrs. Freund's house to take a picture of him. Surely that would cheer her.

Peppy sat demurely as he was photographed. No doubt the little, black, fuzzy fellow had once been lively in his youth, but now he sat with his head on his paws staring out into nowhere.

"Poor guy," Mrs. Freund said, "he is so lonesome he could die. He hardly eats or drinks. He sits and stares out the window and whines softly for her." She looked at me beseechingly. "It would help them both if he could visit Mrs. Oldman." I shook my head. Mrs. Freund tried again. "How about just taking him to the courtyard so she can see him from her window?"

"Let's try it," I said enthusiastically. "Come between three and four tomorrow. All the head nurses will be at a meeting and I'll be in charge."

I told her to put Peppy in a shopping bag to pass the attendants at the entrance. Mrs. Freund was delighted. "Aren't we glad she doesn't own a Great Dane or a St. Bernard?"

The next day I could hardly wait for Mrs. Green to leave for the meeting. Visitors ambled into the ward. Everyone had company but Mrs. Oldman.

"Want me to pull your curtains around your bed so you have some privacy?" I suggested, knowing how she felt about the pitying stares from visitors.

"Yes," she muttered.

I closed the curtain, wondering if our plan would succeed and if Mrs. Freund would manage to keep Peppy quiet in her bag while passing by the two attendants at the main entrance. I had not dared to tell Mrs. Oldman of our plan, fearing it might fail.

My heart lifted when I saw the door of the courtyard open and Mrs. Freund lugging her shopping bag. She ambled casually around the flower border, looking right and left with a mischievous expression, as if violating some holy laws. Mrs. Oldman didn't seem to notice I'd blocked her view from the window. Mrs. Freund tapped the window lightly then reached into her shopping bag. I stood back to watch Mrs. Oldman's face. Never in my life will I forget that moment. At once she rose up, her face reddened, her eyes sparkled, and her voice broke as she cried, "Peppy! Peppy!"

"Shush—shush." I tried to keep her quiet. Outside the window Peppy jumped and whined and, before realizing what I was doing, I opened the window and lifted the little dog out of the bag and into her outstretched arms.

Mrs. Freund stood with her shopping bag wide open, beaming as if she'd seen a miracle, or rather, created one.

But then my heart bunched up in alarm for I heard the voice of Mrs. Green. No doubt she was looking for me.

"Quick, he has to go now." I wrestled the struggling dog back into the shopping bag outside the window.

I could hear Mrs. Green's firm step and voice as she shouted, "What do I hear? Is there a dog on the ward?"

Quickly, I grabbed Mrs. Oldman's bedpan and stepped outside the curtain, trying to look busy and professional as I walked past Mrs. Green. "Back so soon?" I asked cheerfully.

"I thought I heard a dog," she muttered, as if questioning me.

I answered with studied indifference. "Maybe a stray dog in the courtyard."

Without a word she followed me out of the ward and into the utility room. I stopped short. The bedpan was empty. I hesitated. Mrs. Green waited. I didn't know for what. I dared not show that the bedpan was empty for fear of blowing my cover. The silence grew, and my thoughts raced. Would I be reported to the director of nursing for breaking the law? I was still in my probation months. My mouth and throat felt so dry, I thought I might choke.

Mrs. Green didn't look at me as she spoke. "Rules and regulations in a hospital are made for a reason. There are exceptions, though, and while I am against secrecy and breaking rules, there are times that it proves a better policy."

I nodded sheepishly. When a patient's call light sounded, I jumped. Mrs. Green said, "Take your bedpan. Mrs. Oldman likely needs it."

She opened the door for me, and I hurried out into the ward, utterly perplexed. Mrs. Oldman had already bubbled joyfully to all about Peppy's visit and how smart he was. I begged the other patients to keep his visit a secret, lest I lose my job. They all kept their solemn bond and that secret made them special friends with Mrs. Oldman. She thrived under their affection. She regained her interest and confidence in the future. She exercised with such eagerness and determination, it shamed people half her age.

Finally, she left the hospital, welcomed by a joyfully dancing and yelping Peppy.

Mrs. Green never mentioned the dog's visit to me, but when I occasionally had to break rules for the sake of a patient, she was always mysteriously absent.

Lini R. Grol

"In obedience school he learned to HEAL."

Reprinted by permission of Benita Epstein.

A Healing Truth

God offers to every mind its choice between truth and repose. Take which you please; you can never have both.

Ralph Waldo Emerson

I was seventeen years old, in my first year of nursing school, and moonlighting evening shifts as an emergency-room assistant. When the ER supervisor said, "Virginia! Take a gurney out to the chopper, STAT," I jumped and shook like an aspen leaf. I had never retrieved a patient from a helicopter before. Four of us rushed two gurneys out to the waiting helicopter.

My head spun as the wind and noise of the whirring blades drowned out orders shouted by the nurses and paramedics. Two piles of oily black rags were placed on the gurneys, and we raced back to the ER as fast as the rough asphalt would allow.

Still in a daze, I slowly realized the black rags were two burn victims, a mother and her nine-year-old daughter. They had been driving through the canyon when an oil tanker jackknifed in front of them and burst into flames, turning the canyon into a fiery inferno. The two had managed to crawl through flames up the side of the canyon where the helicopter rescued them some time later.

These were the first burn victims I'd ever seen. The little girl's left ear was partially burned away. She looked like a horrid pink and black plastic doll. Sickened by the smell of burnt flesh and hair, I initially wanted to just get away from the horror. But by the time we sent them to ICU, I was even more determined to be a nurse.

On another assignment a few weeks later, I was called to special duty to care for an unmanageable pediatric patient in four-point restraints. The charge nurse told me the child was spitting, swearing and biting anyone who came near her. Her family was at their wits' end, yet asked that sedation be used sparingly, since it made her so groggy. The young girl hadn't been bathed for two days.

With a sinking heart, I followed the charge nurse down a corridor that echoed with the child's curses. I opened the door timidly and was struck in the face with spittle hurled by a matted, naked creature hissing under a canvas restraining jacket. The jacket was tangled under her chin and armpits, exposing her defiant kicking and thrashing. A wrinkled dressing partially covered her left ear. In shocked dismay, I realized this haunted creature was the little burn victim I had retrieved from the helicopter.

The charge nurse told me the child had recovered with only a shriveling of her left ear, but her mother had died after three days in the ICU.

"Whatever you do, don't tell her that her mother is dead," she ordered as she handed me the chart in the hall. "Her family is trying to break the news to her gently, but she won't listen."

As I entered the room, the child screamed, "Get out!

Don't touch me!" Then, "Mama, Mama, Mama!" began her litany, interspersed between obscenities. Terrified, I began doing a miserable job of caring for this wounded, furious little animal.

I tried to feed her soup, but she splattered it over us both with her wild head jerks. She chewed paper straws I put to her lips, then sprayed the chewed paper like spit wads. When her father came that evening, I unsuccessfully tried to cover her nakedness, apologizing with crimson embarrassment at her disheveled state. I muttered helplessly to him as I hurried out of the room. He shook his head sadly, more familiar with his daughter's behavior than I cared to imagine.

When her father left later, she yelled, "You're stupid! Stupid!"

I fumbled for another hour attempting to reach past her fury. I inquired about her unopened gifts. I freshened her flowers. I tempted her with candy, and offered to read her stories and to watch television shows. Nothing worked.

After two hours of frustration, she changed her mantra just a bit, "You don't know anything. Nobody knows anything. But I do. I know!" She finally screamed, "Tell me!"

Scared and shaken, I sat two feet in front of her and asked, "Tell you what?"

She eyed me through her tangled, teary mop, then yelled, "You're just like the rest of them. You'll just say the same thing!"

"What? What do you want to know?" I pleaded softly.

For the first time in six hours, she stopped struggling and cursing. She was so quiet I thought she had fallen asleep. Then a small whimper rose from the sheets, and I heard her muffled question, "Is my mother dead?"

The charge nurse's warning flashed in my mind. I didn't know how to answer without disobeying orders and possibly scarring the child for good if I answered truthfully. I remained silent, but the deadly quiet urged me to risk a tentative compromise. Steeling against her next wave of outrage, I asked quietly, "What do you think?"

"I think she is," she said in a low monotone. "I think my mommy is dead. I can't feel her anymore. She's been dead for a long time." I let her words hang in the air. She knew, without a trace of doubt.

I took a deep breath, prayed for forgiveness, and said, "You're right, Hon. Your mommy is dead."

At that, a loud wail rose from the rumpled sheets, a helpless, lonely one that swelled and dropped without fury, without resistance, without hope. I cried for her loss, then for my loss of any hope of becoming a nurse. When they found out I told her, I'd be fired and barred from any nursing school anywhere.

Her wails finally shuddered to hiccups. "My father kept sa-saying she was in hea-heaven. Whenever I asked where she was, everyone said she's in a be-better place." Her voice trailed off into soft sobbing again, and then she added miserably, "I need a bra and I don't want my father to get me one. I want my mommy to. . . ." Her sorrow rose again, breaking both our hearts.

Slowly, over the last two hours of the shift, I undid her restraints, bathed her, changed her sheets and dressed her in one of her new nighties. We opened her gifts and she wrote thank-you cards to her family. We cried now and then, and she let me hold her whenever a new wave of sorrow swelled through her.

Before settling in for her first night of unrestrained sleep in weeks, she read to me the words she had just written on the front page of her new diary, "My mother is in my heart and Virginia is going to be a nurse. She will be a very good nurse."

I fiercely prayed she was right.

When I finished my detailed report that night, the charge nurse patted my hand and said, "Well done, Virginia. Well done."

The child went home the next day.

Two years later, I graduated as a registered nurse— hopefully, "a very good nurse."

Virginia L. Clark

Finding Your Easter Sunrise

The longer I live, the more convincing proof I see of this truth, that God governs the affairs of man.

Benjamin Franklin

There is a stopping point in the North Carolina mountains called Pretty Place. Pull off the main road and follow a dirt one to a clearing, and there stands an open-air chapel on the side of the mountain. Simple concrete benches encompass a stone pulpit. The area is open on all sides so you can see the breathtaking beauty of the scenery. A feeling of reverence permeates the place. People talk quietly, as though in church, in this wonderful place of solitary reflection.

At Easter time about twenty years ago, a group of friends and I decided to attend the sunrise service at Pretty Place. I had always wanted to go but never managed. I was an emergency-room nurse and had to work on this particular Easter Sunday, too, but worked it out to go to the service, and then go to work my shift. We got up about 2:00 A.M. to make the drive to Pretty Place. We arrived in the dark, parked and proceeded toward the chapel. A huge gathering of people collected in and around the chapel. In darkness, a simple nondenominational church service was held including a hymn, a prayer and a short message.

I was content just to sit and enjoy the tranquility, the smell of earth and pine, and feel the coolness of the morning air on my skin. I heard the birds and the sounds of the woods around us and enjoyed the pleasure of being with my friends. The sky lightened as the day broke and a glowing orange ball began to appear as if it was rising out of the earth. One minute there was a gray canvas and the next, a glowing sphere of orange, yellow and pink rose, filling the sky. Then, more quickly than they had come, the crowd took their leave to return to the real world. I headed for work.

I arrived feeling peaceful and ready for the day. The ER was quiet, too. Since there were no patients, I began cleaning and restocking.

I heard the familiar announcement, "patient in the hall," and then the sound of a male voice calling for help in desperation and panic. I entered the hallway to see a man carrying a small, limp, breathless child. Traces of blood and discoloration smeared one side of her pale face. No other wounds were visible. The man handed me the little girl, dressed in a frilly dress, lace-trimmed socks, patent-leather shoes and a crushed Easter bonnet. His words spilled out. He couldn't see her when he backed the family van out of the driveway. She was dressed and ready for church. She saw her daddy leaving. She ran behind him. She only wanted to go with her daddy.

I rushed her into critical care, leaving the father in the hallway. Someone would come shortly to get him to fill out the paperwork and show him to the family waiting room—not the usual waiting room, but the small, softly lit, private waiting room where families and friends await bad news and pray desperate prayers for the lives of their loved ones.

As the call of Code Blue went out over the hospital loudspeaker, a team gathered to do all that was possible to save this child. Her Easter clothes were cut away and she was intubated. We began CPR, started an IV, and gave her drugs to attempt to restart her heart and lungs. It soon became obvious her neck was broken. We continued to resuscitate her, doing everything within the power of man and medicine. We couldn't give up the life of this small child. Often a knowing, an intellectual process, says there is nothing to do, but the heart pushes us beyond this knowledge to try anyway. So try we did.

After the hopeless resuscitation ceased, I slowly removed the tubes with tears in my eyes, a huge lump in my throat and heaviness in my chest. We took care of the details of preparing her body for death and for her family to see her. The emergency-room doctor went to the family room. His words to the father started with, "Your little girl is dead. There really was nothing we could do, but we tried." He talked, trying to explain what had happened. He listened for a little while to give the father a chance to respond.

The cry we heard coming from this man as he was given the news still touches me at the core of my very being. Some of us have experienced the misfortunes in life that enable us to understand the pain and loss this man must have felt.

It's been twenty years since that Easter Sunday. I am married now and have four children of my own. I traded in the job of being a nurse for that of being a full-time mother and homemaker. Not an Easter has passed since that I do not remember that little girl in the arms of her father on that Easter Sunday. I can always recall the pain and agony of that father's cry at the news of the death of his daughter. Now, as a parent, I understand that cry in a way that I couldn't at that time.

Medical personnel must learn to deal with the pain and suffering of others in order to do their job. We witness human misery, loss of limb and life, loss of family and, at times, the horrible unspeakable things that people do to each other. My saving grace is always that when I remember that little girl dying, I also remember the profound experience of being at the Easter sunrise service. I'm glad that on that morning I made the effort to go. I remember the magnificence of that sunrise there on the side of a mountain and the awe I felt taking it all in.

I experienced two opposite ends of the spectrum of human emotion that day—wonder and despair, life and death, joy and suffering, breathtaking beauty and profound sadness. I wrap the beautiful memory of the sunrise service around me to protect me from the hurt I felt at the death of that little girl. That memory of the sunrise was the armor I carried into battle that day as I went to do my duty in the ER.

As a nurse or a doctor or anyone who deals with pain and suffering, we must care for ourselves in order to serve others. We cannot give water to others from an empty well. We must take time to refill the well—to find our Easter sunrise.

Cindy Bollinger

The Old Woman

What one has, one ought to use; and whatever he does, he should do with all his might.

Marcus Tullius Cicero

As a student nurse, I was assigned to give my first bed bath to an elderly woman with emphysema and heart failure. I was told she went in and out of consciousness, and not to worry too much about communicating with her.

I gathered the bath supplies, but the woman didn't move, open her eyes or acknowledge I was there. I thought giving her a bed bath would be like working on a mannequin, as we had often done in class. While I ran the washcloth over her resting face, the warmth of her skin and little ringlets of hair on her forehead made me keenly aware that, although we might not be able to communicate verbally, she was still a human being. I bathed her gently as I would have bathed a baby.

I had almost completed my task when a whisper came from her lips. "You care," she said, barely audibly. I bent down near her face, touched her cheek and asked what she had said.

She repeated, "You care." Her eyes were open. Her voice was crackly and breathing labored, but she had something she wanted to say. "Most of the nurses don't think I notice, but I do."

By then, her face was animated and she went on to tell of events in her childhood and the antics of her grandchildren. She seemed to be having so much pleasure talking and remembering as I finished bathing her. She gave me advice about life, then patted my hand and finally said, "I'm tired now."

I gathered up the bath supplies and looked at her resting, smiling face. The conversation ended as quietly as it had started.

Mitzi Chandler

Communication Is the Key

I like the laughter that opens the lips and the heart, that shows at the same time pearls and the soul.

Victor Hugo

Communicating with our patients can be a real challenge. Do they really understand what we're asking them?

Consider the new patient at the clinic who finished filling out his health history form. The nurse noticed that under "sex" he checked both "M" and "F"—then wrote in "and if I'm feeling strong enough, sometimes on Wednesday, too!"

Then there was the man who was terribly overweight, so his doctor put him on a diet. "I want you to eat regularly for two days, then skip a day, and repeat this procedure for two weeks. The next time I see you, you will have lost five pounds."

When the man returned the doctor was shocked to see he'd lost nearly twenty pounds. "Why that's amazing!"

the doctor exclaimed. "Did you follow my instructions?"

The man nodded. "I'll tell you, though, I thought I was going to drop dead on that third day."

"From hunger?" asked the doctor.

"No, from skipping!"

Another young man called the hospital shouting, "You gotta help! My wife is going into labor!"

The nurse said, "Stay calm. Is this her first child?"

"No!" he cried urgently. "This is her husband!"

Maybe to communicate more clearly, we simply need to ask for what we need.

A patient's wife passed the nurse's station carrying a large, heavy cardboard box. A few moments later, the patient's call light went on. When the nurse entered, the patient asked if she would give the box to his doctor. The nurse was puzzled to see it loaded with old phonograph records. The patient explained, "The doctor said to have my wife bring in all my old records."

Maybe patients just can't hear us.

One man boasted, "I have a new hearing aid."

"What kind is it?"

"One o'clock."

Karyn Buxman

MEDICAL TERMS ILLUSTRATED:

RHINORRHEA

Meeting Her Needs

What we have here is a failure to communicate.

Cool Hand Luke

In 1994, our health department began serving as the primary care provider for thousands of patients who had previously only received public-health type services in our clinics. This switch to a "medical model" in our neighborhood clinics was quite a change not only for the patients but also for the staff who were more accustomed to providing chronic disease follow-up and preventive care, and now were being asked to provide acute care/primary care as well.

Because of this change, I was now a public health nurse in a primary care setting, working with the physician who was trying to meet the women's health needs as best he could. Not having done a lot of women's health previously, he was somewhat disorganized in his visit sequence but usually covered all aspects of care in a thorough, professional manner.

This particular day, the physician was completing a

visit with a new, elderly patient. In his usual quiet way, as the patient was preparing to leave the examining room, he said offhandedly, "Oh, Ms. R., would you like to have a Pap smear today?"

Ms. R. appeared surprised and a bit confused because she was already dressed, had received her prescriptions, and thought her appointment was over.

"Why, yes, Doctor, that would be nice," the patient said.

I realized immediately that a communication error had just been made.

"Ms. R., the Doctor is asking if you want your PAP SMEAR done today—your test for cancer of the womb. You would need to get undressed again for that test," I tried to explain.

Ms. R. looked embarrassed and replied, "Oh, Doctor, I'm sorry. I thought you said PABST BEER! No, I don't want a PAP SMEAR today, thank you."

Judy B. Smith

Rose

True teaching is only achieved by example.

Plato

Rose had been a resident of the nursing home for quite some time before I began to work there. With curly gray hair and a smile that never quit, she wandered the halls in her own Alzheimer's-induced world, oblivious to the tension and swirl of activity that frequented her home. Up and down, back and forth she went—sometimes looking for her coat or her mother or a ride to Mass. Rose's happy-go-lucky demeanor was a treat and we relished her sweetness.

Rose had a knack for lifting our mood at just the right time, even though she had no idea she was doing it. One particularly hectic night when everything seemed to go wrong, Rose came out of her room and sat in the chair across from the nurses' station where I was furiously documenting a fall that had just occurred. I heard her sigh, and without looking up I asked her what was the matter.

Rose lamented, "Did you ever have one of those days

where nothing goes right?"

Oh, yes, I thought, then looked up to see that Rose had taken a pair of underwear and put them on over her head, with one arm through a leg hole. It took all I had not to burst out laughing. She did wonders for my mood.

Another evening while we were preparing the residents for supper, I noticed Rose seemed sad. Putting my arm around her shoulders, I asked what was bothering her.

"I have no money," she said.

Thinking Rose was concerned about paying for her meal, as some of our residents are, I explained that everything was paid for.

"But I have no money to put in the collection plate," she said, her head hanging.

She thought she was at Mass, so I tried to orient Rose to the here and now, but soon realized that she didn't understand. Taking a coin out of my pocket, I directed her to the medication cart with all its recessed spaces to hold supplies. "Here you go, Rose, put your money there—in the box."

Plunk went the coin. The smile on her face was priceless. You would have thought she had won the lottery. Of course, I was also grinning from ear to ear as she hugged me and called me her angel. That was Rose's name for us. We were her angels.

Later that night, I administered her bedtime meds and handed her the apple juice. She exclaimed, "Oh, my highball! Thank you. I love a drink before bed." Again, Rose blessed me with a smile and a hug.

The next evening at the start of my shift, I heard Rose was gone. She had died that morning on her way to attend her great-grandson's high-school graduation. It was a bittersweet time. We were glad for her, but sad for ourselves.

In the hall outside the room where Rose once lived is a

collage of pictures taken at Christmas. There in the middle is our Rose. Her sweet smile and the loving look in her eyes leap from the wall and draw us in as we still hear her say, "You are my angel."

Little did she know she was *our* angel, sent to slow us down and help us see that life's little detours are only temporary. There is always something to smile about.

Susan Pearson

Where Do Babies Come From?

As Mercy Hospital's three-to-eleven nursing super-visor for forty years, I experienced just about every medi-cal emergency. I donned my administrative hat when needed, but loved it most when I donned my nursing one.

Late one evening, I was paged by the understaffed emergency department saying a mom was threatening to deliver her fourth child while en route to the hospital. I hustled to the ER driveway just as a frantic husband sped their car into the ambulance driveway. He jumped out screaming, "The baby is coming! It's coming!"

I opened the door to the passenger's side to find the young mom leaning back in the seat, groaning and push-ing—with three little boys gawking over her shoulder from the back seat. I raised her skirt. There was the baby's head. With one more groan and push, the infant was in my hands. People from the emergency-room staff raced to the car with medical supplies as I heard one little boy gasp, "Now I know where babies come from!"

His little brother responded, "Yeah! From under the car seat!"

Elaine Stallman

Raspberries and Cream

I once worked in a hospice, giving comfort to the dying.
Although I loved the work I did, I often found it trying.
The people that I cared for became like family,
And when they died my heart would break just as easily.

One woman in particular became a dear, close friend.
Her children rarely visited her, especially near the end.
Mrs. Wiggins was quite frail, her body wrought with illness.
At first, she barely spoke to me, content to lie in stillness.

Eventually, we became pals, as I learned more about her.
She had three kids and one great love, who passed on
    long before her.
Her children had no time for her, and she felt so alone.
I tried to make her feel loved, as if this were her home.

She'd tell me stories of her past until my shift would end.
And then the next time 'round she'd tell them all again.
One night I took an early shift and came to sit beside her.
She whispered that her time was close and asked if I
    would guide her.

Her fragile body looked so still, her breath was weak and
   shallow.
I felt the coldness of her hands, her skin was dulled and
   sallow.
I left to call her children, so they'd know the time was near,
And that I'd spend the night with her to guide her through
   her fear.

When I came back into her room, I saw that she'd been
   sleeping.
And from the moistness in her eyes, I knew that she'd
   been weeping.
I leaned close to her face and asked her if she'd had a dream.
She gently smiled and said she'd dreamt of raspberries
   and cream.

I guess I must have looked surprised at such a strange reply.
But Mrs. Wiggins softly laughed and said she'd tell me why.
"When I was just a little girl I had a favorite aunt,
Who'd spoil and treat me like a queen and give me what
   I'd want.

"My aunt would take me out to lunch and order anything
   I dreamed,
And for dessert we'd share a bowl of raspberries and cream.
Oh, how I loved the special taste so smooth and rich and
   pure.
And how I'd so look forward to the times I'd spend with
   her.

"But soon she passed away and I got older with the years.
So busy with my schoolwork and my teenage hopes and
   fears.
And since my parents worked so hard to fund my college
   dream,

We never had the luxury of raspberries and cream.

"The time flew by and I matured and soon was college-
  bound,
Living in a tiny dorm, my freedom I had found!
What little money that I had went towards my books, it
  seems,
So never once did I indulge in raspberries and cream.

"Soon I graduated and took on a full-time job
Working for the minimum for some obnoxious slob.
I met a man who stole my heart and married right away,
And two years later had a child, with one more on the way.

"All through the early wedded years of family love and bliss,
Our finances were way too tight to think of things I
  missed.
And as the children grew and went off to pursue their
  dreams,
How then could I afford to buy my raspberries and
  cream?

"Then my husband became ill and soon my love was gone.
The kids went off to college and I was once again alone.
His pension barely covered the expenses week to week,
So I went back to work again to try and make ends meet.

"And as the lonely years went by I managed to survive,
But never had enough to spare to truly feel alive.
I'd had a check-up for some pain and went in for an answer.
That's when my doctor told me I would lose my life to
  cancer.

"The medicine and treatment cost more than I was insured
  for,

And soon I'd cashed my savings out and spent all I had
   worked for.
So how could I have possibly indulged in such a scheme
As spending money on a bowl of raspberries and cream?

"And now my hour of death is near and all that I can see
Is how my heart breaks with regret for what will never be.
Why do we wait to do the things that make us feel alive?
Why do we give our life away in order to survive?

"And all the times I wanted to I really had the means.
I just didn't think that I deserved my raspberries and cream.
Oh, promise me you'll never wait too long to find your
   dream.
Promise me you'll fill your life with raspberries and cream!"

I smiled and wept and held her hand so tightly in my own,
And then I kissed her on the cheek and begged her to
   hold on.
I ran as fast as I could run to the nearest corner store,
And stocked up on the very things I knew she'd hold on
   for.

When I returned into her room she watched my little
   scheme,
And giggled as I fixed two bowls of raspberries and cream.
We sat and ate together until every bit was gone,
And then I kissed her hand and held it tight as she
   passed on.

Upon her face there was a glow that showed no pain or
   fear,
As she went to that place of peace where God was waiting there.
Her children came the next day to discuss the final plans.

Her daughter saw the empty bowls upon the bedside stand.

I told her, "Seems your mother adored raspberries and
cream.
But rarely could she buy them for she never had the means."
And as her daughter held the bowl her tears fell to the
ground,
"If I'd have known I would have bought her berries by the
pound.

"If I'd have known her time was short I would have come
to see her.
But I was just too self-involved, and now she's gone forever.
Why do we wait to do the things that really mean the most?
Why do we wait to love someone until their memory's a
ghost?"

The children left and I went home and wept myself to sleep,
And dreamed of Mrs. Wiggins and the promise I must
keep.
I woke up to a brand-new day and grabbed the telephone
To call a friend I knew was feeling sad and so alone.

I told her I was on my way, but first must make a stop,
And at the store picked up some things I knew would
cheer her up.
And when I got there she was glad to sit and talk and dream
As we indulged in two big bowls of raspberries and
cream.

Marie D. Jones

5

CHALLENGES

Obstacles cannot crush me; every obstacle yields stern resolve.

Leonardo da Vinci

Now We're Talkin'

I love these little people; and it is not a slight thing when they, who are so fresh from God, love us.

Charles Dickens

It was late at night when they brought him up from the emergency department to the pediatric ICU. He'd been playing outside when he was run over by a car and dragged down the street—by one of his parents, in a tragic accident. I felt intensely sad for parents I did not know.

He was bruised and bandaged and his four-year-old body seemed nearly lost on the adult-size gurney. And he was alone. The horror and guilt of the accident had distanced the parents; they'd gone home. I wanted to pick him up, hug him and assure him everything would all be okay. But instead I held his dirty, uninjured left hand in mine and said a prayer.

For the next two weeks he endured bandage changes and wound debridements on every limb of his body, except the left arm. That one was reserved for all the pokes and pricks necessary for the many treatments he could not comprehend.

And he was still alone. The social worker explained his distraught parents were separated, barely coping. They just couldn't come. No wonder he hadn't spoken a word since admission. Doctors found no "medical" explanation for his silence, yet no one could get him to talk.

Adding to our worries, his fifth birthday was the next day. Would his parents show up? Thankfully, a young resident overheard our concerns. He said he would buy the little guy a present, and we'd all celebrate together tomorrow night.

But why, for heaven's sake, would he buy him a high-powered water gun? We should have left the gift buying to a female. Nice try, but this toy wasn't something practical the child could play with in the ICU. Or was it?

I filled the squirt gun with water and handed it to my little friend. "Any time you say a word, any word, you can squirt me."

He smiled, but rolled over and went to sleep—on his fifth birthday—alone.

At 5:00 A.M. I started the morning routines. Baths, blood draws, linen and bandage changes.

When I went into his room, he woke easily.

Then, "Hi!" he shouted, and blasted me in the face with water. At first, I didn't know whether to be glad or mad.

I sputtered, "What's your name?"

"Jason!" A spray of water soaked my hair.

"How old are you?"

"I'm five now!" He drenched my shirt. "What else do you want to know?"

I grabbed a towel and mopped my face. Now we're talkin'.

Denise Casaubon

THE FAMILY CIRCUS® By Bil Keane

"The school nurse looked through everybody's hair to make sure we don't have any headlights."

Reprinted with permission from Bil Keane.

You Can Do Anything!

Let me tell you the secret that has led me to my goal: My strength lies solely in my tenacity.

                                                    Louis Pasteur

I was a twenty-year-old nursing student in 1968, preparing for a rotation through the pediatric unit. Compared to cardiac units or the operating room, how hard would this be? After all, I'd always cared for and played with children. This rotation would be a snap. I'd breeze right through it and be one step closer to graduation.

Chris was an eight-year-old bundle of energy who excelled in every sport he played. Disobeying his parents' instructions, he explored a neighbor's construction site, climbed a ladder and fell. His broken arm was casted too tightly, leading to infection, sepsis and gangrene. Sadly, his condition required amputation.

I was assigned as his postoperative nurse.

The first few days passed quickly. I provided Chris's physical care with forced cheerfulness. His parents stayed with him around the clock.

As his need for medication decreased, his level of awareness increased, as did his moodiness. When I saw how alert he seemed as he watched me bring in supplies for a sponge bath, I offered him the washcloth and suggested he take over. He washed his face and neck, then quit. I finished.

The next day, I announced he'd be in charge of his whole bath. He balked. I insisted. He was more than halfway through when he slumped down and said, "I'm too tired."

"You won't be in the hospital much longer," I urged gently. "You need to learn to take care of yourself."

"Well, I can't," he scowled. "How can I do anything with just one hand?"

Putting on my brightest face, I groped for a silver lining. Finally I said, "Sure you can do it, Chris. At least you have your right hand."

He turned his face away and muttered, "I'm left-handed. At least I used to be." He glared at me. "Now what?"

Suddenly, I didn't feel so snappy. I felt phony and insincere, and not very helpful. How could I have taken right-handedness for granted? It seemed he and I both had a lot to learn.

The next morning I greeted Chris with a big smile and a rubber band. He looked at me suspiciously. Wrapping the rubber band loosely around my wrist, I said, "You're left-handed and I'm right-handed. I am going to put my right hand behind my back and keep it there by winding the rubber band around my uniform buttons. Every time I ask you to do something with your right hand, I will do it first, with my left hand. And I promise not to practice before I see you. What should we try first?"

"I just woke up," he grumbled. "I need to brush my teeth."

I managed to screw the top off the toothpaste, then placed his toothbrush on the overbed table. Awkwardly, I tried to squirt toothpaste onto the wobbly toothbrush. The harder I struggled, the more interested he became. After almost ten minutes, and a lot of wasted toothpaste, I succeeded.

"I can do it faster than that!" Chris declared. And when he did, his triumphant grin was just as real as mine.

The next two weeks passed quickly. We tackled his daily activities with enthusiasm and a competitive spirit. We buttoned his shirts, buttered his bread and never really mastered tying his shoes. Despite our age difference, we were playing a game as equal competitors.

By the time my rotation ended, he was almost ready for discharge, and ready to face the world with more confidence. We hugged each other good-bye with sincere friendship and tears.

More than thirty years have passed since our time together. I've encountered some ups and downs in my life, but I've never let a physical challenge pass without thinking of Chris and wondering how he would cope. Sometimes I put a hand behind my back, hook my thumb in my belt and give it a try.

And anytime I feel sorry for myself, for some petty grievance or another, I take myself into the bathroom and try once again to brush my teeth with my left hand.

Susan M. Goldberg

"I Am," I Said

Vision is the world's most desperate need. There are no hopeless situations, only people who think hopelessly.

Winifred Newman

The young physical-therapy aide at the rehabilitation center chattered endlessly while we prepared for my session. I'm embarrassed to admit I was too caught up in my troubles to listen to her. As I watched the other patients struggling with their crutches and wheelchairs, my spirit was overcome by a sense of loss.

So much had changed. Only weeks had passed since bone cancer stole my left leg. Recently healed from surgery, I could barely sit in a chair for an hour at a time. Now I faced the difficult task of learning to walk with a prosthetic limb, a process complicated by an old back injury. The slightest activity sent scalding "phantom" pain into my nonexistent foot. As if that weren't enough, chemotherapy had robbed me of my hair and my strength. A wide range of emotions drained my remaining energy: fear, anger and grief, topped off by a huge dollop of self-pity. Worst, though, I was unable to care for my father who had Alzheimer's disease. I had no choice but to place him in a nursing facility and leave with a load of guilt.

When faced with overwhelming problems, we often escape by focusing on minor ones. People are funny in that way. In this instance, I fretted over the loss of my nursing career and the income it provided. Thankfully, my husband handled the finances. Every time the huge bills arrived, we thanked God that our insurance was adequate. Nevertheless, I missed the rapport with my patients and my colleagues. I'd always enjoyed the teaching aspect of nursing and loved seeing the glow of relief when a patient was able to understand his or her illness. It was such fun when the couples in my childbirth classes proudly showed me their new babies, gushing, "Shirley, it happened just like you said it would."

How I longed to believe I would someday return to nursing. The yearning left me feeling ashamed of my selfishness.

I argued, first with myself, then with God. There were so many reasons for gratitude. Countless people had prayed for me. I was still alive, still a child of God, a wife, a mother and a grandmother. I tried to keep a sense of perspective by telling myself that nursing was only a career; it wasn't my identity. "But, Lord, you led me into nursing and gave me a love for it. It's my calling, and I feel the loss deeply. Why have you taken it from me?"

I paid scant attention to the aide's words as I watched an elderly stroke victim attempting to operate a can opener. Nearby, a middle-aged man recovering from knee surgery drooped in despair. Across the room, a handsome airline pilot practiced walking again, following a severe spinal-cord injury. His cheerfulness puzzled me. I wondered what determined a patient's response to loss. What spurred some on when others were easily defeated? Was it merely an inborn character trait, like a strong personality or a deep-seated tenacity? Was it faith? Whatever it was, I wanted it myself.

I'd like to think I fashioned a prayer that touched God's heart. But in truth, I muddled through a jumble of emotions and came up with nothing but a scrambled plea that meant, "Lord, I need help." I expected no reply.

The aide, still valiantly trying to cheer me up, said, "I understand you used to be a nurse."

A fresh load of anger welled up inside my chest. *Used to be?* I felt like asking her what she thought I was now. Before my mind could form a sarcastic response, words came from my mouth. "Yes, I am a nurse." Somehow I felt different, stronger, but I wasn't sure why.

Later, still feeling insulted, I mentally conducted a one-sided quarrel with the aide who had reminded me of who I "used to be." *Wait a minute. I'm everything I've ever been. I have one less leg, but I still have my brain and my heart. I'm not a has-been! God doesn't have any has-beens.*

I carried that thought in my head until the day a familiar scripture came to mind. I located it in my Bible concordance, then turned to Acts 17:28 and read aloud. "In him we live, and move, and have our being." Three words stood out from the rest: "live," "move" and "have." It didn't say that we *had* our being; we *have* it. My life isn't in past tense. I still am. *I am!*

No sudden or dramatic change occurred, but gradually that passage influenced my attitude. It fanned a tiny ember of faith that lay buried under my negative emotions. Over a period of months, that faith grew to the flame it had once been. I gained strength, and with it a sense of my own potential.

A year and a half after my surgery, I returned to the hospital where I had worked for eighteen years. Physically unable to resume my previous role, I became the manager of the hospital's new home-health agency. Though I could work at my own pace, I found that making home visits was painful and difficult. In our rural area, many homes have no sidewalks or handrails at the steep doorsteps. Carrying a heavy bag while walking with a prosthetic leg was not easy, even with a cane. Once inside, I struggled to keep my balance as I bent over low beds to perform sterile procedures. And I loved it.

Though nothing lessened the joy of being a nurse again, I often doubted whether I could continue this work while we waited for the census to grow enough to hire more staff. But the growth was rapid and steady. Soon I hired other nurses to visit the patients while I managed the office. Once again I was teaching patients, this time by phone. Friendships developed between us, though many of us never met in person. The nurses, aides and therapists formed a great team, and when I retired, the agency was thriving.

At my retirement party, a doctor and colleague of many years announced, "I'm astonished at Shirley's accomplishment in this community." I'm sure he knows, as I do, that God had a hand in making the agency the blessing it is to this day. Isn't it strange how God uses the things we focus on, rightly or wrongly, to get our attention? In my case, he used my anger and my love of nursing to draw me closer to him. Now, when I hear Neil Diamond sing that song titled, "I Am, I Said," I smile inside. It was God who brought me from "I Was," to "I Am." Who but he could know the value of one little word?

Shirley McCullough

One Smile at a Time

Most of the important things in the world have been accomplished by people who have kept on trying when there seemed to be no hope at all.

Dale Carnegie

I was working in a Pediatric Intensive Care Unit when I learned about Operation Smile, an organization dedicated to repairing cleft lips and palates for children and young adults, both stateside and in the Third World. One of my patients had been brought back from Colombia by a local plastic surgeon. This two-year-old boy had a defect too severe to repair in his home country. "J" became the sweetheart of the unit, and we nursed him through his surgeries and recovery.

The goals of Operation Smile and the spirit of its team members touched me quite deeply: "saving faces" for children and giving them a new chance in life. I became involved with the local chapter of the organization, and was soon on my way to North Vietnam with thirty-five other medical professionals, including doctors, nurses and anesthesiologists.

As the first Americans to visit Haiphong (sixty miles south of Hanoi) since the Vietnam War, we were honored by our royal reception. Two of the doctors on our team and several Vietnamese doctors had served during the war as enemies. Now we all worked together for a common goal.

Once the work began, it was nonstop. We had six surgeries going at the same time. I worked in the recovery room. The obstacles were constant and intense, making me feel in control and out of control all at the same time. Personally, we had to cope with jet lag, lack of sleep, unusual foods and meager accommodations. Professionally, it was more critical. Frequently, we were without running water or power. Unlabeled oxygen tanks created a Russian roulette. The primitive conditions were as challenging as the language barrier. With only two interpreters for the whole group, we became very creative with sign language.

The team of Vietnamese nurses in the recovery room was great as they took vital signs and tried to grasp our technology. This was a far cry from their usual duties of scrubbing floors and washing toilets. None of them spoke English, but they could comfort the children in their native tongues.

Having been in the Peace Corps, I took most things in stride. But working twelve- to sixteen-hour days started to catch up with me. With only one more day to go, I wasn't sure whether I was going to make it. I felt sick and was becoming emotional. I went to the bathroom (if you could call it that), and cried like a baby and prayed for energy. I was sent back to the hotel shortly after that to sleep for a few hours. They called me back that evening to monitor a child in respiratory distress from a traumatic pre-op intubation. Tired and tense, I did *not* want to be there. Luckily, the anesthesiologist on call with me was experienced with hypnotherapy. He gave me fifteen minutes of his time, and all my fears dissipated. I relaxed into my duties, and the night went smoothly.

The next morning at the hospital was our last and as we packed our equipment, I felt like a zombie, but a relaxed one. My work was done. I wandered back to the ward and found a flurry of activity. Sutures were being removed, people were taking pictures of the children as parents and children said their grateful farewells. There was so much love in the air, it made my heart swell.

When I walked in, the parents smiled and pointed to their children. I went from one bed to another, saying good-bye. There were two kids and two parents in each bed; some of them were crying because we were leaving.

One mother prompted her child to say something to me, helping him where he hesitated. It was obvious that she was teaching her three-year-old some new words. I got the gist of his thankfulness, but Michelle, one of our wonderful interpreters, arrived just in time to deliver his rich message to me. "I am sorry I cannot speak to you in English, but I want to thank you for my smile."

I started to cry, and then someone handed me flowers that probably cost them a day's salary. I cried some more.

It was a privilege to be a part of an effort that changed the lives and hopes of many families. We had repaired 141 smiles—and our country's image of loving service.

Rita Kluny

Do Your Best and the Lord Will Bless

Let us act on what we have since we have not what we wish.

Cardinal Newman

After a year of preparation, Kay was finally on her way. Every year she volunteered to spend her vacation using her professional nursing skills in the mission field. The Trinity Baptist Church in Santa Monica worked for a year to raise funds to send a team of four to Haiti. Joining Kay from California was Dr. Charles Wood, a dentist, and Kathleen Whitney, another nurse. Dr. Miranti, another dentist from New Jersey, would join them to give dental care to hundreds of people who otherwise had no access to care.

On her way to the airport Kay stopped at the Santa Monica Hospital where she'd been working on the cardiac ward. Kay had been caring for a patient who was very interested in her mission trip and touched by the work she was about to do. The patient was scheduled to go into surgery, and Kay stopped to give him extra encouragement. It was needed. He said, "I'm about to go into surgery and I don't know whether I'm going to come through this or not. I want you to take this envelope—I've put a little money in it. Take it to Haiti. It may be that when you're there you'll discover there are some things you need that you hadn't anticipated, like aspirins or something."

Kay objected, "I can't do that."

"I absolutely insist."

"That is very thoughtful of you," Kay replied. She placed the envelope in her purse, assured the patient he would be in her prayers and hurried to the airport. The flight to Haiti was uneventful, but going through customs was a disaster. The group had to bring all their supplies and equipment with them in several large boxes. The customs officials confiscated all of Dr. Wood's expensive portable dental equipment and all the supplies they were carrying in—lidocaine for anesthesia, dressing materials, surgical gloves, inoculation supplies and even baby vitamins. When Dr. Rick Miranti flew in with only one small backpack, the customs officials let him pass without checking it. The four huddled in the airport waiting room, lifting their urgent prayers. His pack included one set of dental equipment and only about fifty ampoules of the anesthetic lidocaine. Since some patients require more than one ampoule, it meant that only a few patients could be helped.

A missionary came to pick them up and on the way to his home they shared their disappointment. For a year they had planned and prayed and worked so they could bring health and relief from pain to many. Now it seemed their trip would be in vain. The four were so discouraged they considered packing up and returning home. Instead, they decided to do all they could. They would open the clinic. The dentists would take turns using the one set of equipment. They would use the anesthetic as long as it lasted—probably an hour or two—then they would have to close the clinic. In the morning they set up what had to be the world's smallest dental clinic. A single table sat in the open air, with only a roof sheltering them from the direct sun. A dentist and a nurse worked as a team at each end of the table, while a long line of hopeful patients waited their turns. No one had the heart to turn them away.

The expert dentists worked quickly. After the nurses prepared the syringe with the anesthetic, the dentist gave the shot, then the necessary procedures. When he finished, he passed the portable equipment to his colleague while the nurse sterilized the single set of equipment for the next patient.

Hours passed. Patients came, were treated and left. Kay frantically continued loading syringes from the limited supply of ampoules in her box.

At the end of a long day, the weary team closed their clinic. "We must have treated over two hundred patients today," Dr. Wood observed. "That's a record for me."

"Thank God we had enough anesthetic," Kay said.

"Where did the additional ampoules come from? Who kept replenishing the box?"

No one.

The entire team recognized they had been part of a miracle.

In the New Testament, Christ had compassion on the multitude and had multiplied the loaves and the fishes until the need was met. This day God in his mercy had kept the anesthetic from running out. They prayed together in thanksgiving.

They had done what they could, and the Lord added the rest.

Now they needed to decide what to do next. By the grace of God they had made it through one day, but should they presume God would continue to multiply the anesthetic as long as they were there?

They were sorely limited in the treatment they could offer since so much of what they needed was wrongfully impounded in customs. In addition to the portable dental equipment, they needed the collapsible, lightweight dental chair. The customs officials said they would release the equipment and supplies—for a large sum of money. The team knew the legal customs regulations, and they knew they were not required to pay this exorbitant amount. Dr. Woods appealed to the compassion of the customs officer, explaining how they had come as volunteers to treat people for free. The customs officer would be doing a service to his people by releasing their equipment and supplies.

His argument fell on deaf ears. After some haggling, one customs official agreed to release all their equipment and supplies for five hundred American dollars. This sum was much less than the amount demanded before, but this was an expense they had not anticipated, and it seemed impossible.

"An expense that wasn't anticipated." The words jogged something in Kay's memory. She told her group about the visit she had made to the hospital on the way to the airport and the envelope the friend had given for expenses that "hadn't been anticipated." "He said it was for aspirins or something we might need," Kay explained. "It's probably only ten dollars or so."

Kay retrieved the sealed envelope, still in her purse. She opened the envelope and pulled out cash—five hundred dollars.

Five hundred American dollars! Exactly the amount needed.

During the next few weeks they ministered with skill and Christian love to hundreds of patients. They took their clinic to school buildings, beaches and remote villages, sometimes hiking to their destination on mountain trails.

It would have been reward enough for Kay to see the relief from pain and suffering they provided so many. "But what I will never forget," Kay recalls, "are the two miracles of lidocaine and cash. I learned that day that when you do your best, the Lord will bless."

Marilynn Carlson Webber

Pony

Faith evermore looks upward and decrees objects remote; but reason can discover things only near, and sees nothing that is above her.

Francis Quarles

I heard his footsteps before I saw him. In his brand-new Christmas slippers, his shuffling feet never left the floor. As I watched him traverse the hall, I had a sudden image of the little engine that could. His gray jogging suit, a recent birthday present, bagged about his tiny frame and a thatch of snow-white hair crowned his head. He looked awfully sleepy and needed a shave—not unusual for 3:00 A.M.

He approached the nurses' desk and asked, "What are they gonna do with that pony?"

Thoughtlessly, I answered, "What pony?"

He ignored my question and began telling me they should put him down at the far end of the meadow and let him eat the yellowed cornstalks left from this year's crop.

I smiled a sad smile and tried to re-orient John as to his

whereabouts. Although pointless, I had a small glimmer of hope that I could make a difference, that I could make John see the reality of the nursing home. So I continued to patiently explain to John that he lived here in room 114.

Finally, I stopped, and as I gazed into his cloudy blue eyes, I suddenly recognized how much better his reality was than mine. He was in a meadow with a new pony. I was trying to place him within the stark walls of an institution.

I patted John on the shoulder, "I think that the far end of the meadow would be perfect for the pony."

He continued shuffling down the hall, smiling.

Mary Jane Holman

Sadie, Sadie, Special Lady

With the fearful strain that is on me night and day, if I did not laugh, I should die.

Abraham Lincoln

Sadie was eighty-seven years old and had been in the hospital for two weeks when I met her. Though she was recovering quite nicely from a heart attack, she was also experiencing some dementia. She was always pleasant and smiling and called me "Honeychild" when she spoke and told wonderful stories from the past. We spent hours together with her talking and me listening. A master storyteller, she disguised her voice to mimic the characters she so lovingly recalled. Her explicit facial expressions always added flavor to her tales.

Sadie's dementia wasn't apparent until she'd ask questions about the recent past or couldn't find her way back to bed from the restroom. On a few occasions, she attempted to crawl into bed with one of her four roommates, causing uproar and much confusion. Sadie became sullen and quiet following these episodes, and I often wondered what she was thinking.

One morning I started my rounds as usual and noticed Sadie was very sad. She seemed to want to tell me something, but had difficulty finding the right words. After a few minutes I ascertained that she had had an "accident" during the night and needed a good bath and a manicure. I spent much of my morning soaking her hands in warm, sudsy water. To ease her embarrassment, I suggested she imagine she was spending the day being pampered at the beauty shop. We laughed together and played along until it came time to do her peri-care. As I soaked her bottom, she became very quiet again and her eyes grew as wide as saucers. I asked if I was making her uncomfortable in any way. She looked up at me and very innocently said, "Honeychild, they've never done this to me at my beauty shop before!"

I bit my lip and told her I certainly hoped not, and then gently reminded her she was still in the hospital. We both laughed until we cried. And laughter was just the medicine Sadie needed that morning to regain her dignity.

Andrea Watson

Lucky

*The only good luck many great men ever had
was being born with ability and determination
to overcome bad luck.*

Channing Pollock

The truth is, we were whining about being tired, and it
was cold and dark as we ran to the helicopter at 0400 that
morning. We had no clue this would be one of those
flights we'd never forget.

After liftoff, dispatch told us to rendezvous with local
EMS at the scene "of a gunshot wound to the neck."
Thoughts of being cold and tired were replaced by waving red flags. First, our EMS is a skilled and sophisticated
service that only requests our presence at unusual events.
Second is the consideration of the structures of the neck.
A bullet in the cervical spine is frightening; a bullet
through the trachea more frightening; a bullet through
the carotid artery or jugular vein most frightening. Is the
patient paralyzed? In need of a surgical airway? Spurting
arterial blood? Is there an internal bleed occluding the

airway? And where is the weapon? More importantly, who has that weapon?

We landed in the street of a neighborhood made up of small older homes. After egress from the aircraft, we approached the scene, noticing it did not have the feel of a catastrophic event. Law officers had the weapon secured. Our patient was under a huge tree on a front lawn. EMS had fully immobilized him and established two large-bore IVs. The heart monitor showed a normal sinus rhythm, and EMS reported stable vital signs. The victim was talking a mile a minute, which afforded us instantaneous information regarding level of conscious-ness and integrity of the airway. Assessment by flashlight revealed no paralysis. In fact, he was gesturing wildly to the extent that someone is able to do when he or she is fully immobilized. Cajoling him to stop talking long enough to peer into his oral cavity was the most difficult part of the assessment. There was no bleeding in his mouth. It was noted his top dentures were missing, which was his only complaint.

Overall, Lucky, as we came to call him, appeared to be quite healthy and spry for a gentleman eighty-nine years of age. He had no allergies, took no medications, and hadn't the foggiest idea when he had his last tetanus booster. As we prepared to transport him, he pleaded with the EMS and law enforcement personnel to search for the missing dentures because the "gol-dang uppers had cost him an arm and a leg."

During the ten-minute flight to the trauma center, Lucky remained in a sinus rhythm with stable vital signs. No symptoms were manifest and certainly shortness of breath was not an issue, as he animatedly relayed his story. A strange noise awoke him while his dog slept next to his bed. "The gol-dang dog never woke up and barked like a watchdog should." Lucky grabbed the .22-caliber pistol he kept on his nightstand and charged into the night. Running out the front door, across the porch, and into the yard, he tripped over an exposed tree root. As he fell, the pistol fired, striking him in the neck. During the melee, he lost his uppers. The gol-dang uppers had cost him an arm and a leg—which remained his chief complaint.

In the emergency department, examination under bright lights revealed an entrance wound in the neck, an abrasion to the hard palate, and a small laceration without active bleeding at the base of the tongue. To everyone's amazement, X rays of the head and neck showed no bullet fragments.

News of such a mysterious event always travels fast. There was already a crowd of "night people" forming in the emergency department when EMS and law officers from the scene arrived, bearing the missing uppers. There was complete silence as the multitude gaped at the sight of the dentures with the .22-caliber slug imbedded into the hard palate portion.

After completing our paperwork, we usually say goodbye and good luck to our patients before departing for base. It seemed prudent to dispense with the good luck part of our salutation to Lucky. Our last impression of him was of a little old man under a heap of blankets with a shock of unintentionally spiked hair (hence the term, hair-raising experience!) sticking from the top of the blankets. Sticking out the other end were his little house slippers that appeared to be older than he was.

As we left the department we could hear Lucky telling no one in particular, those gol-dang uppers had cost him an arm and a leg—the best investment Lucky ever made!

Charlene Vance

Cast-Cutter

Invention is the talent of youth as judgment is of age.

Jonathan Swift

After years of hospital nursing, I loved my new job in a busy family-practice office, performing a wide variety of duties—phlebotomy, spirometries, EKGs. I accepted each as a new challenge and mastered all of them with confidence.

Well, almost all of them.

I was still nervous whenever I cut off a cast. To prove to the patients (and to me!) that the motorized saw wouldn't cut their flesh, I always put my fingertip next to the spinning circular blade. I then explained how the cotton padding underneath the cast snagged the blade and stopped it before it reached the skin. But, in spite of my own reassurances, cutting casts still made me a bit nervous—especially when the patient was a squirming four-year-old boy.

Danny had broken his arm in a playground accident

a few weeks earlier, and I had assisted the doctor in applying his cast. When I rewarded his bravery with double trinkets from the toy chest, Danny and I became buddies. He had complete confidence in my ability to remove his cast.

That made one of us.

With a reassuring smile I fired up the cast-cutter and started cutting the cast, hoping he'd think the trembling was from the vibration of the saw, not my hands.

The motor buzzed and bits of plaster flew as I methodically pressed the whirling blade back and forth along the length of the cast. Danny started to fidget in the chair, and his face flushed.

"Doing okay, Danny?" I asked.

"I'm okay." He smiled meekly. "It don't hurt." But his facial expression and wiggling told me something was making him uncomfortable.

Thankfully, just then, the final part of the cast was cut. I carefully pried it apart with the cast spreader. After showing him the blunt-ended scissors and promising him they couldn't cut his skin either, I began cutting the cotton padding and underlying stockinet. Danny wiggled some more and even winced a bit when I spread the cast further and gently lifted his arm out of the cast.

I gasped to see a long purple streak on his inner arm! My mind raced for a diagnosis. Phlebitis? Necrosis? Had I cut him? There was no blood!

There, inside the opened cast, embedded in the padding, was wedged a purple crayon.

Bewildered, I looked at Danny.

He said, sheepishly, "It itched!"

LeAnn Thieman

CLOSE TO HOME JOHN McPHERSON

"If you get an itch, just turn whichever one of these cranks is closest to it."

The Race

I am only one; but still I am one. I cannot do everything; but still I can do something. And because I cannot do everything, I will not refuse to do the something that I can do.

E. E. Hale

He'd come for minor surgery, a simple patch-up job. A piece of cake, really, unless you have a history of hemophilia and HIV, a legacy of contaminated blood. What started as "routine" spiraled into complications—needles, tubes, a ventilator—trying to sustain a body that would no longer sustain itself.

He came to us for end-of-life care—pale, hunched over, breathing hard, a feeding tube hanging uselessly from his nose. Fifty years of life condensed into a slim chart of medical relevance: an admitting sheet, history and physical, progress notes. Bare facts: prognosis poor. Running out of options. Running out of time.

His family came to him and knelt at the bedside, their faces wet with knowing. Touching. Talking. They wrapped their arms and voices around him in a passionate effort to keep him connected to this world.

"I want to go home," he said. "I want to go home to die."

Health-care professionals often toss around phrases like "comfort care," "supportive intervention" and "the patient's right to self-determination." We say them as if we know what they mean. But what did they mean to this man and this family?

"I want to go home. I want to go home to die."

His family came to us for help in achieving that wish. They knew it would not be easy, as did we. They knew there were no home-care arrangements in place. They knew his blood pressure was fifty-four over zero. They knew home was an hour away; not a vast distance by most standards, but a tremendous journey under these circumstances. They knew, too, that there was a strong possibility he could die in the ambulance.

"It doesn't matter," his family said. "He will know he is on his way." In that knowing, perhaps, lies the ultimate "comfort care."

And so, we, his medical team of nurses, doctors, social workers and more, blended our planning efforts. We were all participants in this last leg of the race. There were discharge orders to be obtained: morphine, oxygen, a home hospice nurse visit. There was urgency, pressure and determination. Voices were raised and minor misunderstandings occurred, but despite the glitches, a major victory was achieved.

Two hours and forty minutes after we began our efforts, the ambulance arrived. Making an exception to policy, they allowed two family members to ride along, in case death came too soon.

Our patient made it home by two o'clock that afternoon. Four hours later, he died a peaceful death in his own house, in his own bed, with his family present and his dog curled up at his feet.

Martin Gray once said: "We never believe enough in ourselves. We are forever ignorant of the resources of life. But life is to dare to break through the walls that we erect before ourselves. To transcend the limits we impose on ourselves. Life is always to go beyond."

I believe each of us in health care has the opportunity to assist people in how they want to live, and sometimes, in how they wish to die. All of us have a stake in that process. When we bring our gifts to the race, when we combine our gifts with those of others, we are choosing "to go beyond." The results can be powerful, extraordinary—even transforming—for ourselves as well as the people we serve.

Anne Riffenburgh

Mr. Jackson and the Angel Pin

The cure for all ills and wrongs, the cares, the sorrows and crimes of humanity, all live in the one word "love." It is the divine vitality that everywhere produces and restores life.

Lydia Maria Child

Mr. Jackson wanted to die. He missed his wife who had passed away five months earlier. They had been married sixty-three years and were blessed with five children—children who were busy with their own lives. In his loneliness, he lost the will to live. He shut himself off from the world, quit eating, closed his eyes and waited to die.

Several weeks later, he was admitted to the hospital. "Malnourished," the diagnosis reported. During the shift change, the evening nurse hastily explained the case to the morning nurse, Freddie.

"He hasn't eaten in the two days he's been here," she said softly. "Hasn't said a word either. He just looks away and stares off at who knows what. The doc is going to put a feeding tube in his stomach if he doesn't start eating. Good luck, Freddie." With that, the evening nurse hurried out.

Freddie looked at the frail form in the bed. The room was dark except for the soft morning light peeping through the semi-drawn curtains. The white sheets accentuated the outline of his body, which appeared to be nothing more than a skeleton draped with skin. The patient turned his head away and stared at the wall, his eyes void of hope, void of life itself.

Freddie could always find a way into the patient's heart. Somehow, she would find the key to unlock his. Gently picking up his delicate hand, she held it in hers. "Mr. Jackson? How about some lotion on your hands, wouldn't that feel good?"

No response. She walked around to the other side of the bed, leaned over and whispered, "Mr. Jackson?"

His eyes widened as he fixed his gaze on the pin she wore—a gold and silver angel given to her for Christmas. Impulsively he reached out to touch it, but drew his hand back. His eyes began to mist and he spoke his first words since being there. "If I had my pants with me, I would give you all the money I have just to touch that pin."

Freddie quickly contrived a plan. "I'll make a deal with you, Mr. Jackson. I'll give you this pin if you will eat something off every tray we bring you."

"No, Ma'am, I couldn't take it. I just want to touch it. That's the prettiest pin I've ever seen."

"I'll tell you what I'll do, I'll pin it to a pillow and put it next to you. You can keep it until my shift ends, but only if you will eat something off every tray I bring you."

"Yes, Ma'am, I'll do what you say."

When Freddie came to check his lunch tray, she found him thoughtfully stroking the pin. He turned to her and said, "I kept my promise, look." He had eaten a few bites off his tray. They were making progress.

When her shift ended, Freddie dropped in on Mr.

Jackson and said, "I'm off for the next two days, but I'll come by here first thing when I get back."

His eyebrows drew together in a small frown, and he lowered his head.

Freddie quickly added, "I want you to keep this pin and your promise while I'm gone."

He brightened a little, but forlornness still hung heavily in the room.

"Mr. Jackson, think about all you have to be grateful for—your children and grandchildren, to start with," she encouraged. "Those grandbabies need their grandfather. Why, who else will tell them about their wonderful grandmother?" She patted his hand and hoped for a miracle.

When Freddie returned, "amazing," was the evening nurse's appraisal. Freddie smiled and went to check Mr. Jackson's vitals.

"There's my angel nurse," he happily exclaimed.

"It sure is, and I've missed you," she replied, noticing the lovely woman who stood next to his bed.

"This is my daughter. She is taking me to live with her," he said. "I'm gonna tell those grandkids of mine story after story." He looked at Freddie and smiled. "I'm gonna tell them about the angel who took care of their grandpa, too."

Now, Mr. Jackson wanted to live. And live he did, thanks to an angel made of silver and gold, and one made of kindness and mercy.

Linda Apple

Will She Ever Smile Again?

I stare quietly at the purple, swollen little face that lies in sharp contrast to the crisp whiteness of the pillow. Her eyes are closed. She lies sleeping. As I silently tend to her care, I despair that she may never smile again, let alone laugh and run with friends.

Her world has been shattered, violently beaten by a person whose job it should have been to love and protect her. Her innocence is lost. For four days she lays quietly in this hospital bed, not speaking, not moving, just silently watching those around her. Her mother sleeps on the makeshift bed beside her.

Satisfied that she is resting comfortably, I move to leave, when her eyes flicker open. Two sad, little brown slits appear, and her gaze moves about the room, coming to rest on me. She says nothing, just silently watches. I greet her by name and remind her of mine, then chat quietly with her about the beautiful day that lies outside her darkened room. As I have for the last four days, I make little jokes and chat happily about different things as I tend her. Keeping eye contact with her, I smile and carry on with the conversation, not really expecting her to reply.

I am aware that outside this room my many other

responsibilities pile up. The ward is extremely busy, and I have other children and families in my care. I should be moving on, but I am drawn to this silent, sad little girl and her unspoken needs.

Quietly, I begin to bathe her eyes and motionless face, hoping to soothe and heal more than just the swollen and discolored flesh. Eventually time moves on, and I explain to her that I need to go, but that I will be back shortly to see her. I make sure she can reach her bell and explain to her that she can ring it if she wants me for anything before I return. I share a last little joke with her about the kitten I know she has at home and turn to put away my equipment.

Then I hear it. I slowly turn back to her. What was that sound? Had it come from her? I find it hard to believe my own ears, but there again she gives a tiny, almost inaudible . . . giggle.

I stand in shock as her remaining crooked little teeth appear in the tiniest, most beautiful smile I have ever seen.

"What's your name again?" she whispers.

Quietly, I sit down beside her and take her hand. I whisper my name.

"Will you be my nurse tomorrow?"

I smile and tell her I would really love that. Happy with my answer, she settles back down on her pillow and dozes back off to sleep.

As I watch her, I notice her face seems softer, more peaceful somehow. A tiny smile still plays on her battered lips—or is it my imagination now? Tears run down my face as I quietly slip out the door.

The healing has begun.

Ana Wehipeihana

6

MIRACLES

A miracle is a work exceeding the power of any created agent, consequently being an effect of the divine omnipotence.

Robert South

"Can I get continuing education credit for stories that
never cease to amaze me?"

Stormy Delivery

It was just an ordinary day. I had tucked our three children in for their naps, fully realizing I needed it more than they did. Plopping into the overstuffed chair, I rubbed my tummy. Only three more weeks and I'd cradle our baby in my arms, not my belly. I whispered, "I can hardly wait." Then I glanced out the window at the blizzard conditions and amended that statement.

I massaged my abdomen again, this time to rub away a subtle uterine twinge. *It's nothing,* I told myself. The doctor had checked me just the day before and my cervix hadn't dilated a bit. The slight twinges gnawed at me. My first labor was only five hours. My second, just one and a half. My third tied that record. The doctors expected number four to break it. That's why I'd been instructed to call at the earliest sign of labor—that and the fact that I lived forty minutes from the hospital.

As I watched the snow pile higher on the streets, something else gnawed at me. I called my husband Del at work and told him about the twinges. "It's probably nothing, but I think I'll call the office and go in for a checkup before the storm gets too bad. If this isn't early labor, the kids and I will just have dinner with my mom."

Tanya, the office nurse was wonderful as always. She always validated my concerns, though I suspect many of them were unwarranted. In her usual, supportive fashion, she agreed with my cautious plan. So I woke the kids and paraded them to the car, ragged blankets in tow. We inched through the swirling snowstorm for seven miles before the first contraction seized my abdomen. In two minutes, a second contraction—then a third—then a fourth, each more intense, bending me over the steering wheel. The baby's head pressed forcefully down the birth canal. Panicked and pain-stricken, I looked into the rearview mirror at my children, huddled in the back seat.

To six-year-old Timmy I said, "If something goes wrong and our baby comes, you'll have to help Mommy catch it.

"And Danika," I wheezed to my four-year-old daughter, "you just press on the horn and don't stop until somebody comes to help us."

Three-year-old Taylor sat bravely, waiting for her job. "Sweetie, you must sit very still and be quiet."

All three of them followed Taylor's assignment, when they watched my hands grip the wheel as I labored through my Lamaze breathing.

By the time we approached the interstate on-ramp, I knew I couldn't concentrate on slowing a labor and speeding a car, all at the same time.

I pulled over. "Lord," I begged out loud, "we're in big trouble here." I gritted my teeth and panted to keep from pushing. "We need help. Please send a policeman our way."

At that very moment, a patrol car passed us.

Timmy exclaimed, "There he is, Mom! Let's go catch him!" By now the patrolman had pulled on to the interstate, so I put the car in drive again and followed in close pursuit. While the rest of the traffic crawled along at twenty miles per hour, the policeman cruised at thirty. Dangerously, I sped as fast as I dared behind him, honking my horn, flashing my headlights and panting.

The policeman drove on.

I pressed the gas pedal to catch up to him, trying to tap my bumper into his. That caught his attention. He stopped. I stopped. Jumping out of his car, he slammed the door, and tramped to mine. But I was already outside, screaming to him through the sleeting snow. "Contractions, two minutes, baby's coming!"

He looked more terrified than I felt.

He explained that he was on his way to an accident just a few miles down the road. He phoned in my emergency, with little hope for immediate attention. I leaned onto the hood of the car and panted to keep from pushing.

"There's an extra ambulance at the accident site," he exclaimed from his phone. "It'll be here in three minutes!"

"Make it two!" I hollered, wishing the freezing snow could somehow ease the searing pain in my abdomen.

"Can I call somebody for you?" the patrolman asked helplessly.

I shouted my husband's work number to him, but his trembling hands couldn't write it down. He scribbled again and again, and finally just dialed the number as I repeated it a fourth time.

Just then, the ambulance and fire truck screamed across the median and to our aid. Before the paramedics coaxed me onto the cart I went to my children, shivering in the back seat. "Just stay with the firemen," I assured them, unable to force my usual it'll-be-okay-smile. "They'll help you."

I breathed with the rhythm of the ambulance siren, and thanked God I was in the hands of EMTs. Still, I prayed harder that we'd make it to the hospital in time.

Little did I know that my husband was joining me in

prayer as he drove too fast down the same interstate. Cautiously, he sped past a fire truck and looked—then looked again at the three little blond heads in the front seat. He waved the fire truck down. "Those are my kids! Where are you taking them?"

The fireman yelled out his window, instructing Del to head on to the hospital; he'd bring the children. Del glanced at the three beaming fire cadets, waving madly from the front seat. He blew them a kiss and jumped back in his car.

The ambulance siren droned as we finally approached the emergency entrance.

"The baby's coming!" I moaned. In a heartbeat, I was on a gurney, with the paramedics jogging alongside, wheeling me into the birthing unit. Dr. Hoffmann greeted me with a nervous smile.

"So, you came special delivery, huh, Debbie?" I could only groan. He squeezed my hand. "Now let's go deliver this baby."

Right on cue, Del ran into the birthing room just as I slid over to the birthing bed. With a gush, my water burst. The only thing scarier than the increased pain was the look on the nurse's face. Dr. Hoffmann's gaze fixed on hers. I knew we were in deep trouble.

"Debbie, the amniotic fluid is badly stained," he said as he worked feverishly over the baby's protruding head. "That means the baby had a bowel movement under all this stress. That's not a good sign." He grimaced as he grabbed the scissors. "And the cord is wrapped around its neck—tight. Don't push, Debbie. Don't push." He turned to the nurse. "I saw a pediatrician in the hall—get him in here—STAT."

As the nurse rushed out, my three kids and the fireman rushed in. I alternated between panting and praying as the fireman talked in a hushed tone to Del, then left.

Dr. Hoffmann said, "Del, I'm going to give Debbie a

local anesthetic before the next contraction. You may want to take the kids out of the room."

As Del escorted them to the door, I heard Tim ask, "Daddy, why do we have to leave before the next trash man?"

"No, Timmy," Del chuckled. "He said contraction, not trash man."

So then I was panting and praying and laughing.

Two more contractions, and Del was back at my side as our baby pushed his way into our world. And with no one to watch our children, they watched the birth of their brother.

I wish I could say the moment was joyous, but baby Ty debuted in critical condition. Danika summed it up, "Daddy, I didn't know babies were born purple."

For the next six days, Ty fought for his life in intensive care. The pediatrician shook his head in dismay. "Everything went so wrong," he said sadly.

"I disagree, Doctor," I argued. "Didn't God give me an office nurse who listened to my concerns and told me to come in? And didn't he send a policeman just when I asked for one? And didn't he arrange for an extra ambulance to be just a few miles away? And didn't he see to it that a fire truck was there for our children? And didn't he put you in the hallway when we needed you? And didn't you tell me that if Ty had been born outside of the hospital, he never would have survived? On the contrary, Doctor, I'd say everything went just right."

On the seventh day we bundled little Ty in his brand-new blanket, and took him home, healthy and strong.

We're still in awe of how that Perfect Plan unfolded. The kids will attest to that as they sum up the events of that day. "You'll never believe what happened! We got to ride in a fire truck!"

Debbie Lukasiewicz
As told to LeAnn Thieman

The Hand of God

Nothing is or can be accidental with God.

Henry Wadsworth Longfellow

In 1966, during the earliest days of kidney transplanta-
tion, I witnessed a series of events where I could clearly
see the hand of God touching a man's life.

I was a member of the transplant team in a very large,
busy hospital. The plan was in place for a man named
Don to donate a kidney to his younger brother, Ray, on
Wednesday the third.

On the morning of Monday the first, Ray was beginning his scheduled kidney dialysis four floors below the
surgery suite. Monday was a heavily scheduled day for
surgeries. I was assisting a surgeon in one room while
another nurse resterilized the transplant equipment used
over the weekend.

At the same time, a man in his mid-thirties entered the
emergency room in cardiac arrest. The intern, who had
just spent the previous month as part of the kidney transplant team, recognized the man as Don. He had worked

with this donor just the week before. When his frantic efforts to save Don failed, the intern continued CPR, hoping to save the kidney until his younger brother was located. His staff called our surgery suite and was stunned to learn that not only were there two surgery rooms suddenly available, but the younger brother was in the building undergoing his weekly dialysis.

The responsibility fell on the nurses in the dialysis unit to explain to Ray that his brother had fallen gravely ill at work and was not able to be revived. With the two brothers side by side in adjoining operating rooms, the kidney was removed from Don and successfully implanted into Ray.

In a big-city hospital, only by the grace of God could two surgical suites be empty on a busy Monday morning, the kidney transplant team be in the OR, the kidney recipient be in the hospital, and the intern recognize the donor at the time of his death.

That day each team member felt they were a part of implementing God's will on this Earth.

Jo Stickley

Reprinted by permission of Benita Epstein.

Forgiven

*Humanity is never so beautiful as when pray-
ing for forgiveness, or else forgiving another.*

Jean Paul Richter

The real power of healing is not about curing diseases.
This was revealed to me by a male nurse who spent a lot
of time with a woman in a nursing home who hadn't been
able to walk for six years. Edward lifted her in and out of
her chair or into the bed, depending on her schedule.

She always wanted to talk about God and forgiveness.
Because Edward had had a near-death experience, he felt
comfortable doing this.

One night it was so late that Edward slipped out without being the one to put her to bed. He was heading for
his car in the parking lot when he heard her call,
"Edward!" He snuck back inside and into her room.

"Are you sure God forgives us for everything?" she
asked.

"Yes, I'm sure, from my own experience," he said. "You
know the gospel song that tells us, 'He knows every lie
that you and I have told, and though it makes him very

sad to see the way we live, he'll always say "I forgive.""'"

She sighed. "When I was a young woman I stole my parents' silver and sold it so I would have enough money to get married. I've never told anyone and no one ever found out. Will God forgive me?"

"Yes," Edward reassured her. "God will forgive you. Good night."

When Edward arrived back at work the next morning, he was told to see the administrator who asked what he had told the woman the night before.

"As usual," Edward explained, "we talked about God and forgiveness. Why?"

"At 3:00 A.M. the woman came out of her room and, with no help, walked the entire length of the nursing home, put her Bible and teeth on the nurse's desk and said, 'I don't need these any more.' Then she turned and walked back to her room, laid down and died."

This is what the soul of nursing is all about, the reason God created a world where we can all be nurses by showing our compassion and empathy for the wounded.

Bernie Siegel

Afraid of the Night

Death is not a failure of medical science but the last act of life.

Patch Adams, M.D.

Death came to call most often in the early morning hours. Sometimes peacefully, taking my patient as he dreamed. Sometimes violently, with a rattle deep in the throat. Sometimes Death came like a refreshing breeze and carried away my long-suffering patient like a buoyant kite cut loose in the wind, leaving her pain behind. Sometimes it was only after much pumping and pounding and fluids and medications and electrical shocking that we allowed Death to come. But, for whatever rationale, it was my personal observation that Death came to call most frequently in the early morning hours, and for that solitary reason I came to dread the night shift.

Until Olga.

Olga was a terminal-cancer patient whose family could no longer endure the hardship of caring for her at home. It was the family decision, with this strong matriarch leading the family, to place her in one of the beds our tiny hospital designated for long-term, palliative care. Olga firmly insisted they pay only for thirty days because she had chosen the fourth of July to be her "freedom day"— her chosen day to die. Her doctor, on the other hand, stated his expectations. Although she was terminal, she would probably live three to six months, and her demise would be a slow and probably very painful process. He gave orders to provide comfort measures and allow complete freedom for family visitation.

The family came faithfully every day, often staying for hours talking or just sitting with Olga and listening to the radio perpetually playing the Christian music she loved. When the song "I Give You Love" would play, Olga smiled broadly and announced, "That's my favorite song. That's the last song I want to hear when I die."

On the night of July third, I came on duty as charge nurse for the night shift. According to report, Olga's family had been in to see her that evening and left instructions for the nurses not to call them if "it happened," as they had all said their good-byes. "Please allow Reverend Steve to sit with her," they said. "He wants to accompany her in her passage." With the warped humor only nurses understand, the evening shift joked, "Olga's vital signs are stable and there's nothing physiologically to indicate her death is imminent. Lucky you. You're going to have to deal with Olga in the morning, and boy is she going to be mad that she's still here!"

But, things are different at night. Night is when we are closer to ourselves, and closer to our cardinal truths and ideas. I checked on Olga and, pulling her covers up around her shoulders, whispered, "Good night, beautiful lady."

Olga smiled and whispered back, "Good night and good-bye. You know, tomorrow is my freedom day." A warm sense of calm settled about my shoulders—a strong but strangely comforting awareness that she might be right, even though it went against logic, reason and educated predications. Though her vital signs were unchanged, I left the room feeling Olga was very much in control of her destiny.

Throughout the night, Mary, the other nurse on duty, and I turned Olga and provided care. Reverend Steve sat holding her hand, and together they listened as the radio softly played one song after another. When we returned to her room mid-shift, Olga did not arouse as we gently repositioned her.

At 6:00 A.M., just as the sun cast a warm rosy glow through the windows, Mary and I returned to her room. Reverend Steve requested we wait just a few minutes as he felt Olga was "almost through her passage." As I stood at the foot of her bed watching this young minister accompanying Olga to her journey's door, I was filled with awe and a sense of envy of the mastery this strong and beautiful woman had over her life. Out of habit, I checked my watch and began counting her respirations, one—two—three. At that moment, a song began on the radio and a smile spread over Olga's sleeping face. "I Give You Love"—four—five—six. . . .

Olga accomplished not one, but two of her last life goals. The Fourth of July *was* her day of freedom from the pain of her disease. And the last song she ever heard was her favorite.

I have often remembered that night over the years and felt that Olga's story should be told. Because this strong and beautiful woman chose not to "rage against the dying of the light," but to accept it—even welcome it—as entry into the light. Because of Olga I have a much deeper appreciation for endings and beginnings, for the cycles of life and death.

And, because of Olga, I no longer fear the night.

Nancy Harless

And the Angels Sang

We judge ourselves by what we feel capable of doing, while others judge us by what we have already done.

Henry Wadsworth Longfellow

"You have an admission that has to be done early. The patient's name is Mr. Flood, and you'll need to get him admitted in time to give his ten o'clock intravenous antibiotic," said the weekend supervisor at our home-care agency.

It was my on-call weekend, and I had prayed for a quiet one. My favorite musical group was in town and scheduled to sing at my church that morning. They were personal friends with whom I had sung years before. I really wanted to see and hear them again.

I had called the supervisor at 8:00 A.M., hoping there were no calls. To my dismay, there were two other calls besides this admission. And Mr. Flood's wife and daughters wanted me there immediately. I reviewed his orders to admit him, administer the IV antibiotic, do wound care. Then I was to teach the family about his pain medication and how to provide for his general comfort and personal hygiene. He had been diagnosed with cancer. Surgery, chemotherapy and radiation were unsuccessful, so he had chosen to go home to spend his last days with his family.

Hoping to finish this admission visit in less than the usual two hours and still make it to church, I pocketed a tape recorder to record the interview and do most of the paperwork later. I'd see the other two patients in the afternoon and spend more time with Mr. Flood on the next visit.

I set out for the patient's house, feeling more annoyed with each mile. Swearing at the devil for interfering with my plans, I asked God to help me get finished in time to see my friends. I arrived at the house and sat in the car long enough to suppress my resentment and summon up the professional bearing I had mastered in my thirty years of nursing. Controlled and smiling, I pressed the doorbell.

Mrs. Flood opened the door and immediately collapsed in my arms in tears. "I can't do this!" she sobbed. "I've never had to take care of anything before. I can't do it! You've got to help me!"

Still crying, she led me into the bedroom where her husband lay quietly in bed, exuding great dignity and self-control in spite of the pain I knew he must be experiencing.

The hospital summary said Mr. Flood was aware death was imminent. He had accepted his fate with a quiet and confident faith. His wife and daughters, on the other hand, were filled with fearful denial. They had refused the hospice referral. Accepting that would mean accepting the fact that their husband and father was dying. They wanted someone who could bring about a miraculous healing. His sister, a former nurse, had come to help with his personal needs, but the family expected greater things from the home-care nurses, who, at this point, could do no more than provide some measure of comfort.

I went into the bathroom to wash my hands before beginning and told myself to be gracious and compassionate. I also reminded God that I needed to get finished quickly, *the music, you know.*

The required admission paperwork, questions and signatures clearly frustrated Mrs. Flood. Her unstated cry was, "Never mind all that, save him for me now! I can't get along without him!" I acknowledged her distress, recognizing it as fear and denial, both normal aspects of the grieving process, and dealt with her interruptions and tears while trying to interview and treat my patient. Mr. Flood, too, attempted to soothe her as he signed the required papers and responded to my many questions.

The tape recorder remained off. Mr. Flood cooperated with my efforts to keep the focus on him, and finally, after four grueling hours, the initial assessment was done.

I went to wash my hands again before continuing his treatments. Alone in the bathroom, I reminded God that I had missed seeing my dear friends and had no idea when I'd have another chance. I was frustrated at Mrs. Flood's weakness in the face of her husband's need and steeped in self-pity over having missed a blessing because of the time spent in offering answers she refused to accept.

Five hours after my arrival, I was finally through. As I packed up my equipment Mr. Flood asked, "Do you always work on Sundays?"

I explained the weekend on-call rotation, telling him that I usually went to church on Sunday mornings, but that today was different.

He said, "I thought so."

Then, though it had never happened with any patient before, I asked if he would like us to pray before I left. He nodded and closed his eyes, waiting for me to start. I said a brief but sincere prayer for comfort, strength and peace for himself and his family.

As I prepared to go, his wife persisted with questions and pleas, crying out for help in a situation she could not bear. Mr. Flood said to her, "Honey, stop that now, and let me say something." Taking my hand he spoke, with tears in his eyes as they sought my own, "I'm glad they sent you today. Not just any nurse, but you, especially. I don't know you, but I feel like Jesus has been here this morning."

I stood face to face with the indignation I had felt in having missed the morning's music. A stillness passed over me, fixing me to the spot as I suddenly realized what had just happened. Rather than granting me the blessing I had asked for, God had chosen to provide, through me, a blessing for someone who needed it much more than I. I realized a far greater gift had been waiting for me through this dying man, and I had almost missed it.

In my car I accepted the fact that this was the service God had in mind for me that day. Backing out of the driveway I fancied I heard the angels begin to sing. Setting off toward the next patient's house, I burst into joyful song in unison with them and let the passing motorists wonder why I was singing, smiling and crying all at the same time.

Mary Saxon Wilburn

A Cherished Angel

The heart of the giver makes the gift dear and precious.

Martin Luther

Cherished is the word I'd use to describe Grandma Madge. Her loving generosity poured out to every friend and family member needing help. Madge was always the first person to take a home-cooked meal to someone who was sick. The treasured time she spent with them surpassed even the healing benefit of her famous German dumplings.

That's why it seemed sadly ironic that friends and family now came to sit at *her* bedside. When Madge had learned about her fatal illness, she'd insisted on remaining at home. "To be surrounded by my angel collection," she beamed.

Madge's colossal collection of angels—fifteen hundred, to be exact—had started with just a few Christmas tree ornaments and an occasional figurine she'd picked up at souvenir shops or garage sales. But, it didn't take long for her sons to discover that contributions to Madge's menagerie were the perfect solution to the "what to get Mom" dilemma. Soon every friend, neighbor, grandchild and in-law bought her an angel for every holiday, birthday and anniversary. It wasn't long before her tiny cottage overflowed with a host of heavenly beings. She proudly displayed many of them year-round on shelves, the coffee table, end tables and on top of the TV. Her choir of angels assembled in the teeny guest room, reserved for musical figurines only. There, hundreds more singing, twirling, dancing angels crowded antique shelves, hutches and bedside stands.

Each November first, Madge began the month-long process of bringing out the rest of her collection. Angels graced her Christmas tree and the floor beneath it, then cascaded everywhere, from the buffet, to the mantel, to the back of the toilet and top of the refrigerator! To Madge, each angel was a reminder of a person who loved her. She inscribed the name of the giver on the bottom of each, along with the date she had received it. She gave explicit directions. "When I pass through the Pearly Gates, make sure every angel goes back to the person who gave it to me."

Now, with a caring hospice nurse and Madge's two sisters staying with her, that loving task seemed imminent. Late one afternoon, her grandson Troy stopped to spend some precious time. Sitting on the edge of the bed, he tenderly caressed her hand. "You've been an angel to us all, Grandma, a true gift from God."

A few hours later, Grandma Madge ascended through those Pearly Gates.

Her sisters, Rene and Gladys, and the hospice nurse, gathered in the living room marveling at how Madge had died with the same dignity, courage and grace with which she had lived. A faint melody interrupted their testimony.

Bewildered, they turned their heads, trying to discover the source of the music. Rene and Gladys followed the hospice nurse to the guest bedroom while the tune grew louder. There on a table, one lone angel played the song "Cherish" from beginning to end. Then it stopped. With trembling hands, Gladys picked it up and read, "From Troy, 1992."

Gladys held the figurine to her chest. "Thanks, Madge, for letting us know you've joined God's heavenly collection of angels."

"Your angel," whispered the hospice nurse, "has returned to the Giver."

Margie Seyfer
As told to LeAnn Thieman

Lori's Wish

Lori came to the hospital with a great attitude. She was such a spunky twelve-year-old you almost forgot to notice her frail little body and blue lips and nail beds. Lori saw this heart surgery as just one more hoop to jump through on her way to becoming a grown-up. In her bag, she had packed all the essentials of a preteen-age girl and an afghan she was crocheting. It really looked quite nice but had a long way to go.

Lori went to surgery with an abnormal but incredibly brave heart. Late in the afternoon, she arrived in the pediatric intensive care unit with all the typical supportive medication and equipment. We knew her many previous surgeries and time on the heart-lung machine had put her at risk for bleeding, and before long we noted an abnormal amount of blood coming from her chest tubes. This continued over the next hour until the surgeon had no choice but to take her back to the operating room. We got her parents to her bedside for a visit before Lori was quickly returned to surgery. A couple of hours later she was back in ICU and the bleeding stopped. The relief in her parents' faces sent me home, tired but reassured.

The next day, Lori's heart was doing reasonably well,

and her lips and fingernails were pink. But she had a lot of recovering to do. Her family was at her bedside as much as they could be, considering the restricted visiting hours so prevalent back then. Lori's condition rapidly declined, however, and her kidneys began to fail. She needed a ventilator. This tube, through her nose and airway, prevented her from talking, but it definitely didn't prevent her from communicating. She still had that spunky attitude. She was very thirsty but, of course, she couldn't have anything to drink. When I dipped a cloth into a little fruit punch just to wet her mouth, her eyes said thank-you in no uncertain terms.

When the charge nurse came to the bedside to ask if I could stay into the evening shift, Lori overheard. I looked back at her and she mouthed, "Please stay." I did. Her urine output declined even further, and when I went home that night, I felt tired and uneasy.

By the next morning Lori was on dialysis. We all continued to hope her kidneys would begin to recover, but each hour of no urine output was devastating. Lori became puffy as the fluid accumulated in her body and stressed her heart and lungs. She slept more. Her spunkiness faded.

Over the next couple of days her condition continued to decline. How unfair it seemed that now, with a repaired heart, Lori had the pinkest lips ever, but the rest of her organs suffered in the process.

Her unfinished afghan stood out as a reminder of her unfinished life.

Still, her parents stood faithfully by. Her mother was five months pregnant, very tired and so devoted. She told us of Lori's biggest wish—to hold her baby sister. She was so sure it was going to be a girl, Lori had named this Christmastime baby Mary Christine.

But Lori continued to fade. The helplessness we felt was overwhelming. On a beautiful sunny August day, we all said our good-byes and Lori died. As her parents left the hospital, I tearfully handed them Lori's belongings and the unfinished afghan.

The next spring, as I walked down the hall, I saw Lori's mom. Joyfully I blurted, "How is the new baby?" I was heartbroken to learn four-month-old Mary Christine also had congenital heart disease. On Friday of that week, Good Friday, Mary had surgery on her weak and poorly formed heart. Sadly, she followed a course so like Lori's— persistent postoperative bleeding, failure of her kidneys and so on. On Easter Sunday morning the outlook for Mary was bleak. I went with her parents to the chapel.

As we sat quietly there, a butterfly glided silently around us. I was mystified. This chapel had no access to the outdoors. Where could this butterfly have come from? The mother smiled through her tears and said, "Lori is here." She paused, then went on. "Last summer, at the cemetery following Lori's funeral, a butterfly landed on my shoulder and stayed right with me and I felt Lori's presence. Then, when we brought Mary home from the hospital on a cold wintry Christmas Day in Indiana, a butterfly entered the house with us! Again, we knew Lori was there. And now, she is here for Mary!"

As they faced the death of another daughter, these parents looked through their sorrow and found peace, knowing their two girls would now be together. We returned to Mary's bedside and within minutes, she slipped away.

Lori's wish had come true. She was holding her baby sister.

Gwen Fosse

By Accident

Our greatest glory is not in never falling, but in rising every time we fall.

Confucius

The instant my horse bucked, I knew I was going to die. As the reins were wrenched from my fingers, I felt myself thrown violently over his head and onto the ground. With sickening clarity, I heard my bones break. I thought of Christopher Reeve.

"Help me," I cried. "Please, someone help me." Searing pain in my chest and back strangled my words into a whisper. *I'm alone,* I thought. *No one heard me.* I raised my head, and the movement sent an electric shock coursing down my right arm. And then the arm went numb.

In a daze, I struggled to my feet and crawled through the arena fence. *You are strong,* I told myself, *and you can do this.* Pain contorted my posture, but I forced myself to walk the distance back to the ranch house. Doctors told me later that I'd done all of this with seven broken ribs, a fractured spine, a bleeding lung and a broken neck.

"Mary, I fell off 'Nate,'" I groaned into the phone. "I

think it's bad. I can't feel my right arm anymore." I'd called my coworkers at the hospital, knowing they would be my lifelines.

An hour later, I lay strapped in the CT scanner with a stiff foam collar around my neck and oxygen tubing in my nostrils. I was no longer a nurse; I was a patient in my own emergency department. An unexpected wave of fear washed over me. Confusion compounded the pain—fear? *Hadn't I conquered fear?* Buoyed by morphine, I let my memory drift back some four weeks.

"Okay, just roll out," Duke commanded. As I crouched in the doorway of the plane, the wind whipped against my face. I squinted down at the ground, thirteen thousand feet below. Today I would prove how strong I was. Today I would be a skydiver, not a cast-off wife and an empty-nest mother.

"Let's do it!" I shouted back from the plane's open doorway. I gave my instructor the "thumbs up" and I jumped.

The jolting stop of the CT scanner table interrupted my memory. I let the medical team, my friends, do their jobs while I was forced to do my own personal evaluation: *Why did this have to happen to me?* In the past eighteen months I'd survived the loss of a twenty-four-year marriage to infidelity, and the ravages of a flood that had threatened to take my home. Was this some sort of cosmic triple play to make me prove how strong I could be? Or three strikes and I'm out? Again, that shadowy fear surrounded my heart. *What was I afraid of?*

I took inventory: I was a single mother, a veteran emergency-room nurse, and a sturdy ranch woman who could haul a horse trailer, stack hay and deliver a foal. The misfortunes of the past two years had required me to stand taller, to be more assertive and, when necessary, to take it on the chin.

And now that chin was tucked into a foam collar, and there were whispers of "spinal cord injury, permanent weakness." I began to realize what that icy, nameless fear was—I was losing control. A strong woman stays in control and doesn't have to fully trust anyone. After all, I'd trusted my husband, and he left; I'd trusted the security of my home, and the floodwaters came. I had to ask myself the big question now: Did I trust God? I prayed to him, I worshipped him, but did I really allow myself to depend on him? A little card on my dresser mirror read, "Let Go and Let God," yet how desperately I'd fought to keep life's reins in my own hands. Now those reins had been yanked from me.

In the following months, as I worked in physical therapy to regain the full use of my arms, I had time to ponder and to pray. I wondered about my need to feel strong. Was it simply armor to ward off other unimaginable hurts? My cavalier leap from the skydiving plane certainly hadn't left fear far enough behind. I began to set new priorities, to evaluate success and survival in different ways. With great relief, I let God take the burdens from my sore shoulders; I began to trust again.

I hadn't been alone that day in my riding arena, and someone had heard me when I cried out. The accident stopped me from being strong, long enough to find my strength.

Months later, I returned to work at the hospital to find I'd become a local legend. The story was told and retold. "She walked into the hospital with a broken neck," they'd say. One day a new employee heard the story—heard that I'd been alone in the riding arena—and he asked me, incredulously, "Who picked you up off the ground out there, after you fell?"

I felt myself take a deep breath—it was warm and alive in my chest. "Who picked me up?" A knowing smile spread across my face. "Think big," I told him, "really big."

Candace L. Calvert

CPR

Blessed is he who carries within himself a God and an ideal and who obeys it—an ideal of art, science or gospel virtues. Therein lie the springs of great thoughts and great actions.

Louis Pasteur

One Sunday morning I heard my minister say if you want result from prayer, pray for thirty days without ceasing. I didn't know why it was thirty days, but I was willing to give it a try. The following became my daily prayer:

I am available Lord to be used by you each day.
Guide me, precious Lord, and lead me in what I say and do.
May my words and actions be a witness that you are living in me.
To the one that is lonely, may I be a friend.
To those with heavy burdens, help me to meet their needs.
Lord I do not want fame or fortune.
My prayer is that you will use me to glorify your name.
I know I don't have much to offer, but I will give you my all.
Guide me to be what you want me to be.
Amen.

On the twenty-first day of this prayer, CPR took on a new meaning for me.

I was working an extremely busy twelve-hour night shift in labor and delivery. I had just sat down for my first break when a phone call came from my friend working in the emergency room. I barely recognized her urgent voice. An eighteen-year-old boy had been brought to the ER for alcohol and drug overdose. The young man was very close to death, and they had done all they could do to help him. The father of this boy was requesting a priest or minister, and they were having difficulty locating one that could come to the ER quickly. My friend stated, "We know you're a Christian, and we need you to come and try to comfort this father. Please help."

Reluctantly, I said I would come down. As I waited for the elevator, my thoughts became very judgmental and frustration welled up inside me. Then I remembered the prayer I'd been praying. I walked into the ER and approached the father. Taking his hand, I silently led him to the chapel. Before I could even say, "I am not a minister," this six-foot, 220-pound man sank into the chair and became a brokenhearted child.

Through his nonstop sobbing he spoke, "Christian, pray for Raymond. I remember the first time I held my boy. I felt so proud, and I just kept saying, 'I have a son.' As the years passed, those tiny feet became bigger and walked away from his family's love and entered a strange, hardened and destructive world. Tonight too much alcohol and an overdose of drugs are taking his life. It's as though he wants to rebel against everything his family stood for. He knew what he was doing was wrong. Sometimes he seemed so afraid, but he wouldn't stop. Now it is too late. Christian, you have to pray for Raymond."

Those large hands trembled in mine and, as I looked into his eyes, I mourned with him. Silence fell between us, as I searched for the words that would comfort this crumbling tower of a man. I felt so inadequate. I wanted to scream, "Lord, it has only been twenty-one days since I began that prayer! I am not ready for this!"

Time was running out, and I knew I couldn't stall any longer. I clutched his hands, now wet with tears, and began to pray. The words came easily, much to my surprise.

I finished praying with him and went to Raymond's bedside. I took his cold, lifeless hand, and once again began to pray. "Lord, I am asking for a miracle, and I know you can do it."

I stayed with them both until Raymond was taken to intensive care. I visited Raymond on a daily basis and continued to pray for him. Eight days passed with little improvement. On the ninth day, I entered the ICU and a miracle had taken place. Raymond was awake and talking with his father.

CPR had taken on a new meaning for me: Christian Pray for Raymond. As I left the ICU with tears falling down my face, I realized, *Today is the thirtieth day of my prayer.*

Now, I not only believe in miracles, I depend on them.

Johnnie Dowdy

Voice in the Night

Hope is a thing with feathers that perches in the soul.

Emily Dickinson

When I was nineteen years old, my friend Hanneke Boogaard was studying to become a nurse at Beatrix Hospital in The Netherlands. There, nursing students work during their study, the same as regular personnel. During her work on the night shift, Hanneke was strangely drawn to one patient in particular, a forty-year-old woman in a coma. Because Mrs. Groensma never had visitors, Hanneke remained at her bedside longer than the others. At first she tried not to admit it, since for her all patients should mean the same. But this woman fascinated her.

When Hanneke heard the patient had no living relatives, she spent even more time with her. She'd learned that people in comas could sometimes hear when they were spoken to. This woman had no one to do that for her, so Hanneke talked softly to her every night. Since she didn't know her, she didn't know what to talk about, so she told Mrs. Groensma all about herself. She explained how her parents had died in a car crash when she was young. For hours she shared her many memories of them. That's all she had to cling to now. How she wished she had a specific personal item to remember them by—the golden four-leaf-clover locket her mother always wore. It was lost during the accident and never found, even though relatives searched the crash sight and nearby ditch. Night after night, she talked and talked and grew more and more attached to Mrs. Groensma.

She would likely never come out of the coma, and she had no one in the world to care for her. Therefore, the time came for her to be transferred to a nursing home where she would eventually die. When Hanneke objected, she was heavily reprimanded for losing touch with her professional attitude and forbidden to contact the patient in the nursing home. Hanneke saw the logic of her supervisors but could not help thinking about Mrs. Groensma often.

Time went by, and Hanneke became a nurse and found a job in the Beatrix Hospital. One day at work, she was instructing a patient when a lady who was questioning another nurse turned and deliberately walked towards her. It was Mrs. Groensma! They found an empty room where they could speak privately, and Mrs. Groensma explained what she was doing there.

She recalled having been in a dark and lonely place, all alone, until the voice of what she thought must have been an angel started speaking, drawing her attention. Later when that voice stopped talking to her, she longed for the sound so much that she started struggling to get to the place where the voice had come from. She came out of the coma and took a long time to recover. Meanwhile she had questioned the nursing home staff. They eventually told her they had instructions to keep away a certain nurse who had made the mistake of getting too attached to her.

As soon as Mrs. Groensma was able, she came to the hospital to find that nurse. When she heard Hanneke talk to the patient, she recognized the voice that had spoken to her during her coma.

Mrs. Groensma took Hanneke's hand. "I have something I want to give you to thank you. I found it fifteen years ago in a ditch and originally wanted to put pictures of my late husband and me in it and give it to my daughter. When she died I was all alone and wanted to throw it away, but I never got to it. I now want you to have it."

Mrs. Groensma handed Hanneke a small box. Inside, sparkling in the sunlight, lay a golden four-leaf-clover locket. With a pounding heart Hanneke opened it to see her parents' photos.

Hanneke now wears the locket day and night and visits Mrs. Groensma whenever she wants.

And they talk and talk and grow more and more attached.

Carin Klabbers

7

A MATTER OF PERSPECTIVE

*He who wishes to secure the good of others
has already secured his own.*

Confucius

Impacting the Process

Early in my nursing career, I worked in an intensive-care unit alongside a social worker of quiet faith. In response to client situations of overwhelming tragedy or senseless accidents, she reminded the nursing team that while only God controlled the outcome of each patient's situation, we could powerfully impact the process through the nursing care we provide. I was privileged to work among nurses who role-modeled this kind of nursing care.

Mr. Nolan was a patient in the intensive-care unit at our regional medical center. I loved my job and enjoyed implementing his challenging, complex treatment regimen. His large extended family was a joy to know: so supportive of him, so appreciative of his care, even as they faced each new hurdle in his declining situation. Mr. Nolan exuded a quiet dignity that confirmed his family's report that he was a treasured husband, father, grandfather, friend and truly a man of excellence.

A recently retired bank executive, he'd had a heart attack while awaiting a coronary bypass procedure. He recovered adequately to undergo the bypass surgery and was admitted as a "routine" case to our ICU. But complications commenced soon after his arrival in the unit.

An extended period of low blood pressure resulted in kidney failure, and he subsequently required hourly peritoneal dialysis. To survive, additional coronary surgery was needed, and eventually a balloon pump was inserted to support his heart function. The balloon pump catheter was threaded through a groin access. Despite every effort to reposition the catheter, circulation to his right leg was compromised and gangrene developed in some of his toes. Finally, the balloon pump was removed, but not before the entire right foot was cold and black.

Each shift brought greater challenges in maintaining Mr. Nolan's stability. While all agreed he was a "lousy" surgical risk, we knew he couldn't survive long without the required foot amputation. In the OR, the doctors found the gangrene had spread internally through the entire leg. Though stunned to receive him back from the OR with a total right-leg amputation, it was heartening to see how rapidly his vital parameters improved once the toxic impact of the gangrene was gone.

Mr. Nolan stabilized somewhat over the next week, yet the numerous medical complications and operations had taken a devastating toll. It became clear to medical personnel, Mr. Nolan and his family that he was failing and wouldn't survive. I came up with a plan that would give a lasting memory to the devastated family and dignity to Mr. Nolan.

When the family called earlier in the shift, I told them to be prepared to wait a little longer to see him when they came to visit that afternoon. Meantime, on top of the demanding nursing care regimen, I set out to accomplish the hygiene care reserved for quieter night shifts. I gave Mr. Nolan a wash, shampoo and shave, and trimmed and styled his hair to look like it had in a picture the family had shown me. I coordinated care to give him extra rest, hoping he'd be more alert when they came. Meantime I got a team of staff and necessary supplies ready to respond on cue.

With news of the family's arrival, the team went into action, assisting Mr. Nolan into a geri-chair. Linens covered the ventilator tubing and dialysis equipment, and the bed curtains were strategically placed to block the family's view of the numerous IV pumps, tubings, monitors and equipment. I put his glasses on him, then welcomed his family into his room.

For the first time in weeks, Mr. Nolan greeted his wife and family sitting up in a chair with a smile and a twinkle in his eye. The family's laughter and tears flowed while I carefully monitored the machines behind the curtains. The preparations for this brief visit had taken every extra minute I could eke out from his complex nursing care time. Yet the memory of the smiles that family shared will stay with me a lifetime.

Mr. Nolan passed away during my next days off. A few shifts later, I was surprised to see one of his daughters waiting at the front door of the ICU as I arrived. She said the family had directed her to come and tell me how seeing Mr. Nolan sitting up, looking like "Dad," rather than a "hospital patient," was a positive memory that made the ordeal of his hospitalization and death more bearable.

Now as a nursing instructor, I teach my students that every nurse must have complex technical skills, high-level knowledge and thinking abilities. Yet I urge them to aim beyond knowledge and skill and recall that while only God controls the outcome for each of their patients, they can, through the nursing care they provide, powerfully impact the process. I urge them to provide the sort of nursing care that considers the memories the patients and their families have forever.

Catherine Hoe Harwood

Just What I Needed to Hear

I have worked closely with nurses all my professional life and have been enormously enriched by their competence and expertise, as well as by the friendships and affiliations we have shared. The first nurse who made a significant difference in my life worked in the newborn nursery at Tripler Army Hospital in Hawaii, where I delivered my first baby in 1968, as a twenty-year-old, pre-medical student and Navy wife. My sailor-husband, Larry, had returned home a few days earlier from a six-month tour of duty in the West Pacific during the Vietnam War. Our nearest relatives resided thousands of miles away. We were overwhelmed with parenthood and totally inexperienced in infant care.

Although everything appeared to be routine after Peter's birth, he soon developed jaundice, due to an incompatibility between his blood type and mine. The morning after his birth, the babies born to the other three women in our rooming-in unit were brought in their bassinets to remain with their mothers. When I inquired about my baby, I was informed that Peter would be kept in the nursery for observation and regular monitoring of his bilirubin level (the chemical that causes the yellowish skin discoloration of jaundice). As a military dependent, I had seen a different doctor at each prenatal visit and did not have a designated personal physician who could answer my questions and calm my fears.

Being a premedical student, I owned a Merck Manual that provided a brief synopsis of common medical diagnoses. Larry brought the book to the hospital so I could read the paragraphs about newborn jaundice. I learned that elevated levels of bilirubin could be toxic to an infant's brain, and that a level exceeding 20 mg% potentially could cause brain damage (a medical belief at that time). Unfortunately, a little knowledge proved dangerous, as I exaggerated the gravity of Peter's condition and was consumed with anxiety. I became obsessed with the results of each bilirubin measurement and fixated on the number 20, which was now linked in my mind with certain brain damage. To make matters worse, the visitation practices of that era did not permit me to enter the nursery or hold my baby.

For a brief hour each day, I could look through a glass window and observe Peter being cared for by capable nurses, while there was seemingly nothing I could do for my son. By the second day of life, Peter's bilirubin level had risen to the high teens, and by day three, the level peaked at 22 mg%. I was asked to sign permission for an exchange transfusion to be performed to quickly reduce Peter's bilirubin level to a safer range. I was frantic with worry and dread. Even if Peter survived what I surmised was a life-threatening procedure, surely he would be brain-damaged, since his bilirubin level had already exceeded the ominous number of 20.

Throughout the whole ordeal, a compassionate, matronly nurse, who took a special interest in our situation, stood out as our emotional anchor and our source of hope. As preparations for the procedure began, this nurse angel gently reassured Larry and me that Peter would be all right. She hurried to my room afterwards to be the first to report that all had gone well. I found out later that she had even baptized our son before the exchange transfusion, in an unabashed act of love.

I was briefly exhilarated when the medical crisis was over, but a nagging thought soon stifled my joy. What about the chance of brain damage?

Even though I was young and the risks were low, I had contemplated during my pregnancy the very real possibility that my baby could have a birth defect or other medical problem. I resolved that I could love him no matter what. Now I wondered whether I was a bad mother for wanting to know his prognosis.

I mustered all my courage to ask the pediatrician on rounds, "Do you think my baby could have suffered any brain damage from his high bilirubin level?"

His answer devastated me. "We won't be able to tell for about a year."

I couldn't handle such uncertainty. I needed a vision of hope after spending Peter's first four days in an emotional wringer. The doctor left my room, unaware that his answer had stunned me.

Shortly thereafter, the wonderful nurse who had offered such optimism yesterday returned to my room. Her benevolent face reflected genuine concern, and I ventured to ask my question again.

"Do you think my baby could have suffered any brain damage?"

"Absolutely not," she shot back.

"How do you know?" I countered.

"You see, when I bang his crib, he startles and throws his arms out, and that reflex proves he is normal."

Her unwavering reassurance was precisely what I needed to hear. I was instantly ecstatic. Bolstered by her words of encouragement, I triumphantly took my baby home and treated him like a normal child.

A few years later, during my pediatric training, I would learn that the arm-flailing response the nurse had described was known as the Moro reflex, a primitive startle reaction of newborns that is present even with minimal brain function. Yet, my nurse had mercifully cited this reflex as definitive proof that my baby would be all right, and I had believed her. I thought about the doctor's answer to my question and realized that his ambivalence reflected his preoccupation with being right, without weighing the impact of his answer on me. Although his response was technically correct, I wondered what might have happened if I had taken Peter home with lingering doubts about his development. Would I have interacted with him differently? Could I have created a self-fulfilling prophecy?

The nurse's answer was based on right motives, at the risk of being proven factually wrong one day. I will always be grateful to her for allowing me to embark on motherhood with unrestrained hope and optimism.

Today Peter is a highly competent and compassionate psychiatrist, and often, when I am with him, I smile and say jokingly, "Just think what you could have been if it weren't for the brain damage."

"Dr. Mom" Marianne Neifert

All Pain Being Equal

Pain is the deepest thing we have in our nature, and union through pain and suffering has always seemed more real and holy than any other.

Arthur Hallam

It was getting close. We all knew it.

"What did the doctor say this morning?" I quietly asked my mom, seated by Dad's bed as he slept fitfully. It was a daily question yet, before she opened her mouth to speak, I could see by the look in her eyes that the news wasn't good. She turned her weary face toward me and whispered so as not to disturb him.

"He's developed pneumonia. One lung showed up completely white on the X rays." She began to cry softly. My heart sank. I still clung to the childlike hope that if I wished hard enough, it would all go away. The cancer, the drugs, the withering body, the suffering and the waiting. The agonizing waiting. I did not want to watch my father die anymore. And I did not want to watch a part of my mother die right along with him. I didn't know how much more I could take.

I drew in a deep breath and motioned for her to join me outside of the room. She nodded and rose to leave but paused a moment. Looking into his sunken face, she softly caressed his cheek with her trembling hand. He did not stir from his drug-induced dreams.

"Let's get some air," I suggested as I placed my arm around her shoulders. We walked past the nurses' station, and for a moment I marveled at the men and women I saw there. Dad's room was just across from the large partitioned area, and I had come to recognize most of the faces over the course of the last month. Warm smiles popped up from behind the desk. That alone amazed me. Smiles. Always smiles. On a floor solely dedicated to the dying and grieving.

Mom and I went for a cup of coffee, and before long, she wanted to return to Dad's room. She was never away long. In fact, the nurses had set up a cot for her so she could spend her nights as close to her husband as possible. I walked her back and decided to stroll the hallway yet again.

I wasn't doing well that morning. I hurt. Yet, my own grief seemed so insignificant and unimportant compared to Dad's and even Mom's. I fought my tears and assured myself that I would be strong for her.

Later that evening after I had run home for some rest, I returned to the care unit. I noticed one nurse who had been there in the morning and was surprised to see her almost twelve hours later. As I approached I could overhear her discreetly talking with a coworker. I didn't catch who they were talking about, but I understood that a patient wasn't expected to make it through the night. I knew it wasn't my father, yet I felt weakened by this even though death was almost a daily occurrence there.

Another life was ending.

When I walked into Dad's room, I was happy to see him awake and talkative. Mom was dressed up, her hair was shiny and styled, and she had put on some makeup. Though her deep sorrow and exhaustion could not be masked, she looked so beautiful. Tenderly she peeled back the covers and cradled his swollen foot in one hand and gently spread lotion with the other.

Deeply moved by this display of strength, love and dedication, I listened to the chatter between them. For a brief moment they seemed to forget all they were facing. I excused myself and stepped out of the room. Once the door was closed, I leaned against the hallway wall for support. Pain racked through me in great waves, and I could not deny my own grief any longer.

I didn't notice the nurse leave the desk and approach me. She was the same woman whom I had seen in the morning. She stood before me, and I looked into her weary face. Without a word, she wrapped her arms around me. I sobbed as she held me and all of my fear, pain and fatigue flooded forth. I grabbed onto the strength and comfort she surrounded me with.

"I . . . I'm so sorry," I began to say.

"Don't be. That's what we're here for," she replied tenderly.

I chuckled through my sniffles. "Like, you don't have enough with the caring of those people who are dying."

"All pain deserves as much comfort as we can give—including yours."

So few words, yet so much meaning. She had held me for a few moments more and when we separated, I felt so tired I could have collapsed. But that wasn't all I felt. Something had shifted within me. The gift she gave me in those moments in the hallway gave me the courage and the strength to face my father's death two weeks later. It got me through the funeral and the weeks that followed as we all tried to determine what life was, now that he was gone.

Most of all, it gave me the ability to acknowledge that although all pain may not be equal, it all deserves as much comfort as we can give.

Corinne Pratz

The Nurse's Best Medicine

Nursing has been called a "rewarding profession," so much so that it's become something of a cliché. But more than that, nursing tests you, asking more of you than you ever thought you could give. Nurses are generally people who know who they are. We come to that knowledge through our reflection in the eyes of our patients.

It is our patients, more than our colleagues, who have made us what we are, by forcing us to rise to the occasion.

You stand by the side of a young girl named Maria, lying on a stretcher. Maria is very depressed. She doesn't speak, sleeps very little and has to be spoon-fed. Her doctor has prescribed electroconvulsive therapy. This is Maria's first treatment and yours, too. You don't want to be here; they say ECT is scary. The doctor pushes a button and Maria's body rises from the table as you hold her arm. She begins to convulse and you want to turn your head away. Do they have to treat mental illness this way?

What made me think I wanted to be a nurse?

Six weeks later, Maria's treatments end. She's ready for discharge. She's eating and sleeping normally. She talks. She smiles, too, and laughs a little-girl laugh, calculated to touch the heart. She is beautiful—and well. She approaches you and takes your hand. "Thank you for helping me." Then you think, *Maybe I am in the right place after all.*

The six-year-old's head is larger than his entire body. You've had a hard time coping with this monster of a disease known as hydrocephalus. You want to run, hide even. Instead, you put your hand under his mammoth head and put a spoon to his mouth. Is there any point in all this? What kind of life does he have? Then, on visiting day, his mother comes. You see the love between parent and child. Then you understand. You're glad you didn't run.

Manny is catatonic, a huge man who looks straight ahead, ever motionless. Every day you pull and tug, trying to get him to move. During his shower, you get as wet as he does. His flat expression never changes. He seems completely oblivious. Does he even know you're here? You can get so frustrated trying to care for a man who offers no help. Would it make any difference if you just turned and walked away?

But then comes that special day with Manny, a day you will remember the rest of your life. You are face-to-face with another man holding a table leg; a man bent on destroying you.

Out of the corner of your eye you see movement. A huge fist stops the man holding the table leg. A massive shoulder crashes into the chest of the one who might have killed you. Weeks later, when Manny is on his way out of your ward, you ask him, "Manny, on that day—why?"

A beefy hand touches your shoulder. Manny smiles. "You helped me—it was time for me to help you." You spend the rest of the day digesting Manny's words. Then you say to no one in particular—"I like being a nurse."

Allan is schizophrenic and self-destructive. You spend

hour after hour trying to see into his world. You can't. It seems so hopeless. Sometimes, it gets so discouraging, you think Allan would be better off dead. But then, wonder of wonders—you connect.

His conversation becomes lucid—he's talking sense! One of his favorite topics: "You know, Donnie, when I get out of here, I'm going to get me a little puppy." He nearly drives you crazy with that puppy talk, he just won't get off it—but at least he's out of his shadow world.

Two years later, you're walking on the hospital grounds. A car horn blows. You look up to see a shiny convertible pulling alongside, a huge dog in the back seat. "How do you like my little puppy, Donnie?" Allan laughs, "At least he was a couple of years ago!" You follow Allan's car with your eyes as it pulls away, and you think, *I almost gave up on him.*

Harry is manic-depressive, a physically powerful, violent man, who spends most of his time in a seclusion room. You're working nights, sitting at a kitchen table, eating a bowl of Rice Krispies. Harry approaches. A lump forms in your throat. He stares at your bowl of Rice Krispies. "Can I have some?" You get him a bowl, a spoon and push the cereal and milk toward him. He scarfs down the Rice Krispies. It becomes a nightly ritual. No more seclusion, no violence. Harry will have other admissions. Your Rice Krispies are not a cure. But everyone asks, "How come Harry never gives you any trouble?" You smile. How do you explain the power of a bowl of Rice Krispies?

So now you sit, looking back at forty-five years. You're content, fulfilled; you've been "rewarded." Did you come to this by your own effort entirely? No. So, you say a thank-you: to Maria, to a hydrocephalic child, to Manny who saved your life, to Allan and his puppy, to Harry and his bowl of Rice Krispies.

They were your patients, you the nurse.

Who helped who the most?
Hard to say.

Don Haines

Always a Nurse

Some people credit their decision to become a nurse to a life-changing event. Not me. I just always knew I wanted to become a nurse. From my early years, I used my (sometimes willing, sometimes unwilling) sisters as patients. My dolls were constantly bandaged and dotted with marks from ballpoint pen "shots."

I loved nursing school and was filled with pride the first time I put on my uniform. I even liked the cap! Graduating from nursing school ranks as one of the happiest days of my life, as does the day I opened the letter announcing I had passed State Boards. At long last, my dream had come true. I was a nurse!

After graduation I worked in a psychiatric hospital, a nursing home, a telemetry unit and doing private duty with sick children. My satisfaction and confidence in doing assessments, starting IVs, learning medications, and relating to patients and their families confirmed my career choice.

When our first child was born, I quit working outside the home. I loved being with my new baby. Then several months ago, I realized it had been almost three years since I had worked as a "real" nurse. Sure, I continued to read

nursing journals and attend a nursing workshop occasionally, but the advances and changes in technology,
medications and procedures were overwhelming. Could I
ever find my place in nursing again?

I began to doubt my career choice. Had it been a mistake to spend so much time, not to mention money, on a
career I was going to practice for only a few years? Did
what I learned in school so long ago really matter? Could
I ever be a "real" nurse again?

A few days later, our three-year-old took a fall down the
front steps. With my heart pounding, I assessed him for a
potential head injury. His pupils were equal in size, he
was alert and annoyed at my assessment, and his motor
abilities appeared normal as he chased his little sister
across the yard.

I breathed a sigh of relief, and several other events from
the last few days popped into my mind. I remembered the
phone call from my mom, and my explanation to her what
a stroke was and how it might affect her friend.

I thought of the evening before, when I reassured our
neighbor, whose husband had just returned home from
the hospital after having a serious heart attack. I told her
she could call me anytime, and I'd be right over. We
hugged, and through her tears she said, "I'm so glad to
have a nurse next door!"

And I recalled another day when I counseled my father-
in-law on the importance of taking the whole course of
antibiotics he'd been prescribed, and not stopping the
medication when he felt better.

As I looked back, I realized I don't have to work in a big
hospital or know all the details of the latest high-tech procedure to be a nurse. I use my education every day, and
will continue to use it every day of my life. My career
choice was the right one.

I am, and always will be, a nurse.

Shelly Burke

A Nurse Named Gloria

He deserves paradise who makes his companions laugh.

The Koran

"It's a boy," the doctor said in a weak, agitated voice.

After his wan proclamation, came silence. There were no comments about how beautiful the baby was, no questions about what his name would be.

Even the baby was silent.

I dared not ask what was wrong, though I knew there was something. Doctors and nurses huddled at the end of the delivery room. They worked with frightful efficiency, brandishing a menagerie of medical equipment to prod my baby to breathe. Within minutes they whisked Ethan to intensive care. Soon, the physicians rendered the diagnoses—meningitis, pneumonia—massive, life-threatening infection.

My husband and I began what would become a routine—visiting the intensive-care unit to spend time with our son. As we sat at his bedside, we couldn't help noting that he wasn't the baby we'd imagined. His tiny arms were restrained and his head shaved to accommodate piercing intravenous needles. Swaddled in a latticework of tubes and needles, his breathing was performed by the whoosh of a ventilator. More machines beeped and hummed an odd lullaby.

Because of the equipment, we couldn't hold Ethan. Because he was sedated, we couldn't even look into his eyes. Still we went, and the first tenuous days melted into weeks. Ethan was our son, and we couldn't have loved him more if he'd been the rosy Gerber baby of our dreams.

Despite our love, the neonatal intensive care unit was a grim place. We parents wandered the corridors, yet we rarely spoke to each other. Dark circles ringed our eyes, and our faces had "Why me?" expressions. Instead of talking with each other, we spoke to doctors, steeling ourselves for depressing conversations where words like *brain damage* and *seizures* were used with alarming indifference.

To escape, I cried and ate big bags of M&M's. And I prayed like I never had before, my faith bolstered by my need for a miracle. Mostly I waited and hoped for my baby to get better, while the days faded into each other.

One day, however, was different. I started my hospital visit like all the others, by scrubbing my hands with pink disinfectant soap. As I dried them, I noticed they were raw and bleeding from frequent washing with harsh antiseptic. Next I grabbed a sterilized cotton gown and pulled it over my head. The gown felt scratchy and the sleeves were too tight over my winter sweater. Even the color annoyed me—the sunny yellow seemed too cheery for mothers of sick and dying babies. I would have been more comfortable in drab gray or murky blue.

I trudged down the familiar hallway, barely noticing the piquant smell, a mix of alcohol and baby powder. I looked away from murals of smiling bunnies that seemed out of place in this somber setting. I walked by rows of isolettes and their small occupants, premature infants wrapped in cellophane to keep them warm, newborns with birth defects, and older babies who would never have a home outside the hospital.

At the nursery door, I braced myself to see Ethan and hear the day's report of his condition. I knew it wouldn't be promising. At two weeks, Ethan was still on the ventilator, still racked with seizures, still poisoned by menacing bacteria.

Then I heard it. A sound I hadn't heard since the day Ethan was born. *Laughter.* It was not the polite, tinny laughter of visitors who were trying to relieve tension, but real laughter. Boisterous, robust and loud. It was coming from Ethan's nursery. The sound was so alien, I wasn't sure whether I welcomed it or felt threatened by it. Why would anybody laugh here, of all places?

I peeked inside the door to see a group of parents and nurses standing at one end of the nursery, gathered around a nurse named Gloria.

"Good morning!" Gloria called as I walked in the door. "It's great to see you. How are you doing today?"

"I'm okay," I said in a bland voice, still mystified by the cheery atmosphere.

Gloria grinned and waved me inside as she continued her one-woman show. I knew Gloria; she had taken care of Ethan. She had struck me as competent, sensitive and happy. But, tonight she looked positively radiant, as she regaled the listeners with funny stories of hospital life.

I wondered, at first, whether the babies were safe, since all the nurses appeared to be playing hooky. But I knew the nurses would notice the most subtle beep or buzzer while they had one eye on Gloria and one on their small charges. I joined the group and listened to Gloria's impromptu performance. Though I can't remember any of the stories she told, I remember how I felt while listening to her. At first, I smiled. Then, slowly, I dared to chuckle. Before long, I was laughing along with the crowd.

Initially, a pang of guilt pierced my heart. How could I laugh, when Ethan was fighting to live? But as I watched Gloria, these feelings dissipated. Her broad shoulders heaved and her frizzy, dark curls bounced as she entertained us. Her black eyes sparkled, and her lips turned up in an engaging smile. It was impossible not to be enchanted by her joyous spirit.

The more I laughed, the lighter I felt. My depression lifted, freeing my spirit from suffocating sadness. I welcomed the sliver of light, the brightness of hope. Nothing had changed with Ethan, yet I knew that whatever happened, I could handle it.

Gloria's one-woman laugh-fest marked a turning point in Ethan's hospitalization. After that night, I sought out Gloria whenever I visited the hospital. If there was bad news, I wanted to hear it from her. When test results came back from the lab, I wanted Gloria to decipher the numbers for me. When the time came to hold Ethan, to feed him and care for him, I wanted help from Gloria.

Gloria did help, with those tasks and more. She helped Ethan fight off the microscopic intruders that ravaged his body and the miracle I prayed for became a reality. But Gloria helped heal me as much as Ethan. Through the healing power of humor, Gloria gave me the will to smile and the courage to hope.

Lisa Ray Turner

CLOSE TO HOME   JOHN McPHERSON

E: CLOSETOHOME@COMPUSERVE.COM   4-28

www.uexpress.com

McPHERSON   © 1997 John McPherson/Dist. by Universal Press Syndicate

"We're conducting a study on the healing power of humor. As Boppy performs for you, let us know the precise moment that you feel the kidney stone pass."

Dumbo

*Of all the joys that lighten suffering Earth, what
joy is welcomed like a newborn child?*

Caroline Norton

I was the nurse caring for the couple's newborn first child after his cesarean birth. Since the mother was asleep under general anesthesia, the pediatrician and I took our tiny charge directly to the newborn nursery where we introduced the minutes-old baby to his daddy. While cuddling his son for the first time, he immediately noticed the baby's ears conspicuously standing out from his head. He expressed his concern that some kids might taunt his child, calling him names like "Dumbo" after the fictional elephant with unusually large ears. The pediatrician examined the baby and reassured the new dad that his son was healthy—the ears presented only a minor cosmetic problem, which could be easily corrected during early childhood.

The father was finally optimistic about his child, but was still worried about his wife's reaction to those large protruding ears.

"She doesn't take things as easily as I do," he worried.

By this time, the new mother was settled in the recovery room and ready to meet her new baby. I went along with the dad to lend some support in case this inexperienced mother became upset about her baby's large ears. The infant was swaddled in a receiving blanket with the head covered for the short trip through the chilly air-conditioned corridor. I placed the tiny bundle in his mother's arms and eased the blanket back so that she could gaze upon her child for the first time.

She took one look at her baby's face and looked to her husband and gasped, "Oh, Honey! Look! He has your ears!"

Laura Vickery Hart

Bringing the Cows Home

For health and constant joy in life, give me a keen and ever-present sense of humor; it is the next best thing to an abiding faith in providence.

G. B. Cheever

When I was a teenager I worked at a nursing home as a nursing assistant. Although the hours were long and the duties not always pleasant, I developed an understanding, respect and love for the residents. Elmer, a patient with Alzheimer's, was a favorite of mine.

Elmer was transferred from a facility cited by the state for inadequate care. He had no relatives to watch out for him—no one to care. Faded blue eyes, glistening with the dewdrops of old age, stared vacantly past the world around him. Inadequate care had left him bent at the hips and bent at the knees. Like a child's zigzag line of indelible ink on the wall, the damage could not be erased. His wasted legs belied the muscles that once strained in the fields in the hot summer sun. Although his arms remained as strong as the mules he once drove, he could not conceive the limitations of his legs. We were forced to keep him in restraints.

But Elmer's mind, unencumbered by the confines of reality, remained free to enjoy the pleasures of his past. Elmer still smelled the sweet of the evening dew on the new-mown clover. He still wiped the sweat from his favorite horse as they ploughed the frosty ground in the early spring. But Elmer no longer combed the fields and swamps looking for his cows. That chore was mine.

The first evening as I readied Elmer for the night, he asked, "Did ya bring the cows home?"

"Yes," I replied, "I brought the cows home, Elmer."

"How many?"

"Ten."

"Well, ya missed three. Best go back and find them before nightfall. They won't be safe out there."

The next night Elmer again asked about the cows. "Bring the cows home?"

"Yes, Sir, I did."

"How many?"

"Thirteen."

"Gosh darn girl, ya missed two. Go back to the swamp and get the others. They won't be safe out there."

And so it went, night after night. I was rarely able to predict the number of cows that would bring the desired response—"good girl." Sometimes I was sent to the neighbors to return a few cows because they "surely aren't ours." Sometimes I was told to wait out the storm before I went looking for a lost calf. Same time, same place, same station—but *never* same number of cows.

One night I arrived to find Elmer's bed empty and unmade—not a good sign in a nursing home. I cried out, "Elmer." No response. I ran to the nurse's station and asked if Elmer had died. He hadn't.

"Has he been moved?"

"No, he hasn't."

"He's not there," I worried out loud.

"He has to be. He can't go anywhere; he's tied in."

Running back to his room, the nurse and I called, "Elmer! *Elmer!*" Searching his room, I noticed his restraints were tied below the bed rails rather than through them. The crossed part, the part that should have been under the bed, was on top. I knelt on the floor and looked under the bed. There, suspended in his restraints, hung Elmer.

"Get the cows home?" he asked patiently.

Susan Townsend

The Crisis of Today

The crisis of today is the joke of tomorrow.

H. G. Wells

As a new registered nurse, I'd been assigned to work evenings in an intensive-care unit in a small rural hospital. Back then, as now, staffing was short, and I was the only R.N. working that shift. It was a quiet evening with only five patients, all of whom were sleeping or resting. I told the two L.P.N.s to go grab some supper in the cafeteria and bring me back something to eat. Leaving me to cover the unit, they hightailed it out of there before I had time to rethink my lousy decision.

I pored over my paperwork, the rhythm of the beeping monitors playing their familiar tune in the background, when my nursing radar picked up an unusual noise that flagged my attention. *What the heck was that?*

I looked up from my charts into the room across the hallway to see a cardiac patient standing beside his bed. *Hmmmm, not a good idea.* Then suddenly, before I could even complete that thought, *whoom!* His feet shot out from under him, his gown flew into the air, and he disappeared from sight!

Yikes! I leaped from my chair, shot across the hallway, bolted through the door and into the room. As I made my dramatic entry, I spied a giant puddle of greenish brown fluid spreading across his floor. *Nursing diagnosis: greenish brown liquid . . . body fluids . . . oh no! Poop!*

Too late! I was already hydroplaning across the spillage, arms and legs flailing to keep me upright. Always the optimist, my mind raced ahead with positive thoughts: *I'm going to glide across this mess, land on both feet and save the day!*

This, unfortunately, did not happen. Instead, my feet skidded across the fluid and then, *whoom!* I landed so hard on my backside, my head bounced off the linoleum. *Ouch!* I shook the stars off and rolled over to look for my patient. Spry thing that he was, he was trying to get up. *Boom!* He fell again. I tried to jump up to help him. *Wham!* I slipped again. He tried to pull himself up. *Whoom!* I scrambled for balance. *Wham!* With arms and legs splayed in every direction, we looked like Bambi and Thumper skidding on ice.

After what seemed an eternity, our eyes met, and I realized he was laughing. "It's probably not what you think," he said with a wink, and motioned to our putrid puddle. A Styrofoam cup lay tipped beside it.

Totally discombobulated, I couldn't understand what he was trying to tell me. "Huh?"

He shook his head as if to apologize. "I was hoping to hide my tobacco juice before you made rounds."

It took a minute to sink in. *Is this the good news or the bad news? Tobacco juice or poop: Which would I rather be wrestling around in?* To this day I'm still not sure. But once I knew that my patient was okay, I was able to see the humor in the situation, and we both enjoyed a good laugh together.

Lesson #1: Life's curveballs, plus time, equals humor. If there's a chance that you'll be laughing about something later, try to shorten the time frame. Laugh about it sooner.

Lesson #2: It's to your advantage if you can laugh at yourself before others do. By the time I walked out of that room with greenish brown slime painted all over my crisp white uniform, everyone else immediately saw the humor in the situation. Since I was already laughing, my colleagues laughed with me instead of at me!

Lesson #3: The closer you are to tragedy, the odder your humor becomes. Nurses have to be able to laugh at some of the tough stuff or we burn out and leave this wonderful profession.

Nurses can find the silver lining and the humor in the most bizarre places—thank God!

Karyn Buxman

"To help you better understand this good cholesterol/bad cholesterol thing, Nurse Bowman and Nurse Strickling are going to do a little skit for you."

The Assessment

Asssuredly I say to you, unless you are con-
verted and become as little children, you will by
no means enter the kingdom of heaven.

Matthew 18:3

I have been a nurse for twenty-three years in various
areas of nursing, but the story of this child, who I will call
"Tommy," has always haunted me.

I worked in a temporary shelter for abused and
neglected children, ages birth through seventeen years. I
sat on the floor in the lobby listening to the sketchy information the police officer provided. Tommy hid behind the
officer, only cautiously poking his head out every once in
a while when he heard his name spoken. He gripped the
policeman's finger with one hand and held a raggedy
stuffed bear with the other.

I opened a bottle of bubbles and blew them in the air
around me, all the while watching Tommy out of the corner of my eye. Slowly, he peered from behind the police
officer to watch bubbles cascade through the air and
silently pop on the carpet. Tommy took two small steps,

but still held on to the officer's finger. He looked up at the adults standing by him and seemed surprised that no one noticed he had moved. He let go of the officer's finger and hugged the raggedy bear to his chest with both hands. Stealthily, he walked across the room and knelt down about three feet from me. His face was upturned as he focused on the bubbles floating in the air.

This was my first chance to assess his physical condition. I knew his trust in me was only a temporary truce while he remained fascinated with the bubbles.

Tommy's bright red cheeks were smudged with dirt and stained from tears. I realized this redness on his cheeks was the shape and size of a hand—angry welts slowly rising in the form of fingers. His left eye, almost swollen shut, was discolored red and purple. The other eye, big and brown, lined with long, dark lashes, was still intent on the bubbles. There was a freshly scabbed cut below his cracked and edematous lower lip. A crusted, linear abrasion encircled his neck. As Tommy reached to catch a bubble before it hit the floor, I noticed a small circular blister on the palm of his right hand, evidence of a burn likely made from a cigarette.

I sat silently with Tommy and the bubbles, trying not to show the emotions I felt for what he must have suffered and the anger I had for the man who had done this to him. The rest of the assessment would have to be done when his clothes were removed for a bath and Tommy was not ready for that.

Shyly, in a voice barely above a whisper, he asked to blow the bubbles. Soon the room was filled with them floating in the air and Tommy laughing at the simple joy of this game, everything and everyone else temporarily forgotten.

The police officer came and knelt on one knee by Tommy and told him he had to leave. He pinned a toy badge to Tommy's shirt and said Tommy was an honorary sergeant because he was such a brave man today. I watched Tommy stiffen and grow silent once again. His eyes glistened with tears as the police officer shook his hand.

Tommy threw his arms tightly around the officer's neck, the bubbles forgotten. He said, "Tell Daddy I love him."

Rebecca Skowronski

THE FAMILY CIRCUS®   By Bil Keane

"She's listening to PJ's heartbeep."

Reprinted with permission from Bil Keane.

Taking Care of Joey

The tones of human voices are mightier than strings or brass to move the soul.

Friedrich Klopstoch

At 3:00 P.M., the young nurse looked up from her charting at the nurse's station to see the emergency room orderly wheel her admission into room 107. She had hoped to finish her charting and dictate report before he arrived. *And* she still needed a final set of vitals on her post-op tonsillectomy. *And* the ice packs needed to be replaced on the knee in 104. It's a good thing she'd set the room up earlier. She was ready for the admission—bed linens turned down, water pitcher filled, pediatric nightgown on the bed.

The nurse scribbled her signature on her unfinished charting and hustled to 107 to greet her patient. The ER phone report said six-year-old Joey had been removed from a violent home situation that afternoon and was being admitted for evaluation of injuries resulting from physical abuse. She was relieved to see the little boy walk from the wheelchair to the edge of the bed. That was a good sign—his injuries didn't seem severe.

The nurse bent to Joey's eye level and smiled. "Welcome to pediatrics, Joey. We're going to take really good care of you here." The small boy forced an uncertain smile.

"I have a few things I have to finish up real quick, then I'll be back to get you all settled in." Joey sat stiffly on the edge of the mattress, his hands folded in his lap. The young nurse reassured him with another smile. "It won't be long." With that she rushed out of the room, and so did the orderly—but not before handing her two pages of orders from Joey's doctor. X ray STAT . . . lab work STAT.

At the nurse's station, she dialed X ray with one hand while filling out pharmacy requisitions with the other. The charge nurse walked in. "Did you see your admission is here in 107?"

The young nurse took a deep breath. "Yes, I saw him. But until I get the X rays ordered, the drugs from pharmacy and the supplies from central service, I can't take care of him, can I?" She smiled weakly. "And I still have post-op vitals due in 110 and an end-of-shift report to dictate."

The charge nurse said, "I'll check the post-op vitals. You can give oral report later. Right now, prioritize and just do what's most important first."

The young nurse held the phone receiver to her ear with her shoulder and dialed the lab, while stamping central service requisitions. That's when her colleague handed her the other phone. "It's admissions. They say there's a discrepancy about the age of your new patient in 107. The social service form says he's six and the police report says he's five."

The nurse groaned. "I'll ask Joey when I admit him."

"They say they can't complete the admission, which

means they can't fill the doctor's orders, until they know."

The young nurse heaved a sigh and pushed the intercom button.

"Joey?"

He didn't answer.

"Joey?"

Silence.

"Joey, I know you're in there." With false patience the nurse said sternly, "Joey, answer me."

She could barely hear the small, quivering voice. "What do you want, Wall?"

With a lump in her throat, the nurse put down the phone, put down the forms, put down her stethoscope and went to 107 to do what was most important. To take care of Joey.

Donna Strickland
As told to LeAnn Thieman

Pennies from Heaven

Only the person who has faith in himself is able to be faithful to others.

Erich Fromm

Arriving early at the hospital one morning, I stopped by the cafeteria for some juice and a danish. The total came to $1.96. I got four pennies in change. Four pennies to rattle unsettlingly in my scrub pants pocket.

After finishing breakfast, I proceeded to the newborn intensive care unit. In the course of the next shift I would have four different infants entrusted to my nursing care, four precious pennies from heaven dropped into my pocket.

Upon entering, I surveyed the large, open unit. Against the far wall halfway down the left aisle, two nurses stood. One of them talked softly and patted the other on the arm in a consoling ritual. I looked down upon the warming bed beside them. On it lay a tiny, sickly, ghastly gray-colored infant hooked to a high-frequency ventilator. One thing surprised me. She kicked like there was no tomorrow.

My eyes moved up to the monitor screen overhead. Heart rate normal. Blood pressure borderline, but I had seen worse. Then I saw the oxygen saturation reading. It read 30 percent. Normal is above 90 percent. I stared at the tracing several seconds, wondering if it was a mistake or an artifact. It held steady at 30 percent.

Thirty usually means you are dead, not kicking.

I walked over to the bedside. Dehlia, the consoling one, turned and said, "You want to sign up for this baby? You'll be taking her to the morgue."

I nodded. "You know me. I'll take my patients wherever they need to go."

Pam, the baby's nurse through the night, eyed me sharply. Although my shift had not yet begun, she started to give me report.

Baby Camille was a twenty-five-week-gestation infant, a transport from an outlying hospital. She was delivered by emergency cesarean section the previous night after her mother became seriously ill with an infection. An ambulance team had brought Camille immediately to our unit. Throughout the night our doctors and nurses had tried everything for Camille, but her lungs were simply too immature to function. Now, we were just waiting to see if the father could come to see her before we removed her from the ventilator and allowed her to die. The father had remained at the other hospital with his critically ill wife.

I looked down at Camille again. Still gray, still kicking. I glanced back up at the monitor. The oxygen saturation now read 28 percent.

The attending neonatologist came over, just off the phone. "That's it," he told us. "The dad's on the way, but he doesn't want us to wait. Take her off the vent and stop the IVs." I reached up to turn off the monitor as well.

Dehlia asked if I wanted to hold Camille as she died. It

was just after 7:00 A.M., and the baby was now my responsibility. I deferred to Pam, who readily agreed. We brought over a rocking chair and bundled Camille in her arms.

Off the ventilator, Camille died quickly. Pam said she wanted to stay until the father came. She and another nurse took the now-still body, wrapped in a pink blanket and wearing a knitted cap, to the bereavement room to bathe and dress her.

Upon his arrival, the father was taken back to the bereavement room, where he held his daughter while Pam and the doctor talked with him. As Pam finally prepared to go home, I went in to introduce myself. I asked the father what I could do to help. He said he just wanted time to be with his firstborn child. I left him, showing him where I would be and promising to check back soon. I knew he felt guilty, having stayed with his wife while having to let his infant daughter be taken away alone. What a choice.

Returning to the unit, I found I had been assigned a second baby. This one was a large, full-term infant of a diabetic mother, on our unit for observation. Another nurse offered to cover for me until my tasks with Camille were done, but I declined. After the wrenching start to my day, I felt good holding the fat, warmly wrapped, squirming boy in my arms while he took his bottle.

I thought of Camille's father, holding his small, wrapped, unmoving daughter only a room away.

After laying my big baby boy back down to sleep, I returned to the bereavement room. I sat, and we talked together, father to father. I told him my first vision of his daughter. "She looked awful," I said, "but she was kicking. She fought to the end."

"That's how she was after the delivery," he told me with a sad, proud smile. "She was always kicking."

He called his family. He asked me to take one picture

while he held her. Then we took Camille back into the unit where, behind the screens placed around her bed, he said his last good-byes. We walked to the elevator. "Thank Pam for me," the father wiped away a tear as we shook hands. "I know everyone did their best, but some things are not meant to be."

Back on the unit, the charge nurse informed me that my other baby would soon transfer back to the regular nursery to be with his mother. After that, I would be taking over the assignment of another nurse who had to leave.

Having a free half-hour, I decided to take a quick break outside to clear my head. A cool drizzle fell as I walked along a small street beside the hospital. By a wooded area, I stood and looked into the trees, absently fingering the four pennies.

Minutes later I returned, ready for my two new babies. One was a little girl, a growing preemie doing well and starting on feedings. The other, inevitably, was a tiny twenty-five-week-gestation infant hooked to a high-frequency ventilator. "He's very unstable and sensitive to stimulation," his nurse looked at me seriously. "His saturation dropped down briefly to the thirties the last time we turned him. Try not to touch him, or he absolutely dies." Then, knowing what I had already been through that day, she caught what she had said. "Oh, I'm sorry. I didn't mean it that way."

"Don't worry, I understand," I grinned and sat back. "I can take my patients wherever they need to go."

The day progressed. My growing preemie little girl took her feedings well, a big step for her. My twenty-five-week boy stabilized on the ventilator. He even tolerated being turned. I was busy enough not to think of Camille.

The shift ended. I walked out the doors to leave. The drizzle had stopped, and the evening breeze at sunset felt light and cool. Before going to my car, a strong urge overcame me. I walked back down the side street. Sad thoughts of Camille returned. Stopping at the woods, I took the pennies from my pocket and looked them over.

Four babies. My four pennies from heaven. I tossed the pennies into the woods, as though sowing seeds. If three of them should sprout and grow, I should consider that a very productive day.

Raymond Bingham

Take a Number Please

It's easy finding reasons why other folks should be patient.

George Eliot

Nurses and orderlies rushed about the maternity ward helping mothers deliver their babies, then more arrived like an endless tide. There was more work than the staff could handle, so they floated some of us in from the recovery room.

We assisted in admitting the patients and doing the preliminary work, as well as looking after the expectant fathers. One young man was not only nervous, since this was their first child, but quite impatient. He repeatedly asked how much longer it would take. His constant pacing was making the young momma-to-be nervous. Finally we were able to convince him to go to the waiting room and get something to drink and relax, because it would be a while before she was ready to deliver.

After a while I went to the waiting room to give the expectant father an update on his wife's condition. As I talked with him, another nurse came into the room and announced to the husband of her patient that his wife was about to deliver.

The young man with whom I was talking walked over to the nurse and said, "Excuse me. I don't mean to be rude and I have tried to be patient, but I was here way before he was."

Naomi Follis

"McGuire! Party of two!"

Reasonable Resignation

Do your best every day, and your life will gradually expand into satisfying fullness.

Alexander Graham Bell

When I was the nursing administrator in a community hospital, I had made it my custom to follow an adult or a child partly or entirely through hospitalization. Usually, I chose someone because his or her condition was unusual, a nurse asked me to, or because the person presented a problem in interpersonal relations. Mary met all the criteria. She was a loud-voiced, henna-rinsed, aggressive woman gushing profanity. Soon after her first admission to the hospital, I heard about her and the staff's despair in trying to care for her.

The first time I visited Mary, I had to remain on the threshold because the moment she saw my unfamiliar face, she called out, "I don't want any visitors!" When I asked if she needed anything, I received a sharp "No!" I could advance into her territorial limits only as far as she permitted. It took a week of daily rounds to be allowed at her bedside.

Mary had a blood dyscrasia, which meant an undetermined and fragile future. Denying she was sick at all, Mary angrily insisted she would go back home and be normal again. Mary's husband and daughter lovingly and anxiously visited her and suffered her emotional outbursts.

Gradually, Mary began to talk with me. About two weeks after we became acquainted, she invited me to sit by her bed. As we discussed her background, she recounted her career as a writer, and I saw her come alive and appear almost well. An experience she shared one day became the turning point in our relationship. During World War II, Mary had visited a Japanese internment camp in this country. She was to write a story for her big New York City newspaper about the conditions there. At the camp, she found herself outside one of the internees' cabins. She stopped to watch an old gentleman patiently tilling the soil of a small garden plot where flowers bloomed brightly and vegetables grew. She noticed the peaceful, thoughtful and calm expression on his timeworn face.

Mary interviewed the man and learned he had been a successful businessman before the war. She felt compelled to ask how he could maintain such composure in light of the circumstances. Quietly, he responded, "I am not in control of the situation, but I can make the most of my life by providing both beauty and work for myself. I accept life with reasonable resignation."

Mary recalled that story pensively. Until that moment, she said, she had forgotten all about that part of her experience. Why did she remember it now? She stopped talking for a few minutes then asked if she could rest.

Mary went home twice during the next two months. Each time she returned, I visited her daily. It was easy to see her behavior changing. Now loud profanity subsided; she talked about her writing. Whenever depression weighed heavily upon her, she discussed "reasonable resignation," and her indomitable spirit rebounded.

During her fourth admission, the once-aggressive, blustery, brave redhead was clearly losing strength. Now gentler and calmer, she took the lead in our daily conversations, which included people, God and death.

It became my habit to say good-bye each Friday until my return on Mondays. If I was leaving town for any long meeting, I let Mary know. When I went to a four-day seminar, I told Mary a week in advance. The day before I left, I dropped by to see her. I knocked, then stood on the threshold as two nurses cared for her, their faces etched with sorrow. Mary saw me. "I don't need you anymore."

I could only manage to say, "I'll see you again," and quietly shut the door.

The seminar was held in an idyllic setting in central California and my room was on a cliff overlooking the Pacific Ocean. After it had rained all night, the sudden stillness of the storm's ebbing woke me Monday at 4:30 A.M. I felt compelled to go outside on the balcony. Just as I reached the porch railing, the clouds parted and the moonlight burst through. I felt a tremendous sense of release. It was all so breathtaking that, for the first time in my life, I cried for joy.

When I returned on Wednesday morning, I found, as I had surely known in my heart, that Mary had died early Monday morning. She left behind not only a saddened family, but also a hospital staff crushed by her death— crushed because, on the one hand, they were distressed at their early misunderstandings and, on the other hand, overwhelmed by Mary's courageous reasonable resignation.

Sylvia C. Chism

Black Stockings

Every generation laughs at the old fashions, but follows religiously the new.

Henry David Thoreau

There weren't many things I hated in this world as much as I hated black stockings. And yet I tolerated them for three long years when I was a student nurse in Milwaukee in the 1940s. Our student uniform was as attractive as a shroud. Shapeless, sand-colored, white-collared, short-sleeved and belted, the dress sagged halfway between my knees and ankles while other eighteen-year-olds wore knee-length skirts. The two lumpy patch pockets always bulged with pens, scissors and notepads. We even had to wear cotton undergarments to prevent sparking an explosion of anesthetic gases in the operating room. I tolerated cotton slips, but I detested black stockings. Those, and the black shoes we students were required to wear with the uniform, were the final indignity.

Sister Emma said we had to have black stockings before

we went on the hospital floors in our sixth week. My folks and I searched the stores in our spare time, but black stockings were as rare as chocolate bars during the war. By the end of the fifth week, I still had none. In desperation, my mother dyed six pairs of tan cotton hose black. I was ready.

My first patient contact: evening care for three patients. This meant helping them with their toileting needs, washing their hands and faces, and brushing their teeth. We, who had never touched a stranger, had to wash backs and give back rubs with rubbing alcohol and talcum powder. Even worse, everyone knew we were only "probationers," with hairnets, not nurses' caps, on our heads. I tried to do my assignments perfectly, but other patients turned their signal lights on and doctors stopped me in the halls, asking questions. I was so nervous, my underarms were wet with perspiration. My first three hours on duty seemed as if they were three years. Somehow, all my patients ate their suppers, and I finished their care. The head nurse inspected the ward, found dust on the base of one overbed table, but said I was adequate, and dismissed me for the evening. I hurried back to the nurses' home.

Safe in my room, I kicked my black shoes off. The linings were damp. I peeled my garter belt and stockings off. My feet were black as coal! I tried to scrub the color off without luck. With only five minutes before study hall, I dried my gray feet, threw on some clothes, ankle socks and saddle shoes, and dashed downstairs.

For two months my feet ranged in color from dead black to ash gray. The black dye oozed from the stockings, to my feet, to the lining of the shoes until everything was a dirty gunmetal color.

By December, things had settled down, but the life of a student nurse in the mid-forties was far from glamorous. The meals were mostly starch, and there was never enough food to satisfy the appetite of a growing girl; I hid jars of peanut butter in my dresser and ate it by the spoonful. It was routine to work eight hours, go to class for three or four more, and then to study. On my two half-days off I slept or studied, living in constant fear that I'd never learn enough to be a good nurse. But I was becoming more skillful with patients, practicing first on our mannequin, and my feet slowly faded.

Meanwhile, my father scoured the city during his lunch hours until he found some black rayon stockings in a hosiery store downtown and gave me three pairs as a Christmas gift. How I treasured them; they didn't dye my feet.

During our second year, we met students from other hospitals, most of whom were also plagued with black stockings, except for those from a fancy Eastside hospital; they wore white shoes and stockings. Our class agreed that our uniform would be far more attractive without black shoes and stockings, and we petitioned the director of nursing. She refused to listen. "Tradition," she said.

Counting down our 1,095 student days and looking forward to graduation, we dreamed of white stockings and fashionable short skirts.

One evening, a visitor handed me a package and thanked me for caring for his wife during her pneumonia crisis. He gave a similar package to every student on the unit, and the head nurse said we could keep them. Inside the box were three pairs of the first nylon stockings I had ever seen—black, but sheer as cobwebs and seamed up the back. Our grateful visitor owned a hosiery store. I wore my precious black nylons every Sunday until graduation. Meanwhile, our class bought fitted, short-skirted uniforms and the much-desired white stockings and shoes, saving them for the big day.

On August 28, 1947, our class of twenty-one paraded proudly in crisp, tailored white uniforms, white stockings and shoes, and starched white caps to receive our school pins on graduation day.

The following month, a young Frenchman named Christian Dior showed his first collection, "The New Look," featuring longer skirts, about halfway between the knee and ankle. His models pranced down the runway wearing sheer black stockings with their pumps.

Sometimes you just can't win.

Elsie Schmied Knoke

8

BEYOND THE CALL OF DUTY

There are risks and costs to a program of action. But they are far less than the long-range risks and costs of comfortable inaction.

John F. Kennedy

My Mission of Hope

Never doubt that a small group of committed citizens can change the world. Indeed, it is the only thing that ever has.

Margaret Mead

When I was in my late teens, a young priest gave me a prayer card inscribed with the words of Cardinal John Henry Newman, a nineteenth-century cleric. Titled "I Have My Mission," it read in part:

God has created me to do him some definite service:
He has committed some work to me, which he has not
    committed to another.
I have my mission . . . I am a link in a chain, a bond of
    connection between persons.
He has not created me for naught. I shall do good. I shall
    do his work.

The words struck a chord deep within me. The prayer card became one of my most treasured possessions, and I carried it with me for years. The priest also told me about

Mother Teresa, the nun who was working with the "poorest of the poor" in India and I longed to do something meaningful with my life.

A few years later, after I married, I began taking evening classes at a local community college. I started with psychology classes, then took a course that was ostensibly sociology but focused very much on the war in Vietnam. I invested a semester of hard work, earning an A in that class, as I did in most classes, but I took away far more than a good grade.

I soon became active in antiwar demonstrations and in the presidential campaigns of antiwar candidates. I read everything I could, trying to make some sense of America's involvement in Vietnam—but the more I read, the less I understood it.

By this time I had two children and was pregnant with my third; education and motherhood became my equal passions. I continued to enroll in classes, and in a burst of confidence took an intensive biology class. The idea of becoming a nurse grew within me. When I passed that class, I knew I was on my way. I took chemistry and passed that exam, too, with the second highest score in the class. Ultimately, I completed my nursing degree.

Meanwhile, the war in Vietnam dragged on. I felt helpless, fighting for a cause that most people didn't seem to care about. Gradually the thought struck me that perhaps I could make a single, small contribution by making a difference in the life of one person. Recalling a magazine article I had read about the plight of poor, unwanted children in Vietnam, I asked my husband how he would feel about adopting one of them.

We not only adopted one child, but applied for adoption of a second and third. When the process grounded to a halt, it seemed the children would never be released to us. After several frustrating months of waiting, I decided to go to Vietnam and attempt to untangle the paperwork.

Arriving there in November of 1973, I was immediately enthralled by this amazingly vibrant country and its people. On my second day I was invited to work with a nurse at the To Am ("warm nest") Nursery, founded by Rosemary Taylor, an Australian social worker who had been working in Vietnam since 1967. That evening I was greeted warmly by Elaine Norris, a volunteer American nurse.

Elaine was obviously exhausted. The influx of orphaned and abandoned children was increasing daily and this center was overflowing. They had no more room inside and were accommodating the extra babies wherever they could, even outside on the open porch.

The villa's living room had become a makeshift intensive care unit, filled with very sick babies. Many of them were receiving IV fluids from bottles hanging from nails driven into the walls. Nothing in my training had prepared me for such a sight, and the enormity of the task ahead took me by surprise. Nervously, I confided in Elaine that I wasn't sure I was competent to help with so many babies. Elaine smiled and assured me I would learn quickly. We talked while diapering, feeding and caring for the infants. At last, bone-tired, I crawled into bed. As I drifted off to sleep, I listened to the night's serenade: babies crying, gunfire in the street below and explosions in the distance.

I woke before dawn to find Elaine working in one of the rooms. Quietly, she pointed to a tiny baby boy and told me she'd been up all night nursing him. The baby was scheduled to travel to a new family soon, but he wasn't going to make it. The sight was traumatic for me. Before that moment, I had never seen a baby die. I stayed with Elaine, and we lovingly comforted the tiny boy until he passed away. By then I was crying so hard, I was sure I couldn't continue to work. The emotion was too much for me. But I couldn't leave the nursery because Elaine was exhausted after a full night's work. She needed me to get back in control.

I urged her to rest and told her I would take over while she slept. Alone, I gazed about the room, frozen by the awesome responsibility I had just agreed to take on. Suddenly, I was in charge of a house full of babies. There was no doctor and no other nurses, only the Vietnamese staff, who spoke little English. There was nobody I could turn to for advice or guidance; it was up to me to make the decisions.

A childcare worker soon approached me with an infant in her arms. She pointed to the child's forehead. I saw his flushed face and felt his forehead; he was burning hot with fever. Together we sponged the baby with cool water, and slowly the fever diminished. When he was sleeping soundly, the woman gently slipped him into a crib.

I followed behind the workers as they made rounds, quickly seeing how well these women knew their small charges. Though we couldn't converse, we communicated through the needs of the babies. A nurse pointed to one whose IV had infiltrated. The area was red and puffy. I knew what was needed, but there was no doctor to do the job. I'd have to do it alone. My hands shook as I pulled out the IV needle and correctly reinserted it into the tiny girl's vein. It was the first time I had ever started an IV, and I was relieved when I saw the fluid begin to flow into her vein. I fretted, checking the IV every few minutes, and was amazed that it continued working well.

As I went from child to child, my nursing skills came to the fore, and I knew what had to be done. No sooner had I finished with one child than another would need my attention. The hours blurred into a constant round of nursing each baby. I started recognizing the individuality of each one, and soon could identify them as the unique little people they were.

Finally, I looked up to see Elaine smiling and watching me, looking refreshed and rested. "You're a natural," she told me.

"I have my mission."

At last I had found the "definite service" for which I had been created. I returned to the United States only long enough to retrieve my children and husband and never returned to America to live again. The work in Vietnam in 1973 was the beginning of my lifetime commitment to children in Vietnam and India. I eventually opened my own organization—International Mission of Hope.

Cherie Clark

[EDITORS' NOTE: *Cherie Clark was instrumental in implementing Operation Babylift to help rescue three thousand orphans from Vietnam in 1975. From there she journeyed to India where she worked with Mother Teresa. She returned to Vietnam in 1988 where she continues to minister to needy children today.*]

The Heart of a Nurse

*You must give some time to your fellow men.
Even if it's a little thing, do something for
others—something for which you get no pay but
the privilege of doing it.*

Albert Schweitzer

My husband worked as an orderly at a nursing home in
a nearby town. There were two ways patients left his full-
care unit: by going to the hospital or dying. Most had no
visitors so my husband tried to fill that void with a
friendly word or smile for each of the people on his floor.

Easter was approaching. My husband felt sad that there
would be little to designate the holiday for his patients
and wondered what we could do to help. He had been out
of work some time before finding this job, and we were
struggling financially. Still, what could we do to make
Easter a little more pleasant for the patients? What could
we give them?

I looked around our apartment with plants in every
sunny window. "Let's give a plant to every patient," I

suggested.

We bought Styrofoam cups and filled each with some stones on the bottom, potting soil and a plant cutting. When we were done we had thirty potted plants, and I still had windows filled with greenery.

After church on Easter, we took our toddler and headed for the nursing home. One of the nurses found us a utility cart and we wheeled the box of plants around, stopping in each room, greeting each patient by name. Our son, dressed up in his Easter clothes, handed out the plants. Out of respect, he called each resident Grandpa or Grandma, though he knew they weren't his grandparents. They all smiled while we spent a few minutes talking with each of them and wishing them a Happy Easter. Some of them might not have usually celebrated Easter, but we felt our visit transcended religion. Our little boy enjoyed the pats on his head and kisses on the cheek. It was the best Easter we'd ever spent.

Later that week there was a nursing strike. The floor was manned by a skeleton crew and per diem nurses. My husband and the other orderlies were pressed into service to help. It was near the end of his shift and he was exhausted, when one of the substitute nurses hurried out of a room. "Mr. Peterson is dying," he overheard her tell the head nurse. There wasn't much they could do for the old man other than make him comfortable. After the nurse gave him the medication, she returned to her station. On a normal day one of the nurses or certified nurses' aides would sit with a dying patient and offer whatever comfort was needed. This day there was no one extra to perform this humane service.

"I'll stay with Mr. Peterson," my husband offered.

"Your shift's over, and we can't pay overtime," the head nurse said.

"I'll stay. No problem," my husband said again.

It was a long time before he could tell me the rest of the story. He sat down next to Mr. Peterson. The plant we'd given him at Easter bloomed next to him on the night-stand. He recognized my husband. "I'm dying, son," he said in a low voice.

My husband fought back tears. "I'll stay with you awhile."

The old man asked, "Pray with me?"

My husband had no idea what religion Mr. Peterson practiced, but he took the man's gnarled hands in his and prayed with him for God's grace. He stayed with him for hours, talking and praying until the man slipped away with a smile on his face.

"I felt the spirit of the Lord in that room," he told me. "I know Mr. Peterson is with God."

My husband wasn't a trained nurse, but surely that afternoon he had the heart of a nurse.

Beatrice Sheftel

Nurse Puss 'n Boots

Do all things with love.

Og Mandino

It was Christmastime in 1979, and I lay recovering from "female surgery" in a hospital in Virginia. To make matters worse I got stuck with a wacky nurse. And she was mean as a viper. Her short, chubby body waltzed into my room each morning, waking me and shouting, "Time to get up, Missy! Get up and get outta that bed before you catch pneumonia. You've got to move about, or else!"

I didn't like her much, and I let it be known. Besides, it was plain she didn't like me. She frequently quipped, "I'm just doing my job, and I intend to do it by the book, Missy. By the book."

Outside the snowfall piled higher and higher and half of the nursing staff was unable to get to work. But of course Nurse Puss 'n Boots made it. I called her that because she came in every afternoon with her white boots on, covered with snow and stomped around in them all day. I could see her from my window trotting through the white flakes every day at 2:30 on the dot. *What was it about this particular nurse that intrigued me so?* I wondered.

I was sure she didn't have a life outside the hospital. She was domineering and mean and always eager to start her shift, as if it was so wonderful to be stuck in a hospital with sick people every evening. Sullenly I asked God, *Must Christmas come this year? And must I spend it with this gruff nurse?*

Christmas Eve came and I was devastated that my husband and baby boy were stranded at home, an hour from the hospital. There was no way they could drive through the snow-packed interstate. I lay in my bed in a deep state of melancholy imagining how little "Bradley Boy" would look when he opened his train.

To make matters worse, Puss 'n Boots came marching in and noticed my sadness. "Well, Missy. You'll just have to do better than this. You'll have to take what comes," she insisted. I made a face at her when she turned and walked out the door. I could hear her at the nurse's station. "That's right—by the book, always by the book." I groaned and covered my head with my pillow.

At seven o'clock sharp, I heard Christmas carolers in the hallway, singing "O Holy Night." I smiled in spite of myself and walked to open my door. Shocked, I stammered, "I'm dreaming! Ol' Puss 'n Boots put something in my ginger ale."

"Nope. No dream," my husband beamed. "Thanks to your nurse, I'm staying in the hotel one block away." Nurse Puss 'n Boots had arranged for her husband to drive his Jeep to our town the day before and pick up my husband. Not only did she bring him to me, but she paid for his hotel room for a few days, until I could be discharged. I stood gazing at the mean nurse, now turned heroine. She even smiled at me, as I stood with my jaw dropped open in marvel.

I learned this extraordinary nurse and her wealthy husband did generous deeds for many people. She didn't even have to work, but chose to fulfill her life with nursing. My husband adored her. "She's tough, like my old drill sergeant," he said. "We need more nurses like her."

Today, as a nurse, I trot through snow in the hospital parking lot wearing white boots in honor of my favorite nurse. I called her hospital to inquire about Puss 'n Boots and to tell her how she had inspired me. They said she had passed away in her sleep at home—her generous heart stopped beating.

If I know Nurse Puss 'n Boots, she's standing at the gates of heaven right beside St. Peter with her ink pen and chart. She's grabbing each lost soul who tries to slip through the cracks, saying, "By the book, Missy! By the book!"

J. C. Pinkerton

The Pinning

The future destiny of a child is always the work of the mother.

Napoleon Bonaparte

**Northern Oklahoma College invites you to
attend their Nurse's Pinning Ceremony
Friday, May 7, 1999.**

I was the first member of our family to graduate from college and I had waited for this moment all my life. As we assembled in the auditorium, I joked with my family and friends that I was finally graduating. My two-year degree took me ten years to complete while I raised a family and worked as an L.P.N.

The final weeks of school had been so busy and life so hectic, I could hardly believe this moment was actually here. In my new dress and shoes, I didn't look too bad next to all those younger nurses. Then my best friend Dru came with the news—Ronnie may not make it on time. How could my husband, who had supported me so faithfully all these years, be stuck at work and miss this?

My mom had been my first choice to pin me, because she had always been there for me on this journey. But she declined, saying my husband and sons should share in this moment—a moment already bittersweet. My son Jesse was in the Navy, stationed in Chicago, and couldn't attend. Now, with Ronnie stuck at work, my mom and son Clint would have to do the honors. The script had been written for my pinning weeks before, and now it would be changed—again.

My nursing buddies knew my disappointment, as I had spoken often of missing my Navy boy, especially with this being Mother's Day weekend. As my turn approached to cross the podium, I looked around the auditorium to catch a glimpse of my husband, but to no avail. I did see Dru poised to capture the moment on film, but I couldn't hear my script, only my name when I caught the line . . . "will be pinned by her husband and two sons."

There in front of me, coming my way, was my handsome husband, son Clint, and Jesse, fresh off a plane in Navy attire, with smiles so broad and a hearty "Surprise!"

My whole class and all the instructors cheered wildly as the pin I had worked so hard for was lovingly placed.

Dawn Koehn

Last Rites

*M*usic *is the universal language of mankind.*

Henry Wadsworth Longfellow

I took care of Sam on med-surg for about nine months during his frequent admissions for end-stage liver disease. Sam, a World War II veteran with a caring wife and family, had slipped into a coma for nine days and was not expected to recover. On a slow Sunday afternoon, Sam's family had left for the day. When I went to check on him fifteen minutes later, I knew by his breathing he was about to pass on. I walked into the hall looking for other staff members, since we were all quite close to Sam and his family. Just outside the door stood Father Charlie, the Catholic priest who made rounds every weekend. I asked him to give Sam last rites. He checked the chart outside the door and informed me in a kind way that he could not, because Sam was not Catholic. He offered to come in and say a prayer, though.

Entering the room he said, "Oh, I know this man. We're both veterans and have had many discussions." He took

Sam's hand. "Do you mind if I sing a song?"

I was so surprised at this request but, of course, said, "No, go right ahead."

Father Charlie started to sing, "Mine Eyes Have Seen the Glory of the Coming of the Lord."

To my astonishment, Sam, who had been in a deep coma all these days, had tears streaming from both eyes. As Father Charlie sang the words, "Glory! Glory! Hallelujah!" Sam took his last breath.

Jacqueline C. Hadeland

Heroes

*Conscience is the root of all true courage; if a
man would be brave let him obey his conscience.*

J. F. Clarke

I served as an army nurse in Vietnam from February
1967 though February 1968. It was a chaotic, trying time,
encompassing two infamous Tet offensives. Tet and the
months right before were times of enemy buildups and
especially high casualties for Americans.

Although nurses were generally assigned to large base
areas, because of overwhelming casualties, many nurses
and medics found themselves in quite primitive places
with less than the best protection.

I was sent to AnKhe because of my surgical training
and also administrative background. AnKhe was the base
camp for the elite First Cavalry. Casualties were especially
heavy, so a first-aid station was converted to a 100-bed
hospital. Eight nurses worked under tents without suffi-
cient medical equipment.

Small miracles occurred there every day. Mayonnaise

jars became chest drainage bottles. With some crude addi-
tions, they also became suction machines. Corpsmen from
a previous war taught us all to suture and perform surgeries. None of us required much sleep nor became ill. So
we worked impossible stretches of time to treat as many
as were brought in by helicopter.

We had so many surgical patients they were forced to
lay on the tent floors after surgery. All the cots were full.
Supplies and surgical instruments had to be shared.
Antibiotics were long ago used up. Guys were dying for
lack of supplies. Then the angels came.

Two corpsmen reported to me one morning. They had
been assigned here as punishment. Well-educated men,
both had just been released from the stockade. Seems
they refused to "hump ammo"—to load 200-pound
rounds of artillery pieces, after seeing what the results
were. It is still unclear why medics were in an artillery
unit in that capacity, but they were. They came to AnKhe
humble and beaten down, but not without integrity. "We
will do anything—absolutely anything to save lives,
Captain. No matter how risky."

They seemed sincere and almost as desperate as me. I
called their bluff.

The only way in and out of AnKhe was by air, and the
flights were too few and far between. The road was mined
several times daily. Many vehicles were blown up.
Needed medical supplies could not be legally obtained,
let alone transported in.

I briefed them on the risks and the need for supplies.
With great guilt and fear and uncommon prayer, I sent
these two to almost certain death, over the road, off the
record, unauthorized, to get supplies however they
could.

Five long days went by. I began mentally writing the
letters to their families.

But angels were with them. They returned with an intact truck loaded with penicillin, surgical instruments, a real suction machine and even a steel litter on real wheels.

What a faith moment when they drove in! I'll not recount how they got the supplies, but many lives were saved because of their effort and grace from on high. And as a result, all were reenergized to continue our breakneck schedule.

So heroes come out of stockades, angels do roam the battlefield, and there is a God, even in war.

Rhona Knox Prescott

$\overline{9}$

THANK YOU

In helping others we shall help ourselves, for whatever good we give out completes the circle and comes back to us.

Flora Edwards

A Piece of Paper

Hope is life and life is hope.

Adele Shreve

For twenty-five years, I have been involved in emergency nursing; the last fifteen years as a flight nurse with over five thousand patient flights. Along the way, I have collected many diplomas and certifications, and they are displayed on my office wall. One piece of paper on that wall means more to me than all the others. It reminds me why I am a nurse—because I can make a difference in the outcome of a person's life.

Every weekend, Lake Havasu, a popular reservoir on the Arizona–California border, is full of skiers, boats and alcohol. Unfortunately, when all of these mix it can become a deadly cocktail. One Labor Day weekend, our AirEvac unit was called to transport a patient badly injured in a boating accident to a trauma center in Phoenix. A pilot, respiratory therapist and I quickly loaded our equipment into our twin-engine plane and lifted off for Lake Havasu City. Within forty minutes, we landed at the airport and raced to the hospital.

Our patient was a twenty-eight-year-old man who was badly injured when his boat collided with another, and he was thrown into a propeller. I first saw this man, who I'll call John, as the nurse on duty gave me a quick report while we prepared him for transport. John was already secured to a backboard. His color was ashen, and I could see fear in his eyes. As I introduced myself to him, he whispered, "I am going to die." This was quite possible, because the propeller had thrown John into the boat, breaking his ribs, partially severing his right arm, puncturing his chest cavity and collapsing his lung. Now a tube was protruding from his chest to help him breathe. His arm was wrapped tightly to his chest with an ace bandage to prevent further bleeding. His abdomen was firm, tender to the touch and slowly becoming distended from internal bleeding. We put John on our stretcher with oxygen and a heart monitor and moved him to an ambulance. Our pilot was waiting for us at the airport, and we quickly loaded John into the plane and headed back to Phoenix.

During the flight, we administered a large amount of blood. We had taken blood from the hospital in hope that it would help sustain him during the flight to Phoenix. Since blood is kept refrigerated, giving that much cold blood would add another insult to John's already weakened body. To warm the blood, the pilot, respiratory therapist and I sat on each one-half-liter bag. John remained awake and continued to moan, "I hurt all over."

The respiratory therapist looked at me. "Maybe you should give him some morphine," she suggested.

But John's hope for survival was surgery, and we were still over forty minutes away from the Phoenix hospital. Many times I had given pain medicine to help a patient wait out the long minutes until we reached the hospital, but John was different. His condition was so critical that he needed to stay awake and will himself to live. I wasn't going to take away his chances with sedation. As I leaned over John, our eyes met and I said quietly, "I want you to feel the pain. I want you to hang in there and fight for your life." He nodded and closed his eyes.

On takeoff from Lake Havasu, our pilot had radioed the air traffic controllers in Phoenix that we had a patient on board. This is known as a lifeguard flight, which means that we have priority over other airplanes to land. Because of the wind direction that day, the air traffic controllers at the Phoenix airport had all the planes landing from east to the west, but our pilot requested special clearance so we could land "straight in" from west to east, shaving precious time off of our flight. As we taxied to the AirEvac hanger, I could see a helicopter waiting to take us to the hospital. We loaded John into the helicopter while the engines were running, saving the time it would have taken to start them.

When we landed at the trauma center minutes later and unloaded John on the helipad, he was no longer responding to my voice. Time was running out. As the elevator doors opened, the trauma team was waiting for us. I gave the surgeons a quick summary of what had been done for John and his response to our treatment. He was taken immediately into surgery, and I returned to base.

I followed John's progress and spoke with those caring for him. They were amazed he survived. The surgeons had found five liters of blood (over 85 percent of his total blood volume) inside his abdomen. Aside from his other injuries, he had ruptured his spleen, which was removed, and extensive surgery was required to repair his arm. During the operation, he received seven and a half liters of blood. Despite so many hours in the operating room, John had made it and his prognosis was good.

I wanted to see John again in a more stable setting to say, "Way to go, you did it." Two days later, I visited him in the intensive care unit. He was sedated and had a tube down his throat to help him breathe. As I walked in, he saw me and smiled. I was surprised he remembered me. After giving me a hug, he mouthed a "thank you" and pointed to the pictures of his three sons taped to the end of the bed.

Then he took a piece of paper and slowly wrote on it, "I remember you, you talking to me, saying to hang in there everything will be okay. Thank you, I owe you my life."

John went home two weeks after his accident.

And that is the piece of paper I proudly framed and hung on my office wall.

Sherri Sorenson

The Call

The difference between perseverance and obstinacy is that one often comes from a strong will and the other from a strong won't.

H. W. Beecher

I'd rarely dealt with residents and interns, and the thought of being responsible for them unnerved me. I resolved to put my best foot forward and be the coolest head in the hospital. Working with them, I was factual, objective and confident. Maybe a bit too confident for the senior resident, who didn't seem to like me.

When I confided this to a coworker, she offered, "You don't make it easy for him, Virginia. Oh, he's impressed, all right, but he's just waiting for you to do something so he can take you down a few notches."

One afternoon I admitted a seventy-five-year-old man with congestive heart failure. Our new patient was a big, barrel-chested man, about six feet tall, with white hair and large hands gnarled with arthritis. His strong, regal voice boomed through the unit. But he was in trouble. We tried to dry his lungs and pump up his heart, but he grew progressively worse. At 7:38 P.M., he coded.

After we worked on him for about forty minutes with every approved and experimental drug available, his heart was unresponsive. For the umpteenth time, his rhythm wobbled to nothing on the oscilloscope.

Suddenly, I began shouting his name over and over. I didn't even know I was doing it until the resident shook my shoulder and said sarcastically, "Shouting won't bring him back to life. He can't hear you. He's dead."

I cringed at the image of me leaning over the dead man, calling into his ear. I was mortified to realize I was acting like a rookie, especially given the scientific fact that he was no longer alive. I tried to say something in my defense but couldn't explain why it was so vital for me to keep calling his name.

Disgusted, the resident turned away to record the time of death.

Then I saw the heartbeat start up again on the monitor. "He's back!"

Within minutes, to everyone's amazement, the patient stabilized.

I went back to the nurses' desk, still perplexed by my irrational behavior. Apparently my coworker was, too. "Why did you keep yelling at him?"

"I—I don't know. I just had to," I admitted, helplessly racking my brain for a reason. "I just couldn't help it. . . . "

I was even more bewildered the next afternoon when I reported for duty and the day nurse told me the patient had been furious with me all day and wanted to see me the minute I came on duty. I groaned as I walked dispirit-edly toward his bed, wondering again what had come over me to make me act so foolishly that I angered this grand, old gentleman.

I pulled back the curtain around his bed to see him glaring at me. "So you're the one who wouldn't let me go!" he challenged.

"Yes, Sir," I said in a low voice.

"Did they tell you I was going to sue you for malpractice?"

"No, Sir."

"Do you think you're God? Why did you think you had the right to call me back?" He held his hand up to keep me from interrupting. "I was on the way out, and it was the most beautiful thing I'd ever known. But someone kept calling me and calling me. I was so mad I hollered at you all night!"

I stammered, "I'm so sorry. I didn't know what I was doing. Will you please forgive me?"

"Oh, my God, yes!" he said huskily. "Without you, I wouldn't have known my granddaughter loved me. See, I thought she never wanted to see me again, but when she heard I was in the hospital she tried all night to get a flight, but couldn't get here until this morning. And," his voice choked, "if you hadn't called me back I would have died thinking she hated me. But she loves me. She told me today. Imagine that. And I have a great-granddaughter, too!" He paused, then added, "All I wanted was to stay in that beautiful light, but I'm glad you didn't let me. I'm glad you didn't give up."

He chuckled at the equal measure of relief and embarrassment chasing across my face. He closed his eyes and said with a sigh, "I guess neither one of us knew what we were doing, eh?"

I nodded in mute acknowledgment.

The grand, old man died later that same night with his granddaughter at his side.

I don't know what overtook my objectivity that evening so long ago when I relied on something beyond science, beyond myself. But I've come to depend on it in a large way—especially when I need to come down a few notches.

Virginia L. Clark

Love in Your Hands

Love is all we have, the only way that each can help the other.

Euripides

The old man lay all alone
and stared out through his haze.
I knew his eyes were almost gone
and wondered at his gaze.
Perhaps he saw his childhood
on carefree running legs.
But his legs were long-since lost
to diabetes' grasp.
To change his bed and bathe him
was my only task.
Not wanting much to startle him
I called out softly, "Sir."
He stirred his body toward me
glazed eyes focused near.
"Who's that? I don't know the voice.
What you doin' *here?*"

Name spoken, "I just came to help
to fix your bed and such."
"Watch out! Don't hurt me none,"
he shrank back from my touch.
"Them other ones, they's rough you know,
they jerks and pulls me 'round.
And sometime I gets afraid
they'll drop me to the ground!"
I couldn't lift him all alone
not causing fear or pain.
No one around, and so I went
to get the lifting frame
We talked and slowly did
the things we had to do
Refreshed and dressed
he grasped my hand
And said, "Son, God bless you.
Some folks is rough and short, and mean
and though you be a man
I wanna tell you somethin'
You got love in your hands."

Ken Cyr

Silent Angel

A thousand words will not leave so deep an impression as one deed.

Henrik Ibsen

Christmas Day, 1967. I'm a patient at the Ninety-Third Medical Evacuation Hospital near Saigon, Vietnam. Today I'm semi-alert, but unable to sleep and agonizingly scared. The constant aching pain in my arms and a pounding headache make me tense. I feel helpless. My spirit feels empty, and my body feels broken. I want to be back home.

It's impossible to get in a comfortable resting position. I'm forced to try and sleep on my back. Needles, IV tubing and surgical tape are partially covered by bloodstained bandages on my arms.

Two days earlier, my squad's mission was to secure the perimeter of Saigon for a Christmas Day celebration featuring Bob Hope and Raquel Welch. While on a search-and-destroy patrol, near the village Di An, we were ambushed on a jungle trail by a small band of Vietcong guerillas. My right thumb was ripped from my body by AK-47 assault-rifle fire and fragments from a claymore mine grazed my face and neck.

This medical ward has twenty-one sick and injured G.I.s, and one recently captured, young-looking Cambodian. Restrained, he lays severely wounded in the bed next to mine. I'm filled with anger and hostility. As an infantry combat veteran, I've been brainwashed to despise the Communists and everything they represent.

The first hours are emotionally difficult. I don't want to be next to him. I want to have an American G.I. to talk with. As time passes my attitude changes; my hatred vanishes. We never utter a word to each other, but we glance into one another's eyes and smile. We're communicating. I feel compassion for him, knowing both of us have lost control of our destiny. We are equals.

The survival of the twenty-two soldiers in the ward depends on the attentiveness and medical care from our nurses. Apparently, they never leave our ward or take time off. The nationality, country or cause we were fighting for never interferes with the loving care and nourishment necessary to sustain us. They are our life-keepers, our guardians, our safety net, our hope of returning home. It's nice to just hear a woman's voice. Their presence is our motivation to get well so we can go home to our wives, children, moms, dads, brothers, sisters and friends.

Christmas is a special day, even in a hospital bed thousands of miles from home. Today the nurses are especially loving and gracious. Red Cross volunteers help us write letters to our families. All of us still need special attention plus our routine shots, IVs, blood work and I swallow twenty-two pills three times a day. Even on Christmas, life goes on in our little community, like clockwork, thanks to the dedication of our nurses. They never miss a beat, always friendly and caring.

There's a rumor that General Westmoreland and Raquel Welch will visit our ward today and award Purple Hearts to the combat wounded. I'm especially hopeful it's true because I would receive the commendation. The thought of meeting Raquel Welch and General Westmoreland gives me an adrenaline boost that lasts throughout the day.

By early evening we realize they aren't coming. Everyone is very disappointed, especially me. The day's activities cease quickly after a yummy Christmas dinner and most of my wardmates slip off to sleep by seven or eight o'clock.

It's impossible to sleep. The IVs in my arms continue collapsing my veins one by one. I'm pricked and probed by what feels like knives, not needles. My arms are black and blue after many failed attempts to locate a vein for IV fluids. I occasionally doze off, only to be awakened by the agonizing pain of another collapsed vein and infiltrating fluids. My arms are swollen to twice their normal size. This pain is worse than my gunshot wound.

It's eleven o'clock Christmas night. The ward is silent. My comrades and the Cambodian warrior sleep. I'm tense and suffering.

To avoid waking anyone, I silently signal a nurse. She comes to my side and gazes into my tearing eyes. Quietly, she sits on the side of my bed, embraces my arm, removes the IV, then lightly massages my swollen, painful arms.

Gently, she leans over and whispers in my ear, "Merry Christmas," and gives me a long, tender hug. As she withdraws, our eyes connect momentarily. She has tears running down her cheeks. She felt my pain. She turns and moves away, ever so slowly back to her workstation.

The next morning I wake slowly. I have slept through out the night and feel rested. I see while I slept a new IV was inserted in my arm. The swelling is gone. Suddenly, I remember the nurse coming to my side in the night and my Christmas present. I'm thankful and think of her kindness. I look toward the nurses' workstation to see if I can see my angel nurse, but she's gone.

I never see her again, but I will forever honor her compassion toward me on that lonely Christmas night.

Duane Shaw
Dedicated to Peggy Ferrera

Child's Praise

God gave man work, not to burden him, but to bless him; and useful work, willingly, cheerfully, effectively done, has always been the finest expression of the human spirit.

Walter R. Courtenay

Several years ago, I presented a lecture to a large group of parents on the theme of my book, *Traits of a Healthy Family*. In the lecture, I mentioned how children serve as a primary support system for parents—that, in fact, when a child thanks or praises a parent, it means more to the parent than when a spouse does the same.

After my lecture, a young mother came up and handed me the following note. I don't know her and I never saw her again, but I treasure her story:

Besides being a wife and a mother, I work part-time as a nurse in labor and delivery. One evening while my husband and I were getting the children ready for bed, I was called in to work and ended up working through the night. I came

home exhausted and depressed at the thought of taking care
of the kids by myself for the long day ahead. As I was stand-
ing in the kitchen feeling a little sorry for myself, my three-
year-old, Jacob, came and stood in front of me. He looked up
at me with an expression of awe on his face. "Mom, you're
really a nice lady."

I was a little surprised. "What made you say that, Jake?" I
asked. He answered, "Because you go and help ladies have
babies in the dark."

Suddenly, the day ahead didn't seem so long.

Dolores Curran

Ministering Angels

As night and nature took their stance among a unit of weakened children, I took mine as a pediatric oncology nurse one placid evening. The late hours slipped away and, if someone quietly drew near to a child's door, the sound of honest slumber would tickle the ear. I glided from bed to crib to bed again, appraising the quality of comfort these children so deserved. Tucking in little toes; rescuing brown teddy bears from the bed's fierce side-rails and returning them safely under their companion's arm; quietly humming, "Sleep, sleep, sleep . . . tender warrior. Your Father loves you and he's whispering, 'Well done.'"

A girl of seven years lay under a blanket of cotton blue. Her face was that of a darling with lengthy raven lashes and rose-colored lips. My hand reached for hers, and I held it closely as I silently offered thanksgiving for the precious gift of a child in tranquil stillness. I kissed her bare head, then quietly turned to leave when I heard, "Miss Allison?"

I knelt alongside her, gently reaching for her hand once again.

"I want to be what you are when I am grown."

"Oh, Dearest, you will be a wonderful nurse one day. Of that, I am sure."

"No," she whispered. "It is an angel that I want to be. I want to be an angel."

Allison Leigh Usher
In honor of Bethany Garrett, age 7

A Gift from Nana

It is the will and not the gift that makes the giver.

Gotthold E. Lessing

On the morning of March 22, 1995, my sister-in-law went into Los Robles Medical Center to be induced into labor. My husband and I arrived at the hospital in the late afternoon to be there for the exciting event. When we got to her room, everyone present seemed to be in a state of shock.

At the change of shifts, the head nurse, Charlotte, noticed my sister-in-law's last name and immediately paused. The last name brought back a memory of a woman she had once cared for twenty years ago at a hospital fifty miles away. Consequently, she decided to assign herself to my sister-in-law's care that evening. She entered the room and hesitantly asked my brother if he knew of a JoAnn. Stunned, he answered, "Yes, she was my mother."

Although we were excited for the birth of our niece, we could not forget that the next day would be exactly twenty years since my mother had passed away after battling cancer. Charlotte's eyes grew wide as she realized that she was assisting in the delivery of JoAnn's first grandchild.

To our amazement, Charlotte actually remembered my father, brother and me, and throughout the evening she shared several endearing stories of the friendship she had developed with my mom for over a year. The commonality of having children the same age made their relationship especially close.

Well past midnight, my sister-in-law was not making progress, so a C-section was performed and Kylee Ann entered the world. For the first time in twenty years, the sadness I so often felt on this day, the anniversary of my mother's death, was replaced with the joy of new life.

Two days later, as Kylee Ann was being discharged, Charlotte came in holding a delicate white porcelain figurine of a large bird perched on a branch looking down at a smaller bird.

"Your mother gave this to me as a thank-you gift when I took care of her twenty years ago. I've cherished it all these years. Now I pass it on to Kylee Ann"—a gift from her Nana.

Terri Murcia

Thank You, Mrs. Dickenson

We judge ourselves by what we feel capable of doing, while others judge us by what we've already done.

Henry Wadsworth Longfellow

Patients may not be aware of how they can affect the lives of hundreds of people.

After my first year of night duty, I felt overworked and underappreciated as I worked five nights per week on a very busy med-surg floor. We often had fourteen patients each, and that was before IVACs, IV admixtures, unit dose medications and Pyxis distribution. In other words, we were very busy. Every two hours, patients had to be turned, deep-breathed and coughed. Surgical dressings had to be checked and marked. Without computerized or checklist charting, head-to-toe assessment had to be documented every two hours on every patient. I did my best, but as a "new grad" I felt overwhelmed and very inadequate to meet the needs of my patients.

After an especially difficult night, my clinical coordinator announced she wanted to see me in her office. My heart sank to my feet. I was doing the best I could to care for my patients, do all my charting and care planning, and maintain my composure while on duty. I finished counting the narcotics with one of the oncoming nurses and reluctantly dragged my body into her office, prepared for my reprimand.

The clinical coordinator closed the door behind me and asked me to sit down. This was too much for me. I could feel a lump in my throat; my eyes misted. She reached into her drawer and took out what looked like a letter.

"Do you remember a Mrs. Dickenson in room H723-B?"

"No, I don't really remember a Mrs. Dickenson in that room. Was there a problem?" I asked, fighting back tears. The name didn't stand out to me. I could barely remember names from one week to the next because of the high turnover of patients.

"Well, maybe you should read this then," she said, handing me the letter.

In very shaky handwriting was written the following:

Dear Head Nurse on 7 Hamilton,

I was a patient on your floor in the recent past. I'm sorry, but I don't recall everyone's name, but one name stood out to me. It was my night nurse. I remember her soft, comforting voice in the dark. She was the cool hand on my fevered forehead. She diligently checked on me every couple of hours and made sure that I was comfortable and well cared for. I thank her from the bottom of my heart.

Sincerely,
Mrs. Dickenson

I was stunned. I had expected a scolding, but instead received one of the greatest gifts I'd ever been given:

words of thanks from someone's heart.

Fifteen years later, I still carry those words in my heart. I orient new night nurses according to them and practice them as I treat every patient. That thoughtful letter has guided many hands during the night over many years.

Georgann Phillips Schultz

There for Me

Should you shield the canyons from the windstorms you would never see the true beauty of their carvings.

Elisabeth Kübler-Ross

May, 1998

When the call came, I knew she would not live through the morning. I watched as her frail body struggled one last time, finally giving up the two-year battle with chemotherapy, radiation, fatigue and pain caused by the breast cancer she had fought so hard to overcome.

Then a steady touch wiped her brow and held her hand. A soothing voice whispered in her ear with patience, tenderness and love. This touch, this voice provided me, too, the comfort I needed to ease the pain of the inevitable passing of my mother.

May, 1999

The loud ringing of the phone brought me out of the deep sleep I needed so desperately.

My husband had been diagnosed with cardio-myopathy. For five years we had coped with the ups and downs of Jim's health and, finally, the decision to put him on the heart transplant list. As we waited for a heart, we lived our life as fully and normally as possible. He had been on the waiting list four years when he began to rapidly fail. An electronic device was surgically implanted to help his heart function until a transplant could be done.

The months after the device was implanted were the most physically and mentally challenging time of my life. I felt helpless as he fought to recover and gain enough strength to return home, and rejoiced when he finally did. The infection had caught us by surprise; his return to the hospital devastated me.

The phone message cut deep into my heart. Jim had suffered a stroke. He lay in the hospital bed as if asleep. I could hear the surgically implanted ventricular device pumping loudly in his chest. I watched the monitors and prayed the stroke had caused minimal damage.

Then, there she was again. She walked in the room and sat beside me, holding my hand and wiping my tears. She spoke quietly, giving me hope that somehow he would recover, and courage to face the fear if he didn't. As the day wore on, she quietly listened as I told her that no matter what, I would take him home and tenderly care for him.

She gripped my hand as I learned it was a massive stroke, causing irreversible damage. My whole world stopped in that single moment. I insisted I would not leave him there—I would take him home. Through the following agonizing hours she tenderly sat by my side, as I made irrational plans.

I will never forget the determination in her eyes as she finally stood with me by Jim's bedside, and calmly and quietly explained that the husband and father I knew and loved for almost thirty years was no longer here—he was in a better place, free of pain and suffering. With her at my side, I held my Jim's hand, stroked his cheek, and realized I needed to face the inevitable.

May, 2000

My heart filled with love, pride and sadness as she walked toward me with her diploma.

Love, because she was the glue that had held me together during my darkest hours.

Pride, because she had learned to unselfishly give comfort where there is pain, courage where there is fear, hope where there is despair, and acceptance when the end is near.

Sadness, because her beloved Grandma and loving father were not physically here to share this happy moment.

As I looked at my daughter's college diploma, with the R.N., B.S.N. behind her name, I knew that college had given her technical knowledge and life had given her that special something to lead her in her chosen path.

Now she will give the world all the comfort, wisdom and strength she has given me.

Carolyn Gavalas

To the Nurses of the World

Work is love made visible.

Kahlil Gibran

You evangelists of encouragement, you are so much more than you know.

You have never let what you couldn't do stop you from doing all you could do.

You are salespeople; your briefcases are filled with a product called hope.

You are explorers, knowing that once you have gone as far as you can see, you will still see farther.

You are singers spreading the melody of consideration.

You are lawyers making a case for life.

You are authors helping others add more pages to their book of memories.

You are comedians dispensing the medicine of laughter.

You are magicians creating real miracles that inspire patients and families.

Like King Arthur and Joan of Arc, you are warriors battling against the villains of negativity.

Dorothy would have reached Oz much faster in the company of one nurse.

For no one can practice your profession unless they already possess a brain brimming with wisdom, boundless courage and a heart filled with love.

You are living proof that humanity is created in the image and likeness of God, and the name of that God is Love.

John Wayne Schlatter
Previously appeared in Chicken Soup for the Surviving Soul

Who Is Jack Canfield?

Jack Canfield is a bestselling author and one of America's leading experts in the development of human potential. He is both a dynamic and entertaining speaker and a highly sought-after trainer with a wonderful ability to inform and inspire audiences to open their hearts, love more openly and boldly pursue their dreams.

Jack spent his teenage years growing up in Martins Ferry, Ohio, and Wheeling, West Virginia, with his sister Kimberly (Kirberger) and his two brothers, Rick and Taylor. The whole family has spent most of their professional careers dedicated to educating, counseling and empowering teens. Jack admits to being shy and lacking self-confidence in high school, but through a lot of hard work he earned letters in three sports and graduated third in his class.

After graduating college, Jack taught high school in the inner city of Chicago and in Iowa. In recent years, Jack has expanded this to include adults in both educational and corporate settings.

He is the author and narrator of several bestselling audio- and videocassette programs. He is a regularly consulted expert for radio and television broadcasts and has published twenty-five books—all bestsellers within their categories—including more than twenty *Chicken Soup for the Soul* books, *The Aladdin Factor, Heart at Work, 100 Ways to Build Self-Concept in the Classroom* and *Dare to Win.*

Jack addresses over one hundred groups each year. His clients include professional associations, school districts, government agencies, churches and corporations in all fifty states.

Jack conducts an annual eight-day Training of Trainers program in the areas of building self-esteem and achieving peak performance. It attracts educators, counselors, parenting trainers, corporate trainers, professional speakers, ministers and others interested in developing their speaking and seminar-leading skills in these areas.

For further information about Jack's books, tapes and trainings, or to schedule him for a presentation, please contact:

The Canfield Training Group
P.O. Box 30880 • Santa Barbara, CA 93130
phone: 800-237-8336 • fax: 805-563-2945
e-mail: *speaking@canfieldgroup.com*
Web site: *www.chickensoup.com*

Who Is Mark Victor Hansen?

Mark Victor Hansen is a professional speaker who, in the last twenty years, has made over four thousand presentations to more than two million people in thirty-three countries. His presentations cover sales excellence and strategies; personal empowerment and development; and how to triple your income and double your time off.

Mark has spent a lifetime dedicated to his mission of making a profound and positive difference in people's lives. Throughout his career, he has inspired hundreds of thousands of people to create a more powerful and purposeful future for themselves while stimulating the sale of billions of dollars worth of goods and services.

Mark is a prolific writer and has authored *Future Diary, How to Achieve Total Prosperity* and *The Miracle of Tithing*. He is the coauthor of the *Chicken Soup for the Soul* series, *Dare to Win* and *The Aladdin Factor* (all with Jack Canfield) and *The Master Motivator* (with Joe Batten).

Mark has also produced a complete library of personal empowerment audio- and videocassette programs that have enabled his listeners to recognize and better use their innate abilities in their business and personal lives. His message has made him a popular television and radio personality with appearances on ABC, NBC, CBS, HBO, PBS, QVC and CNN.

He has also appeared on the cover of numerous magazines, including *Success, Entrepreneur* and *Changes*.

Mark is a big man with a heart and a spirit to match—an inspiration to all who seek to better themselves.

For further information about Mark, please contact:

Mark Victor Hansen & Associates
P.O. Box 7665
Newport Beach, CA 92658
phone: 949-759-9304 or 800-433-2314
fax: 949-722-6912
Web site: *www.chickensoup.com*

Who Is Nancy Mitchell-Autio?

Nancy Mitchell-Autio is the Director of Story Acquisitions for the *Chicken Soup for the Soul* series. She graduated from Arizona State University in May 1994 with a B.S. in nursing. After graduation, Nancy worked at Good Samaritan Regional Medical Center in Phoenix, Arizona, in the cardiovascular intensive care unit. In September 1994, Nancy moved back to her native town of Los Angeles and became involved with the *Chicken Soup* series. Nancy's intentions were to help finish *A 2nd Helping of Chicken Soup for the Soul* and then return to nursing. However, in December of that year, she was asked to continue on full-time as part of the *Chicken Soup* team. Nancy put nursing on hold and became Director of Story Acquisitions, working closely with Jack and Mark on all *Chicken Soup for the Soul* projects.

Nancy says that what she is most thankful for is her move back to L.A. to be there for her mother, Linda Mitchell, during her bout with breast cancer. Out of that struggle, Nancy coauthored, along with her sister, Patty Aubery, *Chicken Soup for the Surviving Soul: 101 Stories of Courage and Inspiration from Those Who Have Survived Cancer.* Little did she know that the book would become her own inspiration when her dad was diagnosed with prostate cancer in 1999.

Nancy also coauthored *Chicken Soup for the Christian Soul, Chicken Soup for the Christian Family Soul* and *Chicken Soup for the Expectant Mother's Soul.* She will also be coauthoring the upcoming *Chicken Soup for the Grieving Soul* and *Chicken Soup for the Sister's Soul.* Nancy resides in Santa Barbara with her husband, Kirk Autio, dogs Kona and Cora and three cats. She is expecting her first child on October 1, 2001.

You may contact Nancy at:

P.O. Box 30880
Santa Barbara, CA 93130
phone: 805-682-6311
fax: 805-682-0872
e-mail: *nautio@chickensoup.com*

Who Is LeAnn Thieman?

LeAnn Thieman is a nationally acclaimed professional speaker, author and nurse who was "accidentally" caught up in the Vietnam Orphan Airlift in 1975. Her book, *This Must Be My Brother*, details her daring adventure of helping to rescue three hundred babies as Saigon was falling to the Communists. An ordinary person, she struggled through extraordinary circumstances and found the courage to succeed. *Newsweek* magazine featured LeAnn and her incredible story in its *Voices of the Century* issue.

Today, as a renowned motivational speaker, she shares life-changing lessons learned from her airlift experience. Believing we all have individual "war zones," LeAnn inspires audiences to balance their lives, truly live their priorities and make a difference in the world.

After her story was featured in *Chicken Soup for the Mother's Soul*, LeAnn became one of *Chicken Soup's* most prolific writers, with stories in seven more *Chicken Soup* books. That, and her devotion to thirty years of nursing, made her the ideal coauthor of *Chicken Soup for the Nurse's Soul*.

While health organizations were an obvious "niche" for her keynote addresses and seminars, her audiences have grown to include all walks of life. Now cattlemen, contractors and corporate America appreciate her message! One CEO summed it up best when he said, "I'm going to live my life differently after hearing you today."

LeAnn and Mark, her husband of thirty-one years, reside in Colorado where they enjoy their "empty nest." Their two daughters, Angela and Christie, and son Mitch have "flown the coop" but are still drawn under their mother's wing when she needs them!

For more information about LeAnn's books and tapes or to schedule her for a presentation, please contact her at:

6600 Thompson Drive
Fort Collins, CO 80526
phone: 970-223-1574
e-mail: *LeAnn@LeAnnThieman.com*
Web site: *www.LeAnnThieman.com*

Contributors

Linda Apple lives in Springdale, Arkansas, with her husband, Neal. They have five children and one grandson. Linda is an inspirational speaker and writer. She is Women's Touch Ministry director at Christian Life Cathedral, in Fayetteville. Her mother, Freddie Diehl, is a retired nurse. You can contact Linda at 501-521-5683 or by fax at 501-521-8198.

Barbara Bartlein, R.N., M.S.W., is a professional speaker, author and consultant. A motivational humorist, she presents across the country and has appeared at the Comedy Club. Her column, *Success Matters,* appears in numerous publications. Her latest book *Why Did I Marry You Anyway?* is scheduled for release in 2002. She can be reached at *balance4u@aol.com.* Or visit her Web site at *www.successmatters.org.*

Raymond Bingham, R.N.C., is a certified neonatal intensive care nurse. He also works as a technical writer at the National Institute of Nursing Research. Ray is married and has three children and two cats. He enjoys writing essays and short fiction. He can be reached at *rjbrnc@aol.com.*

Linda C. Bird, F.N.P., received her bachelor of science degree in nursing from Michigan State University and M.S.N. from South Dakota State University. She is working as a family nurse practitioner and also has an interest in alternative medicine. She can be reached at P.O. Box 5703, Salem, OR 97304.

Cindy Bollinger, R.N., is a full-time wife and mother. She and husband, Bruce, have four children, Marc, Zachary, Tyson and Emily. "Finding Your Easter Sunrise" is her first attempt to write professionally, and she is very happy to see it in print. Her interests include her family, quilting, reading, traveling and studio art classes. She can be reached at *bbollinger@mailbox.sw.org* or 118 Twelve Oaks Drive, Temple, TX 76504.

Barbara A. Brady, R.N., is a retired recovery room and geriatric nurse living in Kansas. She graduated from St. Luke's Hospital, Chicago, Illinois. She volunteers as a reading tutor and enjoys writing. Her recent novel, *A Variety of Gifts,* is about a retired nurse. You may reach her at 785-271-9090 or *emmerris@aol.com.*

Kathleen Brewer-Smyth, R.N., Ph.D., C.R.R.N., is an educator, consultant and freelance writer. She holds master's and Ph.D. degrees specifically in the study of neuroscience nursing from the University of Pennsylvania. At the time of this publication, her most recent funded research is evaluating neurologic and neuroendocrine correlates of violent criminal behavior of female prison inmates. She has published and presented extensively on topics related to neuroscience nursing and violent behavior. She has held positions as clinical specialist, staff development educator and as a university faculty member, and has practiced in critical care, outpatient and rehabilitation settings. Kathleen can be reached at P.O. Box 9194, Wilmington, DE 19809.

Shelly Burke, R.N., B.S.N., and her husband have two children. Shelly keeps her hand in nursing by teaching Lamaze and CPR classes. She also writes and is currently working on her book *Home Is Where the Mom Is* which will be published in the fall of 2001. You can reach Shelly at *sgburke@megavision.com*.

Karyn Buxman, R.N., M.S.N., C.S.P., is a highly sought humorist and nationally recognized expert in therapeutic humor. She is available to liven up your next meeting or event. To find out how, or for more information on her latest book *This Won't Hurt a Bit!* Call 1-800-8Humorx, e-mail her at *Karyn@humorx.com* or visit *www.Humorx.com*.

Tricia Caliguire and her husband, Greg, are producers of information products, showing people how to make the best use of who they are, where they are, with what they have, to make a better life for themselves and the people around them. Contact Tricia at *Tcalig@aol.com*.

Candace L. Calvert is an ER nurse, mother of two, and writer of inspirational essays, humor articles and fiction. She swapped her riding boots for chili-pepper red dancing boots, and "Two Steps" and twirls across country-dance floors with husband, Andy. She is currently at work on a novel. You may e-mail her at *wintrblaze@hotmail.com*.

Denise Casaubon is a registered nurse and paralegal. She is the president of a teeny tiny corporation, d.b.a. DNR Medical-Legal Consultants. DNR provides expert witness and research services to attorneys and compliance consulting services to health care facilities. Please visit DNR's Web site at *www.dnrconsultants.org* or e-mail her at *Casaubon@qwest.net*.

Mitzi Chandler, L.P.N., writes poetry, inspirational pieces, children's stories and humor. She has worked as a nurse in St. Louis and Chicago, and has presented programs on the effects of family alcoholism on children. At present, she is busy and happy being a grandmother and traveling with her newly retired husband.

Sylvia C. Chism was a nurse administrator for many years in southern and central California, Reno and Baltimore, Maryland. She taught nursing at a university and worked with deaf college students. Sylvia also led workshops in leadership, self-esteem, therapeutic touch and spirituality. She is a member of health ministry, healing ministry, a commission on aging and is a published writer.

Cherie Clark, was evacuated twice with orphans during the final days of the Vietnam War. Cherie then went to Calcutta where she met and worked with Mother Teresa. She founded the International Mission of Hope, a charitable organization. Cherie resided in India for twelve years and returned to live and work in Vietnam in 1988. She is the author of the book *After Sorrow Comes Joy*. Contact her at *CherieIMH@aol.com*.

Virginia L. Clark, R.N., C.C.R.N., is a poet and writer who retired from her twenty-year nursing career in 1987. She now lives in Taos, New Mexico, and writes columns, news stories and features for local publications. Her poetry manuscript *A Child's Book of Shadows* should be available fall 2001. Please contact her at *vlclark4@juno.com*.

Dolores Curran is a parent educator and writer who has lectured extensively on family topics, both nationally and abroad. Her books include *Traits of a Healthy Family, Stress and the Healthy Family, Working with Parents* and *Tired of Arguing with Your Kids?* She resides in Littleton, Colorado.

Ken Cyr, R.N., Ph.D., is a clinical psychologist. Besides poetry, he has written books on weather and behavior; attention deficit for teachers, parents and children, and investigating sexual abuse. Signed copies of *Love in Your Hands* are available. Contact Ken at *Kcyrphd@yahoo.com* or fax him at 210-690-0611.

Kathleen Dahle commenced her nursing training at N.D.S.U. in Fargo, North Dakota and received her B.S.N. from Moorhead State University in 1984. Since 1988, she has worked as a legal nurse consultant. Kathleen resides in Fort Worth with her husband and four very busy children. Please contact her at *kdahlek@aol.com.*

Johnnie Dowdy is the mother of one son, and grandmother to two boys. She is an R.N. supervisor and has been in nursing for thirty-two years working trauma and OB.

Elaine Gray Dumler, a corporate presentation skill trainer, spent a lot of time with nurses and discovered their true healing power. Within eighteen months of Rondi's battle for life, she lost her other sister, Nancy, to cancer. Elaine, husband Larry and son Bryan live at 6460 W. 98th Ct., Westminster, CO 80021 or call 303-430-0592.

Christine Ehlers, B.S.N., received her B.S.N. with an H.A.S. minor from the University of Central Florida in May 2001. She hopes to pursue a career in emergency nursing. Christine enjoys fishing, traveling and spending time with family and friends. She is a member of Alpha Delta Phi Sorority. You may e-mail her at *Cehlers12@aol.com.*

Benita Epstein has cartoons that appear in hundreds of publications such as *The New Yorker, Reader's Digest* and *Better Homes & Gardens.* She has three cartoon collections: *Suture Self, Interlibrary Loan Sharks and Seedy Roms,* and *Science of Little Round Things* (McFarland & Co. 1-800-253-2187). Contact Benita at *BenitaE@aol.com* or visit her Web site at *www.reuben.org/benitaepstein/.*

Joan Filbin received a degree in nursing in 1980. She works in a newborn intensive care nursery in North Central Wisconsin. As a teacher/speaker for women's groups, she has been frequently asked if she has written any of her stories. She has recently returned to school to pursue a long-overdue dream to write. Please reach her at *filbin@stjosephs-marshfied.org.*

Naomi Follis graduated from Purdue University Calumet Campus School of Nursing, and has a diploma from Long Ridge Writers Group. She resides in Oklahoma City where she pursues her study of Native American history and art, and writes poetry and short stories.

Janie K. Ford graduated from Brigham Young University in 1978 and has been a flight nurse in Southern California for seventeen years. Her hobbies include American history, horses, sports, travel and partying with her family. She is a motivational speaker for youth and adults. She can be reached at 714-528-0268 or *janiekford@yahoo.com*.

Gwen Fosse, R.N., has worked with children with heart disease, witnessing many advances in their care for nearly forty years. She thanks her husband, three daughters and parents for allowing her to pursue her "heart" life. She also thanks the colleagues, children and families who have been her teachers. E-mail her at *fusses@aol.com*.

Carolyn Gavalas is laboratory manager at Virginia Gay Hospital in Vinton, Iowa. She enjoys her four dogs, traveling, reading, needlework, stamping, genealogy, attending concerts, bingo, collecting bears and her backyard pond, gazebo and garden. She and her late husband, Jim, have a daughter, Stephanie.

Nancy B. Gibbs is a weekly religion columnist and freelance writer. Her writing has appeared in books by Honor Books and Guideposts Books. She has been published in numerous magazines and devotional guides. She is a pastor's wife and mother of three grown children. Nancy may be contacted at *DAISEYDOOD@aol.com*.

Susan M. Goldberg, R.N., has worked as an OR nurse for the past thirty years. She completed her B.S. degree in organizational management twenty-seven years after graduating nursing school. Susan is the surgical services instructor at a Westchester, New York, hospital, and teaches college nursing courses and self-esteem workshops. You may contact Susan at *Harmony51480@aol.com*.

Viola Ruelke Gommer, R.N., M.S.N., is a retired nurse educator and nurse executive. As a board member of United Methodist Fellowship of Health Care Volunteers, she now shares her knowledge, skills and faith within the United States and in other countries—Haiti, Bolivia, Guyana, Zimbabwe and the Dominican Republic. She is a dynamic speaker and inspiring teacher. Vi also offers guidance and training for persons interested in becoming volunteers in mission. She is proponent of Comprehensive Community-based Primary Health Care. CCPHC empowers individuals and communities to become responsible for their own health promotion and illness prevention. It moves persons from hopelessness to hope. You can reach Vi at P.O. Box 313, Sweet Valley, PA 18656. You may e-mail her at *vgommer@aol.com* or call 570-477-5841.

Lini R. Grol is a retired registered nurse, trained in her homeland in The Netherlands, before coming to Canada. She has published, internationally, poetry, fiction and folktales with scissors-cut illustrations in periodicals, anthologies and books. Her latest books are *A Matter of the Heart,* 1998 and *Lake to Lake,* Lini Grol's NIAGRA, 2001. Her poems are broadcast and are on cassette and CD. She has won prizes for her stories and scissors-cut illustrations. Her WWII poems are read at Remembrance Day services.

Jacqueline C. Hadeland, forty-four, has been a registered nurse for seven years. She works for Good Samaritan Medical Center in West Palm Beach, Florida. She resides in Wellington, Florida, with her husband and fourteen-year-old daughter.

Don Haines, R.N., retired from nursing in 1998. He started writing in 1996, thereby fulfilling a lifelong dream. He lives quietly in Carroll County, Maryland, with his wife, Sheila, and their Yorkie, Minnie. The quiet is shattered when their nine grandchildren come to call. They are a welcome diversion.

Nancy Harless is a nurse practitioner now exercising her menopausal zest through travel, volunteering in various health-care projects and writing about these experiences. Most of her writing is done in a towering maple tree in the tree house built specifically for that purpose by her husband, Norm. She is currently writing a book about the strong and beautiful women she has met on her journeys. Please reach her at *datnurse@interl.net.*

Laura Vickery Hart is a registered nurse, international board-certified lactation consultant and childbirth educator in Central Florida. She graduated from Johnston-Willis Hospital School of Nursing in Richmond, Virginia, in 1968 and received her bachelor of science degree in nursing from Florida Southern College in 1997. Laura enjoys reading and spending time with her children and grandchildren. You may e-mail Laura at *ldybg522@aol.com.*

Catherine Hoe Harwood works with a dynamic faculty group teaching nursing at Trinity Western University, a private Christian university in Langley, British Columbia, Canada. She previously taught nursing at University of Western Ontario. Catherine is blessed with two children and a wonderful extended family. She may be reached at *harwood@twu.ca.*

Mary Jane Holman, R.N., works in the intensive care unit at Doctor's Hospital in Shreveport, Louisiana. You may reach her at *mjnick@bellsouth.net.*

Beverly Houseman, R.N., is a retired nurse. She was a childbirth educator for twenty-eight years and is married with two sons and two grandchildren. Beverly enjoys writing, crafting, singing and traveling. She is writing her own book about life with her mentally handicapped son, Rusty. You may contact her at *happyhousemans@mindspring.com.* Beverly also counsels people with pre- or post-abortion syndrome.

Sarah Webb Johnson graduated from Baptist Hospital School of Nursing in Memphis in 1979. She spent seven years working in the intensive care unit at Baptist Hospital. Sarah then pursued a career in public health and school health where she has met her greatest nursing challenges. You may reach her at *wtsbrcj@aol.com.*

Marie D. Jones is an ordained New Thought Minister working toward her doctor of divinity. She is a widely published writer and producer of a line of children's videos called Gigglebug Farms. She lives in San Marcos, California, with her husband, Ron and baby, Max. You can reach her at *mariejones@mac.com.*

Kathryn Kimzey Judkins, L.V.N., has lived in California since 1962. In 1965, she became an L.V.N. Since retiring in 1998, she spends much of her time writing poetry and short stories. Married fifty-four years, she has three children, six grandchildren and two great grandchildren.

Bil Keane created *The Family Circus,* based on his own family, in 1960. It now appears in well over fifteen hundred newspapers and is read daily by 188 million people. The award-winning feature is the most widely syndicated cartoon in America. Check out *The Family Circus* Web site at *www.familycircus.com.*

Carin Klabbers likes to write inspirational stories (she is published in *Chicken Soup for the Gardener's Soul*). She combines her household duties with volunteer work and writes monthly articles for the local newspaper about fair trade. You may reach her at koninginneweg 75, 2g82 AH Ridderkerk, The Netherlands. Her e-mail address is *pmklabbers@HETNET.NL.*

Allen Klein (aka Mr. Jollytologist) is a professional speaker and bestselling author. His award-winning programs show audiences how to use humor to deal with not-so-funny stuff. His books include *The Healing Power of Humor* and *The Courage to Laugh.* You may contact him for information at *www.allenklein.com* or e-mail him at *humor@allenklein.com.*

Rita Kluny, R.N., B.S.N., C.H.T.P., C.H.T.I., H.N.C., is a Healing Touch (energy healing) instructor. She founded the Healing Touch for Babies program, and teaches workshops and consults internationally. She practices Healing Touch seasonally at Omega Institute for Holistic Studies, and was named the 1994 American Holistic Nurse of the Year. Her Web site is *www.healingtouchforbabies.com.* E-mail her at *healingbabies@yahoo.com.*

Elsie Schmied Knoke, R.N., received a bachelor of general studies with honors from Roosevelt University and a master's in management from Northwestern University. She wrote articles and two anthologies for nurse managers. Now retired, she writes essays and short stories. Her novel *Apple Blossom Time* is on *www.enovel.com.*

Dawn Koehn is an OB nurse/sonographer in Enid, Oklahoma. She and her husband, Ron, have three sons. Dawn enjoys reading, gardening, travel and spending time with family and friends. She plans to continue her nursing education at Oklahoma University. You may reach her at *ronniedawn@aol.com.*

Laura Hayes Lagana is a registered nurse, professional speaker, author of a forthcoming inspirational book about caregivers, patients, nurses and is one of the coauthors of *Chicken Soup for the Volunteer's Soul.* She may be reached at Success Solutions, P.O. Box 7816, Wilmington, DE 19803 or by e-mail at *NurseAngel@LauraLagana.com.* You may visit her Web site at *www.LauraLagana.com.*

Debbie Lukasiewicz is the blessed mother of seven children and wife to one terrific man. Baby Ty is a happy, healthy five-year-old. Debbie and Del give thanks daily for all their miracle babies.

Christy M. Martin is a nurse in a small town with a big heart—Chillicothe, Texas. She loves the outdoors and spending time with her two children. She dreams of some day hanging up her nurse's cap and becoming a full-time writer.

Maxine, America's Queen of Attitude, has graced Hallmark products since 1986. When Maxine speaks her mind, more often than not she's speaking our minds, too. With her own nationally syndicated cartoon, Maxine always tells it like it is—and her fans wouldn't want it any other way.

Shirley McCullough's insights come largely from her experiences as a registered nurse, home health agency administrator and community health educator. Please reach her at *smac@ktvd.net*.

Donna McDonnall, R.N., graduated from Immanuel Medical Center, Omaha. Donna recently retired after working eighteen years as a public health/school nurse. She was named Colorado School Nurse of the Year in 1999 and received the Nightingale Award in 1991. She enjoys writing, traveling, photography and her family. You may contact her at *mcdonnal@ria.net*.

Linda McNeil was a physical therapist in her first life. She is now an author, professional speaker and consultant specializing in change, customer service and team building. "Lin" is the author of *7 Keys to Changing: Your Life, Health and Wealth*. You may reach her at 1-800-745-3488 or at *linmcneil@aol.com*. Visit her Web site at *www.linmcneil.com*.

Roberta L. Messner, R.N., Ph.D., is widely published in the nursing and lay literature. She speaks on a variety of nursing and inspirational topics, including the popular *Stories That Shape Nurses*, a presentation that encourages nurses to believe in the power of their own stories. She can be reached at *rlmessner@aol.com*.

Joyce Mueller, R.N., is a retired nurse, mom, grandmom and world traveler. She has lived and worked in Bangladesh, Pakistan and the Solomon Islands. She enjoys her life on the Oregon coast, where she writes fiction, poems and memoirs. Please contact her at P.O. Box 718, Port Orford, OR 97465.

Terri Murcia, born November 26, 1963, received her B.A. degree from Loyola Marymount University in 1985. She has been happily married for twelve years and has a three-month-old son. She walked in the Avon Breast Cancer 3-Day in October 2001 in memory of her mother and grandmother. Please e-mail her at *murcia@earthlink.net*.

Janis Nark, Lt. Col., U.S.A.R. (Ret.), served for twenty-six years in the Army Nurse Corps with assignments that included Vietnam and Desert Storm. She is a highly sought-after motivational speaker addressing the areas of change and stress, who touches the heart, tear ducts and funny bones of all who hear her. She is published in four books and has three presentations on tape, including "Finding Control in the Chaos" and "Tools for Transformation: Change Does Not Equal Stress." You may contact her at *www.Nark.com* or *JanisNark@aol.com*. Her phone number is 828-652-2155 and fax is 828-652-4547.

Marianne Neifert, M.D., is commonly known as "Dr. Mom," is a pediatrician, author of parenting books, national speaker and the mother of five grown children—all born during her medical training. She is a contributing editor for *Parenting Magazine* and writes a bimonthly medical column for *BabyTalk Magazine*. She can be contacted for speaking engagements on parenting issues and life balance at Dr. Mom Presentations, P.O. Box 880, Parker, CO 80134 or *DrNiefert@aol.com*. Visit her Web site at *www.Dr-Mom.com*.

Chris S. Patterson is a "man of many hats." An accomplished chef, his career was cut short by lung cancer, directing him to pursue his loves of drawing and writing. As a survivor, he has established himself as a published freelance cartoonist, illustrator, and published writer of humor and poetry. Please contact him at *Cartoonsbychris@aol.com*.

Susan Pearson, R.N., received her degree from Quincy College in Plymouth, Massachusetts. She is the mother of six sons, and works in long-term care with many wonderful "roses." Susan enjoys writing, gardening and working on her student nurse Web site, the Snurse's Bookmark. Visit her at *www.tripod.com/ susanp/index.html*.

J. C. Pinkerton graduated Stonewall Jackson Nursing School and attended Southern Sem College in Virginia. After a career in nursing, she now enjoys freelance writing. She is constantly researching ancient history, America in the 1800s and children's stories. For more information on J. C. Pinkerton, contact her at *www.angelfire.com/journal/writersdream* or e-mail her at *pinkerton@rockbridge.net*.

Corrine Pratz is a freelance writer with a passion for creating works that make an impact. She has had stories and articles published in magazines, newspapers and online. She is the author of *Color Me Happy!! An Approach to Expressive Arts for Children* and has conducted workshops and seminars relating to various art forms. Her second book *Losing Dad* will be completed in 2001. She lives on beautiful Vancouver Island in British Columbia, Canada, with her four great kids and wonderful husband. She can be reached at Box 1573, Lake Cowichan, BC, Canada V0R 2G0 or through *pratzpro@home.com*.

Rhona Knox Prescott, R.N., L.C.S.W., is a nurse, clinical diplomate in social work and author. She coauthored *Another Kind of War Story: Army Nurses Look Back to Vietnam* in 1993 and has had many poems and short articles published that deal with the combat experience from a nurse's perspective. She graduated from the University of Houston. Her stepmother and daughter have also served with the U.S. Army providing three generations of female military service. Her clinical specialty is trauma counseling. Maureen W. Southorn, her daughter, is also published. Her son, Mike Prescott, works for Executive Books. Marianne Austin, her daughter, is a chemist. You may reach Rhona at *Rhona41@hotmail.com*.

Maryjo Relampagos Pulmano is an R.N. working for Kaiser Permanente in southern California. She thanks her parents for raising her to become a writer, singer and nurse. She thanks her husband, Rayne, son Nathaniel and the Pulmano family for teaching her the true meaning of family. You may reach Maryjo at *mpulmano@lycos.com*.

Zaphra Reskakis, M.S., R.Ph., has a B.S. in pharmacy from Columbia University and an M.S. in clinical pharmacy from St. John's University. She has been published in *Clever, Reminisce, Hellenic Chronicle, Lose Your Identity* and *What's Cooking*. Zaphra is a storyteller, enjoys theater, traveling and being the *yiayia* (Greek for grandma) of Amanda, Brendan, Cory, Nicholas and Michael. You may e-mail her at *yiayiazaph@aol.com*.

Naomi Rhode, R.D.H., C.S.P., C.P.A.E. Speaker Hall of Fame, is past president of the National Speakers Association, recipient of the 1997 Cavett Award and is known for her inspirational, dynamic speaking to both healthcare and general audiences. She is co-owner and vice chairman of Smart Practice, a marketing and manufacturing company, which provides products and services to the healthcare industry worldwide. Naomi is the author of two inspirational gift books, *The Gift of Family—A Legacy of Love* and *More Beautiful Than Diamonds—The Gift of Friendship*. She is also a contributor and coauthor of *Meditations for the Road Warriors* and many other books and publications. You may visit her Web site at *www.smarthealth.com/rhode*.

Anne Riffenburgh received a master's of social work degree from the University of Southern California in 1988. She has worked extensively with patients and families impacted by cancer. Recently she completed *Helping Children Cope with Grief: A Handbook for Parents, Teachers and Therapists*. She may be reached at *anneriff@aol.com*.

John Wayne Schlatter is a frequent contributor to *Chicken Soup for the Soul* and can be seen and heard on the video and audio versions of this series. In 1993, Professional Speaker Network named him Speaker of the Year. He can be contacted at 760-787-9134.

Victoria Schlintz, R.N., M.A., is a registered nurse and has a master's degree in education. She has an emergency nursing background, and currently directs education services at a Northern California hospital. She is also a student at the Graduate Theological Union, Berkeley, California, and an ordination candidate in the United Methodist Church.

Georgann Phillips Schultz, R.N., M.A., lives in Virginia with her husband and two preschool daughters. She writes poetry, picture books and MG fiction for children and moderates three children's writing groups. Her picture book, *Foghorn Hannah*, Munchweiler Press, Spring 2002, starts, where else? In a hospital nursery! You may reach her at *auntgeorge@mindspring.com*.

Margie Seyfer is a nationally known motivational speaker who conducts high-energy keynotes and workshops on attitude enhancement and telephone customer service. She has inspired thousands of people to become more effective in the areas of communication, interpersonal skills and workplace harmony. Please reach her at *seyfermarg@aol.com*.

Duane Shaw is a retired business entrepreneur. He is a highly decorated combat Vietnam veteran and is currently writing a military autobiography. Plans for future books include a men's handbook *How to Love and Treasure Your Partner* and *Post Traumatic Stress Disorder from the Inside Out*. Publisher inquiries welcome. You may e-mail Duane at *djshaw95444@aol.com*.

Beatrice Sheftel received her associate's degree from Manchester Community College, her bachelor's from the University of Connecticut. She is a substitute teacher, freelance writer. She is published extensively online and in regional and national publications. She is completing an inspirational novel and memoir about growing up in Brooklyn, New York. You may e-mail Bea at *bts1ct@aol.com.*

Dennis Sibley is a former United Kingdom hospice nurse who has a master's of arts degree in Death and Society from Reading University. Dennis is chairman of The Buddhist Hospice Trust, which offers spiritual support from within a Buddhist perspective. He can be reached at *dsibley@ukonline.co.uk.*

Bernard S. Siegel, M.D., who prefers to be called Bernie, retired from the practice of general surgery in 1989 to speak to patients and their caregivers. In 1978, he originated Exceptional Cancer Patients, a specific form of individual and group therapy. EcaP is based on "carefrontation." In 1986, his first book, *Love, Medicine and Miracles* was published, followed by *Peace, Love and Healing* and *How to Live Between Office Visits.* Bernie's realization that we all need help dealing with the difficulties of life, not just the physical ones, led to his fourth book, *Prescriptions for Living.* It helps people become aware of the eternal truths and wisdom of the sages through Bernie's stories rather than await a personal disaster. Bernie and his wife and coworker, Bobbie, live in a suburb of New Haven, Connecticut. They have five children and eight grandchildren. Contact Bernie through his Web site at *www.ecap-online.org,* via e-mail at *bugsysiegel@compuserve.com* or by phone at 814-337-8192.

Rebecca Skowronski, R.N., graduated from Mercy Central School of Nursing in 1977. She has two children and resides in Boca Raton, Florida, where she works on a sub-acute rehab unit. Rebecca and her husband, Martin, provide seminars in crisis prevention and stress management. She can be reached at *rls@proactive.net.*

Judy B. Smith received her B.S.N. from the University of Tennessee College of Nursing in 1965. She is certified in community health nursing and case management and currently works as a school nurse. Her nursing practice has also been in hospitals, public health clinics, tuberculosis control, home visitation, nursing education and home health care. Judy has published numerous articles in professional journals regarding nursing and health care and plans to write a book describing experiences as a home visitation/research nurse for teen mothers and their babies.

Sherri Sorenson, R.N., B.S.N., C.C.R.N., received her nursing diploma from Iowa Lutheran Hospital and her B.S.N. from the University of Phoenix. She has been a flight nurse with AirEvac Services in Phoenix, Arizona, since 1986. She enjoys riding and competing in dressage with her two horses. Please reach her at *rn358102@aol.com.*

Susan Spence has been writing all her life but only recently started getting published. She is happily married, has two beautiful stepchildren and works as a veterinary technician. "God has blessed me with the gift of writing and all the praise goes to him." Any questions or comments can be sent to *Arpoet@aol.com.*

Diane Stallings, R.N., has nursed hospital patients for nearly twenty-two years. Currently working intensive care and telemetry, she keeps a journal of inspiring moments and writes short stories. She cares for her husband and two children in Fountain Hills, Arizona. You may reach her at *gdstallings@juno.com.*

Jo Stickley, R.N., has worked many years as an operating room nurse. Besides being involved in the early transplant programs, she served in the armed forces, in research and is now working in the ambulatory surgery setting. She plans to retire in the near future and continue her hobbies of cooking and herb gardening.

Donna Strickland, R.N., M.S., C.S., C.S.P., is a full-time national speaker and organizational development consultant known for her high-energy, content-rich and fun-filled programs. Donna consults with corporate and healthcare groups in the areas of leadership, teams, change, performance management, humor and emotional intelligence. She can be reached at *www.Donna Strickland.com* or by calling 303-777-7997.

F. A. Thompson is a graduate of London University. He served in the British Army and the Indian Army in the Far East during the Second World War. He has worked in education in West Africa and in colleges in England. He writes short stories and articles for shipping magazines.

Scot Thurman is currently an assistant director with the Baptist Student Union in Fayetteville, Arkansas. He graduated from the University of Arkansas with a degree in business in 1992 and graduated from Ouachita Baptist University in 1997. His love lies in helping people grow closer to God.

Susan Townsend is a full-time teacher of emotionally disturbed high school students, and a part-time writer. She and a colleague are currently writing a book about the trials and triumphs of troubled kids. Susan lives in Oshkosh, Wisconsin, and can be reached via e-mail at *morgan@vbe.com,* or by fax at 920-233-3722.

Johanna Tracy, M.S.N., R.N., C.S., received her bachelor's and master's degrees in nursing in Detroit, Michigan. She teaches nursing at Capital Health System School of Nursing in Trenton, New Jersey. Johanna volunteers with the American Red Cross at the local, state and national levels. You may contact her at 215-735-1942 or e-mail her at *HtracyRN@aol.com.*

Lisa Ray Turner is an award-winning author of books and magazine articles. Along with her own writing, Lisa works with clients, teaching writing and doing freelance editing. She lives with her husband and three sons in Littleton, Colorado. She can be reached at *PinkDiva@aol.com.*

Allison Leigh Usher received her B.S.N. in nursing from Texas Tech University in 1999. In Atlanta, Georgia, she worked at the AFLAC Cancer Center at Egleston Children's Hospital. She currently lives in Houston, TX. Please reach her at *ausher@aol.com.*

Charlene Vance graduated with a B.S. in nursing from the University of Tulsa. She is a nationally registered paramedic and certified flight registered nurse. For over twenty years she has practiced nursing in a rotor wing aircraft flying within a 150-mile radius of Tulsa.

Andrea Watson received her practical nursing degree in 1976. She completed her B.S.N. from Eastern Michigan University in 1989. She works in cardiology at W. Beaumont Hospital in Southeastern Michigan. Andrea enjoys traveling, boating and spending time with her husband and two daughters. She plans to pursue her M.S.N. at E.M.U. in the fall. Please reach her at *andrea207@yahoo.com*.

Ana Wehipeihana is a pediatric nurse in New Zealand. She received her diploma in nursing in 1992, and her B.S.N. in 1996. She enjoys diving, water-skiing, wake-boarding, writing and traveling. She would like to become more involved in journalism/writing in the future. Please contact her at *jrwehi@xtra.co.nz*.

Mary Saxon Wilburn is a weekly contributor to *The Times-Georgian* and *The Carroll Star News*, and has been published in nursing and religious magazines. She also teaches writing workshops and is working on two novels. She and her husband, Larry share five children and ten grandchildren. Mary may be reached at *Mnsaxon@aol.com*.

John Wise is a registered nurse and a freelance cartoonist living in Clearwater, Florida. Creator of the *Tales from the Bedside* cartoons and books, he boasts a large collection of rejection slips and letters from the world's most prestigious publications. He can be reached at *jwise2@tampabay.rr.com*.

Permissions

We would like to acknowledge the following publishers and individuals for permission to reprint the following material. (Note: The stories that were penned anonymously, that are public domain, or that were written by Jack Canfield, Mark Victor Hansen, Nancy Mitchell-Autio and LeAnn Thieman are not included in this listing.)

Working Christmas Day. Reprinted by permission of Victoria Schlintz. ©2000 Victoria Schlintz.

Proud to Be a Nurse and *New Job.* Reprinted by permission of Barbara A. Brady. ©2000, 2001 Barbara A. Brady.

Nellie. Reprinted by permission of Joan M. Filbin. ©2000 Joan M. Filbin.

All in a Day's Work. Reprinted by permission of Naomi Rhode. ©1998 Naomi Rhode.

Jack. Reprinted by permission of Kathryn Kimzey Judkins. ©2000 Kathryn Kimzey Judkins.

Olivia. Reprinted by permission of Heather Black and Denise W. Lewis. ©1993 Heather Black and Denise W. Lewis.

A Matter of Believing. Reprinted by permission of Scot Thurman. ©1996 Scot Thurman.

Wake Up! Reprinted by permission of Kathleen M. Dahle. ©2000 Kathleen M. Dahle.

The Night Al Heel Broke Loose. Reprinted by permission of Elizabeth Turner. ©2000 Elizabeth Turner.

Jelly Hearts. Reprinted by permission of Joyce C. Mueller. ©1998 Joyce C. Mueller.

Boarder Baby. Reprinted by permission of Zaphra Reskakis. ©2000 Zaphra Reskakis.

What Day Is Today? Reprinted by permission of Allen Klein and Dennis Sibley. ©1998 Allen Klein and Dennis Sibley.

Fresh Sample. Reprinted by permission of Donna McDonnall. ©2000 Donna McDonnall.

Codes for the Holidays. Reprinted with permission from *RN.* Copyright ©1999 Medical Economics Company, Montvale, NJ. All world rights reserved.

Christmas Magic and *First Injection.* Reprinted by permission of Barbara Bartlein. ©1999 Barbara Bartlein.

A Forever Kind of Love. Reprinted by permission of Christy M. Martin. ©2000 Christy M. Martin.

Taking Care of Joey. Reprinted by permission of Donna Strickland. ©2000 Donna Strickland.

Pennies from Heaven. Reprinted by permission of Raymond Joseph Bingham. ©1999 Raymond Joseph Bingham.

Take a Number Please. Reprinted by permission of Naomi Follis. ©2000 Naomi Follis.

Reasonable Resignation. Reprinted by permission of Sylvia C. Chism. ©1982 Sylvia C. Chism.

Black Stockings. Reprinted by permission of Elsie Schmied Knoke. ©1991 Elsie Schmied Knoke.

My Mission of Hope. Reprinted by permission of Cherie Clark. ©2000 Cherie Clark.

The Heart of a Nurse. Reprinted by permission of Beatrice Sheftel. ©2000 Beatrice Sheftel.

Nurse Puss 'n Boots. Reprinted by permission of J. C. Pinkerton. ©1999 J. C. Pinkerton.

The Pinning. Reprinted by permission of Dawn M. Koehn. ©2000 Dawn M. Koehn.

Last Rites. Reprinted by permission of Jacqueline C. Hadeland. ©2000 Jacqueline C. Hadeland.

Heroes. Reprinted by permission of Rhona Knox Prescott. ©2000 Rhona Knox Prescott.

A Piece of Paper. Reprinted by permission of Sherri Sorenson. ©2000 Sherri Sorenson.

Love in Your Hands. Reprinted by permission of Ken Cyr. ©1990 Ken Cyr.

Silent Angel. Reprinted by permission of Duane Shaw. ©2000 Duane Shaw.

Child's Praise. Reprinted by permission of Dolores Curran. ©1990 Dolores Curran.

Ministering Angels. Reprinted by permission of Allison Leigh Usher. ©2000 Allison Leigh Usher.

A Gift from Nana. Reprinted by permission of Teresa A. Murcia. ©1995 Teresa A. Murcia.

Thank You, Mrs. Dickenson. Reprinted by permission of Georgann Phillips Schultz. ©2000 Georgann Phillips Schultz.

There for Me. Reprinted by permission of Carolyn Gavalas. ©2000 Carolyn Gavalas.

To the Nurses of the World. Reprinted by permission of John Wayne Schlatter. ©1995 John Wayne Schlatter.

Chicken Soup
for the Soul

www.chickensoup.com